TEN STEPS TO BEHAVIORAL RESEARCH

Thomas E. Whalen

California State University, Hayward

UNIVERSITY PRESS OF AMERICA

Lanham • New York • London

4720 Boston Way
Lanham, MD 20706

3 Henrietta Street
London WC2E 8LU England

Printed in the United States of America

British Cataloging in Publication Information Available

Library of Congress Cataloging-in-Publication Data

Whalen, Thomas E., 1938–
Ten steps to behavioral research / by Thomas E. Whalen.
p. cm.
Bibliography: p.
Includes index.
1. Psychology– –Research– –Methodology. 2. Social sciences–
–Research– –Methodology. I. Title.
BF76.5.W47 1989 89–5460 CIP
150'.72– –dc19
ISBN 0–8191–7394–0 (alk. paper)
ISBN 0–8191–7395–9 (pbk. : alk. paper)

All University Press of America books are produced on acid-free paper.
The paper used in this publication meets the minimum requirements of American
National Standard for Information Sciences—Permanence of Paper for Printed Library
Materials, ANSI Z39.48–1984. ♾

To ELLIS PAGE

Whose mentoring, friendship, and scholarship

have inspired me for thirty-five years.

PREFACE

This book grew from the author's need and desire to organize twenty years' teaching notes into a single volume. There was also a notion that students might benefit by viewing other students' research, perhaps even more than by studying the products of professional researchers. Finally, because technology has become such a pervasive part of the research process, I decided to devote considerable space to the utilization of computers in quantitative analysis. The intent here is to enable students to *do* research rather than just read about it.

These are the guiding motifs of the book. The original idea of *Ten Steps* came from a presentation I made to a group of teachers: *Ten Steps to Classroom Research.* I later incorporated the steps into my own teaching and found them useful. Whether there are eight, ten, or twelve steps is a debatable question. I have found ten to be a nice round number.

The book is divided into four parts. Part One characterizes the nature of scientific behavioral research and describes many different varieties and types. The philosophical tension between quantitative and qualitative paradigms is explored. Part Two lays out the ten research steps and illustrates their use with four master's theses. The examples of student research were chosen to show four major types of research--descriptive, correlational, causal-comparative, and experimental.

Parts 1 and 2 of the book are foundational. In my own teaching I have experienced a vast range of prior knowledge and preparation among entering graduate students with repect to these basic elements of research. For some, chapters 1-5 are a refresher for solid undergraduate training; others encounter the material for the first time and require much more time to assimilate it. Depending on the circumstances, some instructors may wish to proceed rapidly through parts 1 and 2, while others may spend considerable time, using parts 3 and 4 only selectively. The latter method may be quite appropriate for many undergraduate programs in psychology and related fields.

Parts 3 and 4 present much new material to most graduate students. Part Three begins with a general description of electronic computers and gradually spirals inward to a specific illustration of SPSS for data handling. As time passes, more and more students will become computer literate at earlier ages. The information in Chapter 6 will become redundant. At present, however, most students at all levels are deficient in their understanding of how computers work. The purpose of Part Three is to foster an appreciation for the machinery of research, the marvelous hard- and software which occupies a large space in the behavioral researcher's tool box.

Part Four provides the rest of the tools--the nitty gritty nuts and bolts that must be fit together to produce quality research. Part Four, in sheer volume of words, constitutes well over half the book. However, not all instructors may choose to spend half their time on these chapters. One alternative might be to have students identify their own types of research, and then if course time is short, to assign only one or two of the last four chapters for reading and later discussion in individual or small-group supervision. My own preference is to cover chapters 9-12 thoroughly. But, pragmatically, that may not be feasible in all programs.

One of the features of Part Four which provides a good reason for reading all four chapters is the unfolding analysis of data on personal happiness. For more than a decade, I have collected data from my own students using the *Happiness Questionnaire* shown in *Appendix A*. I found that students' motivation for data analysis is enhanced when they are analyzing their own behavior. They are especially eager to find out where their social and sexual behavior and attitudes fit on the group continuum, and which behaviors are related to happiness. Instructors may wish to use this questionnaire with their students.

The happiness data are used as a vehicle for illustrating all the major statistical methods in the SPSS package. Examples are given for computing a frequency distribution, standard scores, the Pearson r, multiple regression, canonical correlation, the t-test, ANOVA, ANCOVA, and MANOVA for repeated measures designs. Many of these statistical procedures are also highlighted in student research. Each of chapters 9-12 presents a detailed summary of a master's thesis in which the methods under discussion were used.

A word on writing style: I am aware that we live at a time when gender equity is very important. The liberation of women has been one of the most significant events of the past generation. Various attempts have been made to modify English grammar to cope with this social change. Unfortunately, most of these, including many modifications recommended by the American Psychological Association, lead to very cumbersome language. For this reason, with respect to the use of generic pronouns, I have chosen to retain standard English usage when the gender of the referrent is unknown. When the known gender is female, as is the case among three-forths of the student researchers whose work I have cited, I have used female pronouns as referrents.

Acknowledgments

Many individuals contributed to the publication of this book. I would like to thank professors Robert White, Don Brown, Ted Alper, and David Frey for the research discussions we had over the years. They stimulated my thinking and motivated my continued learning. Jerry Rose, Peter Chamberlain, and Paul Tumolo of the Cal State Hayward Computing Center gave me much of their time and advice toward the solution of computer problems. Dean Arthurlene Towner, my boss for two years, understood my need for writing time and thoughtfully provided it. Dr. Mary di Sibio and Martha Kentfield were most helpful as proofreaders and discussants, and Karen Wells provided valuable technical assistance in the reformatting and enhancing of the SPSS tables. Tessie Wenger and Bette DiSanti provided typing and encouragement.

And, finally, thanks to my family for persevering--my wife Carolyn who read every chapter and kept me going, my parents who constantly encouraged me, and my children, Jennifer and Holly, who one day may read the book and finally understand what Dad does at work. Lastly, I wish to thank Cal State University for the sabbatical year during which I wrote most of the book.

Thomas E. Whalen

Danville, California
March, 1989

TABLE OF CONTENTS

PART TWO: Ten Steps To Behavioral Research

PART THREE: Computers and Behavioral Research

PART FOUR: Different Methods of Behavioral Research

CHAPTER ONE

CHARACTERISTICS OF BEHAVIORAL RESEARCH

Before attempting a definition of behavioral research, it might be worthwhile to consider how research on human behavior fits into the larger scheme of research in general. What exactly is research, and what kinds of research are worthwhile for a graduate student to pursue? Does academic research have to be scientific? If so, what makes it that way? These are all questions faced by the student who must complete a thesis as part of an advanced degree. This chapter will focus on these and other important questions about behavioral research.

Most authorities on research methodology distinguish between research done in the physical vs. the social realm. This is really a distinction between the natural and the human sciences: physics, chemistry, and biology vs. psychology, sociology, and anthropology. This same distinction would apply to the practical derivatives of these disciplines: electronics (physics and chemistry) vs. education (psychology and sociology), for example. Of course, some research fields are not so clearly defined. Medical research contains aspects of both the physical and social sciences. The term "behavioral research" is an inclusive one which generally refers to investigations of human behavior in a variety of settings: the school, the workplace, and the research laboratory, to name a few. The term "behavioral" is not meant to designate a particular theory or school of thought such as the theory of behaviorism associated with J.B. Watson and B.F. Skinner in psychology.

Now, what about the scientific nature of behavioral research? If psychologists and anthropologists refer to themselves as social scientists, does that mean their research is scientific? Is all research in the natural sciences scientific? These questions may seem a bit ethereal, but they are important when it comes to gaining an understanding of where knowledge comes from and the level of confidence we place in it. They are also very important aspects of the current debate over what kind of research is most productive in applied settings such as education. This controversy will be explored in greater detail later.

In his book, *Foundations of Behavioral Research*, Kerlinger (1986) points out that it would not be easy to get scientists and researchers to agree on a definition of scientific research. Nevertheless, he presents the following one:

> Scientific research is systematic, controlled, empirical, and critical investigation of natural phenomena guided by theory and hypotheses about the

> presumed relations among such phenonema (Kerlinger, 1986, p. 10).

This definition seems to imply an underlying methodology used in conjunction with a previously accumulated body of knowledge (theory).

Another authority, Helmstadter (1970), stated that most philosophers of science define science in terms of its one universal and unique feature: method. Before discussing the method of science, however, it is worth considering other ways humans arrive at knowledge.

Some Non-Scientific Ways to Knowledge

Epistemology, a branch of philosophy, is the study of how we come to know things. Epistemologists have described a number of ways humans arrive at knowledge. Let us consider three of these: tenacity, intuition, and authority.

Tenacity

The term "tenacity" is used to designate that knowledge to which we hold tenaciously. It is knowledge we have always believed simply because we have always believed it. Sometimes this form of knowing is referred to as blind tradition. Others may think of it as superstition. Though most of us think we are above such beliefs, it is surprising to see the degree to which many intelligent individuals use the method of tenacity in their everyday lives.

There are two forms of tenacious knowledge: that which is passed on from one generation to the next, and individually discovered knowledge. The former is represented by the common superstitions and stereotypes--the number 13, black cats, women as gossips, etc. Individually discovered knowledge is quite common among sports persons--the lady who always wears pink socks on the day of an important golf match, the fisherman who always baits his hook in a particular, unusual way. B.F. Skinner is said to have induced such knowledge in a pigeon, which, just prior to being fed by the automatic device in its cage, stretched its neck. Later, when the pigeon was deprived of food, it began stretching its neck until it was fed. Thereafter, whenever it was hungry, the pigeon stretched its neck repeatedly until food arrived.

Intuition

The method of intuition has been touted recently by some psychologists and business executives as a useful and underused method for creative thinking. Intuition is the power of knowing immediately and without conscious reasoning that something is true. Undoubtedly, intuition can be a marvelous facility. But what if my intuition does not agree with yours? It was intuition that produced Aristotle's belief that heavy objects fall to earth faster than light ones. Galileo disproved that "fact" many centuries later by applying the scientific method. He conducted an experiment by dropping a 10-pound and a 1-pound weight from the top of the Leaning Tower of Pisa. A crowd of students, professors, and priests looked on as both weights struck the ground at the same time. Followers of Aristotle bitterly opposed Galileo's new theory, and he was forced to leave his post at the University of Pisa over the dispute. Ironically, Galileo himself was later sentenced to prison by the Inquisition for upholding the Copernican theory that the earth revolved around the sun rather than vice versa. A German contemporary of Galileo, Johannes Kepler, is thought to have used intuition to "discover" the eliptical rather than circular orbits of the planets around the sun. In this case his intuition turned out to be correct.

Thus, we can see that intuition can be a valuable tool. An important Christian belief is that every person has the capacity within himself to know best how to treat his fellow man. In other words, an individual knows intuitively the difference between right and wrong. This may be true. Our American forefathers seem to have thought so when they phrased the opening lines of the Declaration of Independence. Intuition may work very well with certain kinds of knowledge but less well with other kinds. For this reason, the fruits of one's intuition need to be checked and validated. As Helmstadter said, "No scientific statement ever begins with the words, 'We hold these truths to be self evident'" (Helmstadter, 1970, p. 9).

Authority

Knowledge based on authority is probably the most commonly used form of knowledge for most individuals. Much of our culture is built upon authoritarian knowledge. In fact, human civilizations could not exist without the method of authority. Much of our educational system is built upon the method of authority. Our religious lives are based upon authority. What you will learn from this textbook on how to conduct research is based more on authority than on the scientific method. Therefore, knowledge based on authority is good and proper, except when the authority is wrong. In the mid-1980's medical authorities advocated a high fiber, low fat diet to prevent heart disease and cancer. Marriage counselors have used methods of therapy based largely on the authority of prominent therapists. Some baseball managers routinely call for the sacrifice bunt because baseball experts say it's the best strategy. The "knowledge" in these examples is based on authority, at least to a considerable degree. It may be correct, but it too requires verification. In the case of the sacrifice bunt, there is already some evidence to the contrary (cf. Niel & Liebert, 1980, pp 7-9). Let us now explore a way of verifying knowledge based on tenacity, intuition, and authority.

The Method(s) of Science

Much has been written about the scientific method, and yet science is still a poorly understood concept. Kerlinger (1986) describes two views of science: the static and the dynamic. The static view, one held mainly by the lay public, is that science is an accumulation of facts and figures, a huge data bank of information. It is the scientist's job to know how to access this data bank and to add to it occasionally through his own research.

The dynamic view of science is one which emphasizes activity: what scientists do, the methods they employ to conduct their research. It is this aspect of science which distinguishes it from other fields such as engineering, teaching, and counseling. In these latter fields, a practitioner typically relies on current knowledge to "engineer" a solution to an applied problem. To the extent that the practitioner makes use of scientific knowledge relevant to his field, he is engaging in one aspect of scientific behavior. Notice that this kind of activity is not far different from going to the library to look up the latest information on a particular subject--a definition of research often subscribed to by the public, the static view.

But what is it that scientists do, the dynamic view? What methods do they use in their research? Not surprisingly, authorities do not completely agree about the procedures of science. But their descriptions are usually quite similar. John Dewey, the American philosopher and educator, listed four steps in the process of scientific inquiry. It should be noted that the ordering of these steps is not crucial. It should also be noted that the term "scientist" is not an exclusive one. As researchers we are all scientists to the degree we are willing to use the methods specified below.

1. Problem-Obstacle-Idea

The researcher is faced with an obstacle, an unknown relationship between phenonema, perhaps a vague sense of discomfort with someone else's theory of behavior. He responds to this emotional uncertainty by grappling with the concepts involved. In the end he is able to formulate a research question.

2. Hypothesis

After more thinking about the problem and his related research question, the researcher formulates a conjectural statement. "Under such-and-such conditions, if A takes place, then B will also be present."

3. Reasoning-Deduction

This step involves the application of a form of logical reasoning. Logical principles existed long before the practice of science, but the use of logic is so intertwined with science that most writers include it as an essential step. What this step implies is that the scientist must deduce a particular outcome from a more general theory. An example may clarify this point. Suppose I have read an article extolling the importance of mentors for women college students. The writer states that influential men can often trace their success back to a mentor, an older helper who showed them the ropes and guided them through the early difficult phases of their career. Based on this notion of the importance of a mentor, might it be that more women would enter college teaching as a career if they had a mentor during graduate school? Does having a mentor relate to higher academic achievement? If an experiment were set up in which certain students spent more office-hour time with certain professors, might this lead to greater motivation on the part of the students and thus greater achievement? Even without an experiment, do students who naturally seek out professors outside the classroom achieve higher grades than other students?

Notice how I have moved in my thinking from a general theory about mentors to a much more specific situation. Perhaps I have become too specific and moved too far away from the concept of a mentor. I may have to retrace my thinking and try again. But the idea is that I began with a rather broad, general problem and gradually reduced it in scope through a series of logical steps to a more specific and testable outcome.

4. Observation-Test-Experiment

This step represents the essence of science. It incorporates the empirical method, knowledge through experience (observation) with a carefully controlled test of the hypothesis. If a scientist believes something is true, he must observe the real world, collect data from his observations, and put his belief to a test. When Galileo simultaneously dropped a cannon ball and a musket ball from the Leaning Tower, he was checking his subjective belief against something apart from himself, objective reality. This was something Aristotle and his followers were unwilling to do.

Two points can be made about Galileo's test. First, it incorporated an experiment, albeit a primitive one by today's standards. Although the use of an experiment is considered by some authorities to be a necessary part of the scientific method, others disgree. According to Helmstadter (1970), "...the experimental approach...is the prototype of the scientific method, the ideal toward which we strive (but do not always achieve) in today's study of human behavior" (p.14). And Kerlinger (1986) stated, "Much valuable social scientific and educational research is preoccupied with the shorter-range goal of finding specific relations; that is, merely to discover a relation is part of science" (p. 10). The relationship between class size and student achievement is a modern educational example.

In Galileo's case, suppose he had been prevented from conducting his crucial test. Suppose he had been told he could not drop two weights simultaneuosly, only one at a time. Could he then have tested his hypothesis? The answer is yes, provided he knew about modern statistical analysis. By repeatedly dropping different size weights and measuring the elapsed times of their descents, and then by calculating the coefficient of correlation between object weight and descent time, Galileo would have arrived at the same conclusion. Actually, according to one account (Babbie, 1975), the results of Galileo's experiment were not one hundred per cent conclusive. The heavier object preceded the lighter one by the width of a few fingers.

The second observation about Galileo's test concerns this last point. What if, instead of a few fingers' width, the two objects had arrived on terra firma a few feet apart? At what point would the difference between them be wide enough to accept Aristotle's theory of falling bodies instead of Galileo's theory? Much of the rest of this book will deal with these two problems: how to conduct controlled research even when an experiment is not possible, and how to know when one's hypothesis has passed the test. If an inverse relation is discovered between class size and students' achievement, how strong must it be to be "significant"?

Before we leave the topic of scientific method, let us consider some other very important characteristics of scientific research.

Other Characteristics of Scientific Inquiry

Science is based on the assumption that all events have antecedent causes. Scientists don't pretend to know the specific causes of all events, but they assume that such causes exist and can be discovered. In one sense, science is a state of mind, a set of values which must be accepted. Accepting the scientific approach often requires a conscious decision.

> The scientific commitment also rests on a belief system that must be accepted on faith. This belief system assumes a reality consisting of objects and events anchored in a space-time continuum which relate to each other according to laws of cause and effect. It can be perceived correctly only by the waking, unintoxicated brain and is to be comprehended by the intellectual analysis of sensory data. According to

> this view, the ultimate test of the validity of any phenomenon is the ability to meet the criteria of scientific evidence, including replicability and the use of controls (Frank, 1977, as cited in Neale & Liebert, 1980, p. 10)

Generalization

Scientists are not the only human beings who believe that events have antecedent causes. But the way in which scientists study causality is somewhat different from the way non-scientists do. How does the method of science differ from other methods of determining causality? Babbie (1975) provides a distinction: An historian, or biographer, or clinical psychologist would generally use an idiographic process for discovering causality, a process of focusing on a single event or person and probing all aspects of that event or person to try to understand causality. For example, a psychotherapist would study the whole person in order to understand his neurotic behavior, whereas a research psychologist would examine neurotic behavior in many individuals in an effort to arrive at a general understanding of neuroticism. An historian might study the civil war in depth to determine its causes, while an historiographer would study many wars to try to establish the existence of a general pattern of characteristics that are common to wars in general. This latter technique is known as the nomothetic approach. The root word "nomo" comes from the Greek word for law. Thus, behavioral scientists are mostly interested in discovering general principles of human behavior which hold true for large populations of individuals.

Parsimony

Scientists attempt to gain the greatest amount of understanding from the smallest number of factors. The scientist works toward the development of theories which are explanatory, but which are relatively simple, elegant models of reality. Realistically, there is a trade-off between elegance and comprehensiveness. The scientist's quest for parsimony often places him at odds with the lay person who interprets the scientist's findings. For instance, if a researcher builds a theory of religious behavior which incorporates only age, sex, marital status, and social class, he might be attacked by a senior citizens' association because he has typecast their church-going behavior. Not all poor old widows go to church regularly, they might say. Religion is a much more personal thing than that. This is true, of course. But it does not negate the fact that these variables are strong predictors of church attendance in the general population.

People don't like to be typed, or grouped, or classified--things which a behavioral scientist must do in order to try to understand general patterns of behavior. What we sometimes forget is that all theories are probabilistic in terms of individuals. This is true in the physical sciences as well. For instance, in genetics the mating of a blue-eyed person with a brown-eyed person will probably result in a brown-eyed offspring, but not always.

The beauty of theories is that they provide normative data about phenomena, which allow the scientist to accurately predict, control, and understand behavior. Thus we can predict voting preferences, traffic fatalities, educational achievement, antisocial behavior, and many other human behaviors with great precision. The benefit of this knowledge is that it gives the individual a guidepost from which to judge his or others' behavior. It allows one to know when he is or is not being determined (predicted). It allows a student, or a teacher, or a therapist to strive beyond the group norm knowingly or to accept the group norm knowingly.

Determinism

According to Babbie (1980), the deterministic nature of the social sciences represents its most significant departure from humanistic examinations of social behavior. Determinism refers to the predictable aspect of human behavior. Taken to its extreme, the deterministic perspective suggests that individuals have no free will, that external (or internal) factors determine how an individual will behave. This philosophy was prominent in the early religious history of the United States. It was the doctrine of Predestination emphasized by the followers of John Calvin.

It is probably the deterministic stance of science which, more than anything else, accounts for the criticism of the scientific method as dehumanizing. This charge has been brought by some humanists who argue that scientists don't care enough about individuals, only about theories which predict their behavior.

Consider for a moment the logic of this argument. Both the nomothetic model used by researchers and the idiographic model used by humanists make the same assumption about causation. That is, the causes of human behavior are determined in some way by antecendent factors. People don't just behave randomly. There are reasons for the way people behave. Now, if there are reasons why some people are more religious than others, or more prejudiced than others, or why a person votes for candidate X rather than Y, how then is a careful listing of all the private, individual reasons for these behaviors any less deterministic than a partial list of a few variables which parsimoniously explains the behavior? If both methods are equally deterministic, then are they not equally humanistic?

Much of the controversy about the method of science among academicians in particular and people in general is probably deeply ingrained in the human psyche and will always exist. In the field of psychology, in particular, there will probably always be a schizm between the tough-minded and tender-minded psychologists. The Watsons, Thorndikes, and Skinners will continue their tradition, and the Fromms, Maslows, and Rogers will continue theirs. It is this writer's belief, however, that much can be gained by bringing these two traditions closer together so that the best characteristics of each can be melded together in an even more powerful model of inquiry. For a more detailed explication of this phenomenon, see Hitt's (1969) article, "Two Models of Man" (in Torrance, 1975). This same division in thinking has continued into the 1980's in the form of a debate between the traditionalists (behaviorists, positivists) vs. the relativists (phenomenoligists, humanists). This topic will be explored further in the next chapter.

CHAPTER TWO

TYPES OF RESEARCH

Behavioral research may be typed under many different classifications. However, contemporary research paradigms are generally classified in one of two broad categories: quantitative and qualitative types. Quantitative models are more traditional and emphasize numerical representation of variables, random sampling of research subjects, and statistical analysis of data. Qualitative models are historically more recent and emphasive the "naturalistic" methods of anthropology, where greater importance is placed on verbal description and interpretation of behavior. This chapter will begin with a section on the vocabulary of research, drawing on the taxonomic work of Helmstadter (1970). This section is followed by two sections describing traditional and naturalistic types of research. The chapter concludes by exploring the controversy between quantitative and qualitative types and recommends a course of action for student researchers.

The Vocabulary of Research

In his book, *Research Concepts in Human Behavior*, Helmstadter (1970) proposed a three-dimensional model called a taxonomy of research in the behavioral sciences. It is shown graphically in Figure 2.1. It was Helmstadter's belief that any study can be characterized if it is described with respect to the three dimensions: breadth of application, level of outcome, and degree of control. Although Helmstadter's model is probably too complex to serve as a working theory of research design, we can learn much about the language of research by studying its features. Let us see how various types of research fit into these three dimensions.

Breadth of Application

This dimension of the taxonomy refers to the extent to which a research outcome can be generalized. The first distinction along this dimension is between pure and applied research.

Pure research, also known as basic research, is often broadly generalizable. The researcher's motive is often simple curiosity. Some historical examples of pure research are Mendel's studies of genetic transmission, the pecking order of hens, and Pavlov's conditioned response. It is pure research which sometimes leads to striking discoveries of great importance.

Pure research is often difficult to finance because of its apparent lack of practical results. In 1975, U.S. Senator William Proxmire presented his "Golden Fleece" award to the National

FIGURE 2.1
A Taxonomy of Research in the Behavioral Sciences

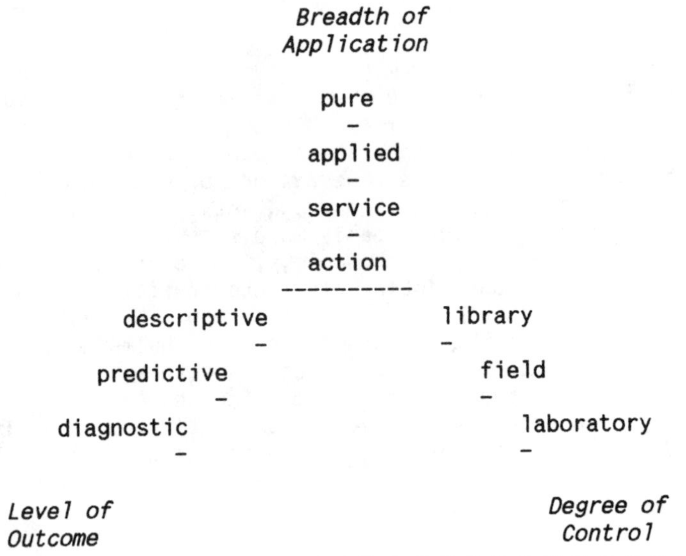

Breadth of Application

pure
-
applied
-
service
-
action

descriptive - predictive - diagnostic -

Level of Outcome

library - field - laboratory -

Degree of Control

Institute on Alcohol Abuse and Alcoholism for a series of studies it sponsored on the effects of alcohol on aggressive behavior in sunfish. Proxmire was fond of pointing out how NIAAA was testing what it means to be "stewed to the gills" or what is really meant by the expression "drinks like a fish." For several years during the 1970's the senator got much political mileage from criticizing such research.

Applied research, sometimes called developmental or product research, has as its motive the solution of a practical problem. Unlike the pure researcher, the applied researcher sets out to solve a specific problem. It is possible that someone looking for a cure for AIDS will find it. On the other hand, a cure may come as a serendipitous result of pure research on an apparently unrelated topic. Because of the high cost of much research, there appears to be a trend away from pure research and toward applied research. Even in the universities, because of the greater availability of funds from outside agencies for specified research, there is movement toward applied research. It should be noted that the distinction between pure and applied research is not always clearcut, and some authorities make no such distinction.

Service research is really a form of applied research in which the initiation of the research is not from the researcher himself, but rather comes from some administrator or practitioner who wants a study done to solve a problem with which he is faced. The motive here is to provide service to someone, usually for profit or recognition. This is not to say that profit and recognition are absent from pure and applied research. But in service research, they are often a stronger source of motivation. An example of service research is program evaluation in education and mental health wherein an outside firm or individual is contracted to evaluate the merits of a funded program. The generalizability of such research is often restricted to a few locations similar to the one in which the evaluation takes place.

Action research is sometimes held in low esteem by scientific purists because of its lack of generalizability. The term action research is used to refer to efforts to bring about in-shop improvement of onsite workers. In this sense, it is similar to a type of program evaluation in which the evaluation is done by the staff of the project rather than by an external agent. The emphasis is on how to make a specific process work better. Action research produces results which are the least generalizable of all because it applies strictly to the local setting.

Level of Outcome

Another way of viewing research is in terms of its level of outcome. This dimension refers to the extent to which causality is a factor in the outcome.

Descriptive research is research which attempts to answer the question: What is the status of X?. Some examples of descriptive research are the status of adult literacy in the U.S., the status of racial integration in Mississippi schools, the incidence of child abuse in San Francisco families. In all of these examples, the emphasis is on determining the existence of a phenomenon and its degree of severity. No attempt is made to discover why the condition exists or how one might predict its occurrence.

Predictive research is that which attempts to investigate a relationship between factors. If it is known, for example, that hyperactivity in young children is related to the socio-economic status (SES) of parents, then school officials, based on their knowledge of SES patterns, can make staffing adjustments to deal with this problem. Notice that predictive research does not necessarily seek the "cause" of a behavior, only a correlate of it. Also, predictive research is not always involved in predicting the future. The relationship between variables discovered through predictive research may or may not be future oriented.

Diagnostic research is an elaborate form of prediction. Its purpose is to explore not only relationships between variables, but cause-and-effect relationships. Some years ago, a relationship was discovered between first grade reading ability and a child's knowledge of the alphabet on entering kindergarten (predictive research). A researcher conducted an experiment in which some children who did not know the alphabet were taught it prior to entering kindergarten. He later compared their first grade reading ability to a comparison group of children who had not been taught the alphabet. He was searching for a possible cause of reading disability in first graders. Unfortunately, his hypothesis was not supported. The causes of reading disability appear to be more complicated than just not knowing the alphabet prior to kindergarten. Nevertheless, this study is an example of diagnostic research. Note that if the researcher's hypothesis had been borne out, then a remedy could have been prescribed: learning the alphabet. This is analogous to a medical diagnosis followed by a prescription to "remediate" a disease. The physician's prescription implies an underlying knowledge of what causes the disease and therefore what remedy may shorten its existence.

Degree of Control

The "degree of control" dimension concerns the degree to which a researcher is able to manipulate the treatment variable(s) in his study. It also pertains to his ability to control (minimize) the effects of extraneous variables.

Library research, which most authorities would not classify as scientific, has the least degree of control. In this type of research, the investigator simply combs the archives in search of information relevant to his topic. The extent to which he includes all sides of an issue is partly a function of the library he uses and also his own willingness to conduct an exhaustive search. This type of research is often conducted in conjuction with a more scientific type. In recent years, a technique called meta analysis has been developed which provides for a quantitative analysis of archival research and allows the investigator to conduct a more controlled, statistical analysis of past research (cf. Glass & McGraw, 1981).

Field research is that which takes place outside the artificial environment of the laboratory, in the natural setting of the behavior under investigation. Much research in education and social psychology is conducted in the field. In terms of control, the researcher is able to select the time and place of observations, but often is not able to manipulate variables. He must await the natural occurrence of such variables as positive reinforcement, punishment, or crowding--whatever his variables of interest may be.

Laboratory research generally allows the highest degree of control. In psychology, the famous animal studies of Pavlov and

Skinner fit into this category. But, of course, many laboratory investigations involve human beings as well.

Traditional Models of Research

Campbell and Stanley's Paradigm

One of the most seminal and influential publications on research methodology in the last generation is *Experimental and Quasi-Experimental Designs for Research* (Campbell & Stanley, 1968). This monograph, first published as a chapter in the *Handbook of Research on Teaching (1963)*, distinguishes between three types of research. Figure 2.2 shows the characteristics of this model. The three research types are juxtaposed with three levels of research control.

Experimental research, similar to Helmstadter's laboratory research, has the greatest control. The researcher is able to assign subjects at random to experimental groups. He is able to randomly assign groups to treatment conditions. And, the researcher has full control over the manipulation of the treatment. If one is studying the effects of crowding on mental tasks, for example, one has the power to set up different degrees of crowding by placing more or fewer people in a room and then measuring the mental performance of subjects (Freedman et al., 1971 as cited by Cozby, 1985, p. 16).

Although experimental research need not take place in a laboratory, in Campbell and Stanley's view many so-called field experiments do not meet the criteria for a true experiment. They are thus *quasi-experiments*. This type of research has some but not all of the features of the true experiment. The quasi-experiment usually occurs in a natural setting. School-based research often fits this category. The researcher must use intact groups of children. They have already been assigned to their classrooms. Sometimes the researcher is able to select a classroom at random to invoke a special treatment, but more often he may have to accept a volunteered classroom. Once he has one or more classrooms the researcher may conduct his experiment as usual. These research conditions are among the most common in education and counseling settings where individuals often choose for themselves which class they will enroll in or which counselor they will seek for help. Special care must be taken in such investigations to avoid confounding the treatment with other extraneous variables. Much of Campbell and Stanley's monograph deals with this problem.

A third type of research is *ex post facto*, "after the fact." With this type, the researcher enters the scene after the treatment has had its effect. Suppose a researcher is interested

FIGURE 2.2
Types of Research and Differences Among Them

Important Characteristics	*Experi- mental*	*Quasi- Experimental*	*Ex Post Facto*
1. Ability to assign Ss to groups	Yes	No	No
2. Ability to assign groups to treatments	Yes	Maybe	No
3. Ability to manipulate treatment	Yes	Yes	No

in the value of a college education. He locates a number of college graduates and measures their success using the criteria of his choice. He then compares these subjects with a comparable number of non-college graduates and draws his conclusions. Note that the researcher has no control over any important factors here. He cannot assign subjects to go to college, the treatment. Nor does he have any control over the kind of treatment a subject got--which college he attended or what he majored and minored in, etc. While *ex post facto* research frequently draws negative criticism from scientific purists, researchers often have no alternative with human subjects. Consider, for example, the host of respectable medical studies on the effects of smoking on cancer and heart disease. With the exception of animal experiments, which are extremely important, all of these studies are *ex post facto*. It is simply not possible to assign human subjects at random to smoking and non-smoking experimental groups. Fortunately, there are now some very powerful statistical procedures which help minimize the confounding effects of extraneous variables and therefore make *ex post facto* research a worthwhile endeavor. We will explore these procedures in later chapters.

Lehman and Mehrens' Classification

The original classification of research by Lehman and Mehrens contained five types: historical, descriptive, correlational, causal-comparative, and experimental. The present delineation contains the final four types of research: descriptive, correlational, causal-comparative, and experimental. Historical research, while of value, is infrequent in behavioral investigations and has been omitted here. The Lehman and Mehrens

4-type model has the potential of incorporating most of the research types previously discussed in this chapter.

Descriptive Research. You will recall that descriptive research is one of the research types in Helmstadter's taxonomy. Lehman and Mehren's concept of descriptive research is similar to Helmstadter's: it is concerned with determining the nature and degree of existing conditions. Lehman and Mehrens point out that many studies cannot easily be classified under only one heading. A single investigation may describe two or more groups of subjects and may even explore relationships between variables, but if its primary purpose is to describe existing conditions, then it should be classified as descriptive.

Lehman and Mehrens (1971) listed four sub-types of research under the descriptive category. These include the *case study*, where an extensive study is made of a few individuals, or a *survey* approach, where many individuals are sampled. These authors also distinguished between *longitudinal* and *cross-sectional* description. In longitudinal research, data are gathered on the same subjects at different points in time. Child growth studies are often longitudinal. In cross-sectional research, data are gathered at one point in time but from different subgroups. These might be different grade levels in educational research.

Correlational Research. Lehman and Mehrens define correlational research as that which is concerned with discovering and/or measuring the degree of relationship between two or more variables. Such research is often conducted for the purpose of making predictions. The general term "correlational", then, would include most varieties of predictive and field research and some evaluation research.

It is helpful to recall that one of the goals of science is the prediction of behavior. The reason prediction is useful is that it helps us to make correct decisions. The more accurate our predictions are, the better are our decisions. Counselors, for example, make predictions about behavior when they recommend that students attend certain colleges or enroll in particular programs. Such predictions are based on relationships discovered in past research. Correlational studies can also be very useful as exploratory investigations which prepare the way for more precise experimentation. To the extent that variables can be eliminated from further consideration in correlational research, this is a useful step in the scientific approach.

Causal-Comparative Research. Causal-comparative research as defined by Lehman and Mehrens is really the same as Campbell and Stanley's *ex post facto* research. This writer prefers the term "causal-comparative" because it connotes a search for causal relationships and also implies a comparison of two or more groups.

Lehman and Mehrens correctly point out that causal comparative research has characteristics of descriptive, correlational, and experimental research. It is a kind of hybrid type that both describes and seeks causal relationships. Unlike experimental research, however, causal-comparative research cannot "prove" cause-and-effect relationships.

Recall that *ex post facto* research was defined as that in which the "treatment" has already occurred, and where the researcher has no control over the assignment of groups or subjects to receive the treatment. The major difference between causal comparative and experimental studies is that in the former the researcher begins with two or more groups of subjects, one in which the variable of interest is present, the other(s) in which it is absent or partially present. The variable of interest can be either an hypothesized cause (treatment) such as social class, divorce, traumatic brain damage, or drug use; or it can be a presumed effect such as delinquent behavior, scholastic success, lung cancer, or mental illness. In either case the researcher makes a comparison between the groups to determine how they differ. If significant differences are discovered among other variables, these other variables become possible explanations for the cause-effect linkage.

While some authorities would call causal-comparative research just another form of correlational research (cf. Cozby, 1985), I believe the distinction between them is quite useful. Research questions posed as relationships typically lead to the use of correlational statistics; whereas, research questions posed as differences between groups often lead to the use of some form of analysis of variance. Though a researcher is not really constrained to this statistical dichotomy, there is a pedagogical advantage in emphasizing the distinction, at least until the student reaches a more advanced level. These ideas will become much clearer in following chapters after detailed examples are given.

Experimental Research. Experimental research includes all types--pure, applied, laboratory, and diagnostic--in which the researcher is able to manipulate the treatment variable. In Lehman and Mehrens' model there is no distinction between experimental and quasi-experimental research. These authors are aware of the advantage of random assignment of subjects to groups but do not consider it to be an essential attribute of experimental research. They are also aware that the experimental method is the *sine qua non* for establishing cause-and-effect relationships, but that it is not a panacea. One might wonder why more experimental research is not conducted in the behavioral sciences. Indeed, correlational and causal comparative studies surely outnumber experimental studies in the published literature.

The reason is that experimental research is often more time-consuming, expensive, and difficult to conduct. It also may lack realism if conducted in a laboratory rather than in a natural setting. Despite these shortcomings, the student is encouraged to be creative in the pursuit of this method. Is is sometimes possible to "elevate" a correlational study to an experimental one with a little extra critical thinking and planning.

Naturalistic Models of Research

Thus far we have been looking at what have come to be called traditional or conventional types of research. The Tesch (1978) and Erickson (1986) models which follow are examples of more recent thinking about research in the behavioral sciences. They are reactions against what their proponents consider to be restrictions and limitations of traditional, scientific research. These newer models are known by a variety of names such as naturalistic, ethnographic, and anthropological. Naturalistic research, as opposed to conventional research, relies heavily on the methods of anthropologists and other social scientists who use an *ethnographic approach* where the researcher becomes an active participant in the research environment. Naturalistic research is more impressionistic than traditional research. Much less emphasis is placed on the testing of preconceived hypotheses. Primary emphasis is given to an accurate description of the meaning which research subjects attach to concepts (variables) of the investigation.

The Tesch Model

According to Tesch (1980), naturalistic research is not a rejection of conventional approaches, but a broadening of our repertoire. It is neither better, nor more valid, nor more ethical; it is merely different. Furthermore, it is not more "human" or more "natural." Nor is it easier or more fun. If anything, it is probably more difficult. The Tesch Model emphasizes two types of research, phenomenological and transformative. These are placed in the context of other types of research in Figure 2.3. Both phenomenological and transformative research are placed in the context of conventional types using standard research vocabulary. Tesch characterizes phenomenological research as basic and predictive, while transformative research is applied and evaluative. Figure 2.3 also adds a third type called "hermeneutic" research, a more theoretical type often used by biblical scholars to interpret historical texts.

Phenomenological research can be traced to the philosophical school that grew out of the thinking of Edmund Husserl around the turn of the century. The purpose of such research is exploratory,

FIGURE 2.3 *
The Tesch Model

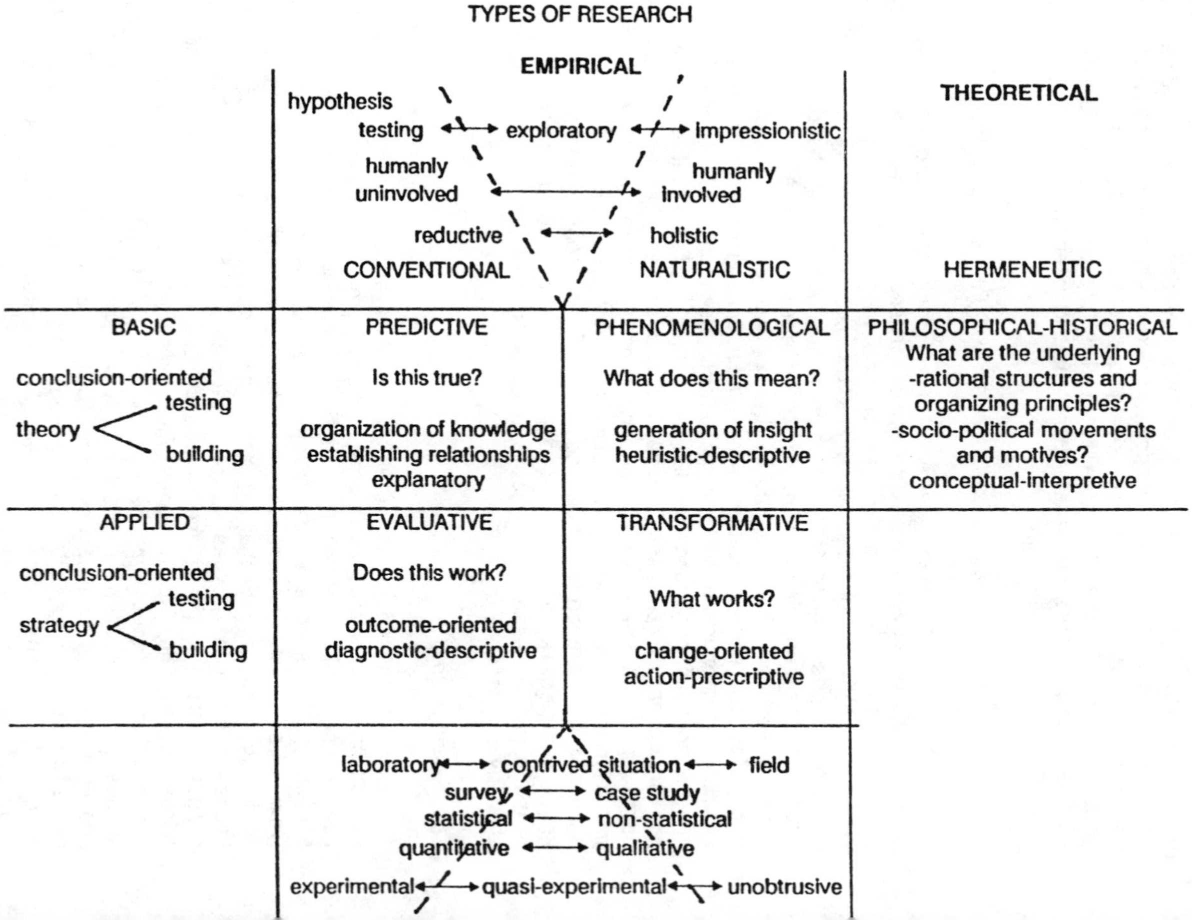

TYPES OF RESEARCH

	EMPIRICAL		THEORETICAL
	hypothesis testing ⟷ exploratory ⟷ impressionistic humanly uninvolved ⟷ humanly involved reductive ⟷ holistic		
	CONVENTIONAL	NATURALISTIC	HERMENEUTIC
BASIC conclusion-oriented theory testing / theory building	PREDICTIVE Is this true? organization of knowledge establishing relationships explanatory	PHENOMENOLOGICAL What does this mean? generation of insight heuristic-descriptive	PHILOSOPHICAL-HISTORICAL What are the underlying -rational structures and organizing principles? -socio-political movements and motives? conceptual-interpretive
APPLIED conclusion-oriented strategy testing / strategy building	EVALUATIVE Does this work? outcome-oriented diagnostic-descriptive	TRANSFORMATIVE What works? change-oriented action-prescriptive	
	laboratory ⟷ contrived situation ⟷ field survey ⟷ case study statistical ⟷ non-statistical quantitative ⟷ qualitative experimental ⟷ quasi-experimental ⟷ unobtrusive		

* reprinted by permission of the author

and the procedure is descriptive. The method is decribed as holistic--not towards maintaining control, but towards the inclusion of all relevant data. The important thing is the experience of the people being studied, more specifically, their own interpretation of the phenomenon and the meaning they subjectively attach to it. The researcher attempts to enter the research setting without presuppositions and strives for insight through the discovery of meaning. Some possible questions for investigation through phenomenological research are: What does having an abortion mean to teenage girls? What does it mean to be an abused child?

Transformative research is defined by Tesch (1980) as a systematic inquiry and action process which aims at positive change in the human condition. The research objective is to evaluate possible procedures which have been devised or will be devised to alleviate an unsatisfactory human condition. The method is not unlike process evaluation; it is an ongoing process during which changes are implemented until they result in the achievement of predetermined objectives. The central question of transformative research is, "What works?" Typical research topics are: How can we best treat children of abusive parents? What is the best way to prevent high school students from dropping out of school?

Erickson's Interpretive Approach

In his recent chapter, "Qualitative Research on Teaching" (in Wittrock, 1986), Erickson attempted to pull together the methodologies of several types of research under the unified title of qualitative (as opposed to quantitative) research. These types are variously referred to by Erickson as ethnographic, qualitative, participant observational, case study, symbolic interactionist, phenomenological, constructivist, and interpretive. Erickson decided to use the term *interpretive research* to refer to the whole family of approaches to participant observational research. While there are similarities between Erickson and Tesch, Erickson is less willing to accommodate and coexist with what he refers to as the positivist/behaviorist point of view, the more traditional scientific approach.

According to Erickson, the theoretical conceptions that define the phenomena of interest in interpretve research on teaching are very different from the earlier mainstream approaches. This statement pertains as well to other topics of research beyond education.

While Erickson's model is indeed interpretive, it is at the same time heavily empirical. One should not conclude that Erickson does not advocate collecting data. Indeed, the voluminous data collected using his approach are often difficult to easily summarize. He advocates a very "labor intensive" approach to research, one in which the researcher spends every day in the field, carefully observing and interacting with the participants. The use of field notes is essential, and they should be given as much time in review as it takes to write them. Video-taping is another common feature of qualitative research. From an economic point of view, this type of research is very expensive.

Erickson's brand of qualitative research has one important characteristic in common with the previously described phenomenological research. The goal is to determine the meaning of events as held by the subjects of the investigation. Erickson believes that the points of view of research subjects, what he calls their "meaning perspectives," are often overlooked in conventional research. He gives three reasons for this: First, the subjects are often relatively powerless members of society, such as teachers and students (his examples). Secondly, the meaning perspectives are often held outside conscious awareness and thus are not explicitly articulated. A third reason is that from a positivist point of view, the subjects' perspectives are regarded as irrelevant, part of the subjectivity that must be eliminated for "objective" inquiry to be done. An important feature of interpretive research, according to Erickson, is its ability to reveal the unexpected. This is accomplished by delaying theorizing until the researcher better understands his subjects.

The Quantitative-Qualitative Debate

At the risk of oversimplifying a complex controversy, one might conclude that the current tension between advocates of quantitiative and qualitative research is another manifestation of the earlier friction between behaviorists (positivists) and humanists (relativists) described in Chapter I. For many years there have been strong philosophical differences between the so-called positivists and relativists. What is the source of these differences and how do they impinge on research methodology?

According to Smith and Heshusius (1986), the quantitative approach has a realist orientation. It is based on the idea of an independently existing reality that can be described as it really is. Truth is defined as a correspondence between our words and that independently existing reality. Facts can be separate from values and beliefs.

Putman (1981), in tracing the history of interpretive philosophy, had this to say about the relativist approach to research:

> The interpretive tradition, based on an idealist temperament, took the position that social reality was mind-dependent in the sense of mind-constructed. Truth was ultimately a matter of socially and historically conditioned agreement. Social inquiry could not be value-free, and there could not be a "God's Eye" point of view--there could only be various people's points of view based on their particular interests, values, and purposes (Putnam, 1981, cited in Smith and Heshusius, 1986, p. 5).

Relativists tend to believe that "truth" is culturally specific. There is no absolute truth apart from the meaning perspectives of individuals within social groups. This is Erickson's philosophy of interpretive research. This "new" philosophy has not gone unchallenged by the positivists. Donmoyer (1986) has questioned the validity attributed by relativists to research subjects' meaning-perspectives. In his view there is no reason to believe that an insider's view of a phenomenon is necessarily more valid than an outsider's view:

> For example, a group of male teachers may indicate to a researcher, and may actually believe, that they entered the teaching profession because they sought creative, socially meaningful work. A group of sociologists, however, might observe that virtually all of the males interviewed were the first generation in their families to graduate from college and might indicate that a simililar pattern has been uncovered in other studies of male teachers. The sociologists might then interpret the subject's choice of professions in terms of social mobility. There is no reason (nor is it likely that further data collection could provide a reason) to believe that the subjects' interpretation of their own action is any better (i.e., any more valid) than the sociologists' interpretation (Donmoyer, 1985, p. 17).

Donmoyer's criticism applies in a situation where the researcher and the subjects of his investigation have different meaning-perspectives. But what about the situation described by Erickson previously, in which the meaning held by the subjects is outside their conscious awareness and not articulated? Positivists would argue that the researcher cannot achieve insight into such meaning without imposing his own view. Furthermore, if the subjects already have a precise meaning, how does the researcher consolidate and summarize all of their somewhat different phenomenological perspectives? Which subjects' perspectives should be given the most weight? Whose are the most representative, the most reliable and valid views?

The crucial distinction about one's underlying concept of reality is the difference which prompts some researchers on both sides to believe that positivists and relativists have incompatible philosophies. However, there is reason to believe that both schools of thought offer valuable ideas and procedures for contemporary behavioral research. Although this book will utilize the traditional research model of Lehman and Mehrens and indeed emphasize a quantitative approach to research, the author encourages students to make liberal use of qualitative data to enrich the sometimes dry residue of statistical analysis. After all, we are conducting research on people. As researchers, we should aspire to a high level of communication about the persons we study, using both verbal and quantitative data to our advantage.

This chapter has presented a number of different types of behavioral research in order to acquaint the reader with the many varieties of research in education and psychology. While it may be possible to conduct research without knowing much about its organization and philosophy, the graduate student who knows how his own research fits into this larger framework will almost certainly make a stronger contribution to the field. The following chapters will link the theoretical knowledge of this chapter to a series of practical steps in conducting research.

CHAPTER THREE

THE PRELIMINARY STEPS

The next three chapters will present a series of important steps in the research process. The intent is to provide an overview and conceptual framework for the more technical chapters which follow. Although this chapter will cover only the first five steps, a synopsis of all ten steps is presented below to give the reader an immediate grasp of the total research process. In keeping with the purpose of this book, the research examples used are based on actual studies conducted by graduate students.

The Ten Research Steps

1. Pose a research question.
2. Define vague terms in the research question.
3. Determine the type of research being conducted.
4. Determine how to measure the variables.
5. Classify the variables according to how they are measured.
6. State the hypothesis or hypotheses.
7. Determine the need for a control group.
8. Determine appropriate statistical procedures for testing the hypotheses.
9. Collect the data.
10. Analyze the data and draw conclusions.

The Definitional Steps: Steps 1-3

Step 1: Pose a research question.

Examples:

A. What are my students like?
B. Is a knowledge of grammar related to writing ability?
C. Why do some students become better counselors than others?
D. Do weekly quizzes promote greater learning?

Each of the questions above was personally relevant to me at some point in my teaching career. Question A, *What are my students like?*, is one all teachers have some interest in. When I first started teaching graduate students, I attempted to answer this question by gathering demographic data from my students. This descriptive process coupled later with a theoretical model of personality led to a revealing analysis of the student dropout phenomenon in graduate school. It is important to note that research questions should be formulated, whenever possible, in the context of behavioral theory. It is through the rigorous testing of theories that greater progress in behavioral research and its applied fields will be made.

The second question, *Is a knowledge of grammar related to writing ability?*, was of special interest to me earlier in my career when I was teaching high school English. I decided to test the pedagogical theory that facility in grammatical analysis (sentence diagramming) produces more effective written communication (student essays). This research became the basis of my own master's thesis.

Question C, "Why do some students become better counselors than others?", was of interest to me and my colleagues in the Department of Educational Psychology at California State University, Hayward. We urged students to explore this question in the context of theories of personality and vocational interest.

The last question, "Do weekly quizzes promote greater learning?", was proposed to me in a rather militant way by some of my students in my first year of graduate teaching. I was fresh out of a Ph.D. program at the time and filled with the then-current theories of learning. One theoretical principle which I incorporated into my teaching was frequent assessment of student progress. My students, many of whom were older than I at the time, objected. They challenged my practice of weekly quizzes, claiming it was not suitable for adult instruction and demeaning to them. I resisted their militancy for a while but finally agreed to put their challenge to a test.

Step 2: Define vague terms in the research question.

Having posed a research question, one is often perplexed by the vagueness of human thought and language. When we ask, "What are my students like?", what do we mean by "like"? Obviously we have something in mind by the term. But what exactly? After some thinking, I decided I was interested in knowing where my students had received their undergraduate degrees, what they majored in, their ages, gender, race, marital status, work status, primary financial support, and place of residence.

Question B above sought the relationship between a knowledge of grammar and writing ability. What is meant by "a knowledge of grammar?" What do we mean by "writing ability?" I decided to settle on a definition of grammar based on a syntactical theory of language usage. I defined writing ability very simply as technical correctness. Although one might quibble with my exclusion of the rhetorical or creative aspects of writing, I had an important reason for focusing on correctness of expression. This will become clearer in the next section on measurement.

For Question C, *Why do some students become better counselors than others?* , the word "why" is obviously quite vague. There are innumerable variables that could be included for investigation here. Which one(s) are we most interested in? How about personality? What personality characteristics do good counselors have? While there is still some vagueness in the term "personality", we have made progress toward greater specificity.

For Question D, "Do weekly quizzes promote greater learning?", the definition of "learning" was crucial. It was decided that learning should be defined in the traditional way--how well students performed on the final exam at the end of the course.

Step 3: Determine the type of research being conducted.

The discerning reader may have noticed that the four research questions presented at the beginning of the chapter represent each of the categories of Lehmann and Mehren's classification system described in the previous chapter. Questions A through D above represent in order the four categories: descriptive, correlational, causal-comparative, and experimental. Recall that descriptive research asks the question, "What is the status of X?" Thus, if one asks, "What are my students like?", one is asking a status question: What is the status of my students?

Question B, "Is a knowledge of grammar related to writing ability?", is clearly correlational. Note the phrase "related to" in the actual question. Now, one might ask whether this question ought to be correlational. That is, is correlational research the most appropriate type to answer the research question? If our interest is mainly in exploring the relationship between grammar and writing ability, then correlational research is quite appropriate. But, what if we're really interested in determining if knowledge of grammar causes better writing? Experimental research would be more appropriate to answer that question.

It is not immediately obvious from the wording of Question C just what type of research might be involved: "Why do some students become better counselors than others?" It should be clear that in order to answer this question, the researcher must do more than simply describe good counselors. The phrase, "better counselors than others," calls for a comparison of some kind. Who should be compared? How about a group of good counselors versus a group of not-so-good counselors. When we make such a comparison, and if we find some variables on which the two groups differ, we are then in a better position to answer the basic question of causal-comparative research: What are some possible causes of X?

Does X cause Y? This is the question posed by experimental research. Do weekly quizzes promote greater learning?

Experimental research does indeed seem the most appropriate type for this research question. Note, however, that this question could be investigated using a different method. If we could find and compare several classes in which weekly quizzes were used vs. classes which did not have quizzes, we might also be able to answer the question. We would now be in the causal-comparative mode. In another variation, if we could find several classes in which quizzes were used at varying time intervals--once a week, twice a week, once a month, twice a month--we could then correlate the frequency of quizzes with student achievement. We would then be conducting correlational research. The reader should contemplate these various designs of research. While experimental research is not always possible or necessary, you should understand that it is the most appropriate in this case.

Measurement Considerations: Steps 4-5

Step 4: Determine how to measure the variables.

While we made some progress toward accurate measurement by reducing the vagueness in our research questions above, further precision is necessary. We must develop what is called an "operational definition" for each variable. Kerlinger (1986) has this to say about the operational definition:

> An *operational definition* assigns meaning to a construct or variable by specifying the activities or "operations" necessary to measure it. Alternatively, an operational definition is a sort of manual of instructions to the investigator. It says, in effect, "Do such-and-such in so-and-so manner." In short, it defines or gives meaning to a variable by spelling out what the investigator must do to measure it (Kerlinger, 1986, p. 28).

The present research questions contain many variables which need operational definitions. Question A, which asks about the status of students, has such variables as race and marital status. While these seem like simple variables, how should they be measured? How many races are there? What is the difference between race and ethnic group membership? Should we ask a student his race directly with a fill-in response, or should we provide him with a set of categories to choose from? In the actual study the researchers settled on five categories: Asian, Black, Chicano, Other Minority, and White. The student respondent was asked to place himself in one of these five categories. It is possible that the researchers offended a native American or a Polynesian by not having a category specifically for them, but they chose to assume that risk in favor of a shorter set of categories.

What about marital status? Again, this seems to be a rather simple variable. How many categories of marital status can there be? In 1975, it seemed reasonable to include five: single, married, divorced, separated, and widowed. A decade later it might be important to include the additional category, living together, or cohabitiation, as it is more politely called. One might also want to differentiate between hetero- and homosexual cohabitation.

In addition to such categorical variables, there are variables which require a different sort of measurement. How does one measure a counselor's effectiveness or a student's knowledge of grammar? These are much more difficult measurement questions. They deal with the concepts of reliability and validity. While measurement is extremely important to research, it is a subject about which separate books are written and additional courses are taught. The student is strongly urged to take a course in tests and measurement or appraisal procedures, whatever the title may be, if he or she has not already done so.

Fortunately for researchers, the thorny problems of reliability and validity are not quite so crucial for groups as they are for individuals. That is, when a researcher measures an ability or trait in large numbers of individuals and then averages the result, this average will be much more reliable than a single individual's score. Since most research involves groups of twenty to thirty or more individuals, we can be pretty confident of our results even though our measurement tools may not be perfect. For a discussion of this and many other important measurement issues, see, for example, the book by Weiner and Stewart (1984), *Assessing Individuals: Psychological and Educational Tests and Measurement.*

Returning to our present example, how can we measure counselor effectiveness? The researcher (Calcagno, 1975) decided to use expert opinion. She first conducted a survey of eighteen counseling faculty members to get their opinions as to what they felt were the most important characteristics for an individual to possess in order to be an effective counselor. Each faculty member was sent a list of 28 counselor characteristics compiled from a survey of research studies dealing with characteristics of effective counselors. From this list, each professor was asked to pick out the five most and five least important characteristics for counselor success. In addition, each faculty member was asked to rank order the group he had selected by giving the most important characteristic a value of +5, the second most important a value of +4 and so on to +1. In addition, other characteristics not included on the list were solicited. A total of 14 completed lists were received from the faculty. These data were summarized by adding all ratings for each particular characteristic. The 28 characteristics were then rank ordered again in order of their cumulative ratings. The top five rated characteristics were

FIGURE 3.1
Counselor Characteristics Ratings

Dr. --------------

Directions:

Please rate the student listed below on the following scale. A rating of "outstanding" is the highest and is given a value of 4, and so on with "fair" the lowest rating receiving a value of 1. Please circle the appropriate rating for each of the five characteristics.

Student	I.D. No.	Out-standing	Excellent	Good	Fair
	Self-awareness	4	3	2	1
	Empathy	4	3	2	1
	Tolerance of ambiguity	4	3	2	1
	Ability to listen	4	3	2	1
	Self-confidence	4	3	2	1

self-awareness, empathy, tolerance of ambiguity, ability to listen, and self-confidence. These characteristics then became the criteria for counselor effectiveness in the study. They were each placed on a 4-point scale from "outstanding" to "fair" and the faculty were asked to rate their students. Though this measurement procedure is more involved than most, its end product shown in Figure 3.1 is certainly quite simple and straightforward.

Another construct that has been the subject of many research studies since the turn of the century is grammatical knowledge. As I delved into this topic as a young teacher, I began to realize that many others had posed the same question as I about the relationship between grammar and writing ability. This is an exhilarating, yet perplexing, reaction in conducting research. It is reassuring to know that one is not alone in the quest for truth. But it is equally disconcerting to know that others have thought your thoughts and may have already found the answer to your question. The purpose of library research is to determine this before you waste your time reinventing the wheel.

Despite the fact that many previous investigators had looked into the relationship between grammar and writing, and had for the most part concluded there was a weak relationship between the two, I decided, with the concurrence of my advisor, that various design flaws in the previous research made a new study of value. One of the major problems with past research was in the measurement of both grammatical knowledge and writing ability. I will not attempt to recount all the details here. Suffice to say that many previous studies failed to use objective measures of either variable.

In order to create a more objective and reliable measure of grammatical knowledge, I took the course of many researchers. I decided to compromise somewhat on my definition of grammar and use a standardized test of English. I chose the California Language Test, Junior High Level. This test contained two sections: (1) Mechanics of English, including capitalization, punctuation, and word usage, and (2) Spelling. It was my judgment that the word usage section of the test came closest to my concept of grammar, but I had to acknowledge that the entire test measured the important components of the junior high curriculum. Thus, for the sake of definitional clarity and potentially greater reliability of measurement, I opted for the standardized test. This is a common decision and one that you should consider in your own research. There is a lot to be said for using standard tools of measurement which have already undergone rigorous development and refinement. One of the biggest problems in behavioral research is the disparity between operational definitions of different researchers who are presumably studying the same variables.

Step 5: Classify variables according to how measured.

Measurement is defined as the assignment of numerals to attributes of objects, events, or persons according to certain rules (Shavelson, 1981). The attributes referred to here are what we call variables. A variable is simply an attribute which can take on different values. Thus, measurement in behavioral research involves the quantification of attributes. Such variables as race, marital status, counseling effectiveness, and knowledge of grammar can be measured in the sense that numerals can be assigned to different categories or levels of these attributes. When we assign numbers to attributes, we create a measurement scale. In behavioral research there are four kinds of measurement scales we must be aware of. These are the nominal, ordinal, interval, and ratio scales.

Nominal Scale The word nominal is derived from the root word meaning *name*. Nominal variables, those which are quantified according to the rules for nominal scales, are also referred to as categorical variables. They are variables such as race and marital status which have discrete categories of membership. Previously, we defined marital status as having five categories: (1) single, (2) married, (3) divorced, (4) separated, and (5) widowed. Notice that this time we also assigned numerals to the discrete categories. Thus a 5-point nominal scale of measurement has been created. It is important to understand that this "numerical" scale has no numerical meaning in the usual sense of that term. That is, the numbers I have assigned to the various categories of marital status do not signify a greater or lesser status to particular categories. Widowed individuals, who received a value of 5, are not greater than or better than single individuals who recieved a value of 1. The numerals used with nominal scales are simply convenient symbols which mean that Category A does not equal Category B does not equal Category C, etc. Notice here that letters of the alphabet have been used to name the categories rather than numbers, a common practice on multiple choice tests. It is partly because of computers that we use numbers to create nominal scales of measurement. Most computer programs have been designed to process numerical rather than alphabetic data.

The important thing to remember about nominal variables is that the numbers we assign to their categories have no intrinsic meaning as numbers. Some other terms used in conjunction with nominal scales are *dichotomous*, *trichotomous*, and *polytomous*. Gender is an example of a dichotomous, nominal variable--female and male. Politics might be scaled as a trichotomous variable--Republican, Democrat, and Independent. Marital status is a polytomous variable because it has several categories of membership.

Oridinal Scale The term "ordinal" signifies an ordered relationship among the categories of an ordinal variable. Recall the variable couseling effectiveness. At one point in the measurement process the researcher requested respondents, professors in this case, to rank order a set of characteristics of good counselors. That is, she asked them to first identify the five most important characteristics and then rank them 1, 2, 3, 4, 5. This is an example of ordinal measurement. Each professor selected his five favorites from the list of 28 and then assigned the numerals 1 to 5 to them. In the case of an ordinal scale the use of numbers has numerical meaning in the sense that a lower number in this case signifies a greater degree of the attribute being ranked--counselor effectiveness. And, a rank of 2 represents a stonger degree of the attribute than a rank of 3, etc.

Two points need to made concerning the ordinal scale. First, and most importantly, although the scale values signify an ordered relationship, they do not necessarily mean that the ranked characteristics are precisely one unit apart in the degree to which they measure the attribute. That is, a given professor, whose top three choices might be ability to listen, self-awareness, and empathy, might see little difference between the importance of self-awareness and empathy; but each of these may rank much lower than ability to listen in his view of counselor effectiveness. The second point is that the numbers assigned to characteristics on an ordinal scale can be reversed. While the researcher here chose to assign a value of 1 to the first choice and 5 to the fifth choice characteristic, she could have reversed the scale values. This is a common practice. Because most individuals attach greater importance to larger values than smaller ones, there is sometimes a psychological advantage to following this practice.

Interval Scale An interval scale is one which contains the properties of the nominal and ordinal scales, and in addition has the property of equal intervals between points on the scale. The famous *Likert Scale* in psychology is an example of an interval scale. Likert (1932) was a prominent social psychologist whose technique for measuring attitudes has become a standard in behavioral research. The Likert scale is a 5-point scale of agreement in which a value of 5 is assigned the response, "strongly agree." A value of 4 is assigned to the response, "agree," and a neutral response receives a value of 3. The responses, "disagree" and "strongly disagree" are given the values 2 and 1, respectively.

Among the present research examples, the variable of counselor effectiveness was ultimately placed on an interval scale. This was done by transforming the original effectiveness variable into five separate variables: self-awareness, empathy, tolerance of ambiguity, ability to listen, and self-confidence. The purpose for measuring these variables was to determine the degree to which counselors possessed these attributes. Each of these variables was placed on a 4-point interval scale ranging from "outstanding" to "fair" (Figure 3.1). Two points should be made concerning this process. First, it might be argued that the ordinal quality of the effectiveness characteristics was ignored when all five of them were given equal weight. Recall that the professors as a group rated self-awareness as most important, followed by empathy, etc. It would be possible to differentially weight responses on the 4-point interval scales if we chose to do so. However, in this case as in most others, the researcher chose not to do so. A second point is that one might also argue about the true equality of intervals on the interval scale. Is the differnce between outstanding and excellent really the same as the differnce between good and fair? The truth is that we cannot prove it is. Some measurement theorists argue that such a 4-point scale is really ordinal. However, this author is not alone in considering such scales as representative of interval measurement. Labovitz (1970) argued that "although some small error may accompany the treatment of ordinal variables as interval, this is offset by the use of more powerful, more sensitive, better developed, and more clearly interpretable statistics with known sampling error" (Labovitz in Nie, et al., 1975, p. 6). The important connection between measurement and statistics will be discussed in a later section.

There are many other types of interval scales. The semantic differential is a 7-point scale used in conjunction with bipolar adjectives to measure an individual's reaction to a concept or thing. The semantic differential was originally developed by Charles Osgood and his associates (Osgood, et al., 1957) to measure the meaning which persons attached to concepts. It was Osgood's hypthoesis that human language contained many redundant words and that it was possible to summarize cognitive beliefs into a few important dimensions. By using a statistical technique called factor anlysis, Osgood was able to reduce meaning to three important factors: evaluation, potency, and activity. Figure 3.2, taken from Mueller's (1986) book, *Measuring Social Attitudes*, shows a typical use of the semantic differential. Once the respondent has placed his check marks or X's in the spaces between the bipolar adjectives, these are converted to the numerals 1 through 7. Sometimes a researcher will actually put the numbers underneath the appropriate spaces on the response sheet. Sometimes different numbers are used. A common variation is to use a numerical scale from +3 to -3 with 0 representing a neutral point. In some applications of the semantic differential, a total score is derived by adding up the reponses for each adjective pair. (Note the need to reverse the scoring for those pairs in

- -

FIGURE 3.2
Sample Semantic Differential Designed to Measure Three Dimensions of Meaning

My Spouse

```
 valuable ----:----:----:----:----:----:---- worthless
    clean ----:----:----:----:----:----:---- dirty
      bad ----:----:----:----:----:----:---- good
   unfair ----:----:----:----:----:----:---- fair
    large ----:----:----:----:----:----:---- small
   strong ----:----:----:----:----:----:---- weak
     deep ----:----:----:----:----:----:---- shallow
     fast ----:----:----:----:----:----:---- slow
   active ----:----:----:----:----:----:---- passive
      hot ----:----:----:----:----:----:---- cold
```

Note: The first four adjective pairs measure the evaluation dimension, the next three measure potency, and the last three measure activity.

- -

which the negative adjective is on the left.) In other applications, only adjectives for a particular dimension are used. For example, an educational researcher might use only those adjectives from the evaluation dimension to evaluate a new curriculum.

There are many other variations of the Likert and semantic differential scales of measurement. The interested reader is urged to check the library for books containing measurement scales on different topics. There are books on psychological attitudes, tests and measurements in child development, and educational tests and measures. Other valuable references are Buros' *Mental Measurements Yearbook* and the 1984 volume, *Test Critiques*, published by the Test Corporation of America.

While there are many ready-made measurement scales available for research use, the student should not be overly cautious and fearful of creating his own. A common question that students have is: How many points should one use on a measurement scale? How about the 10-point scale so often used in the popular media? Generally speaking, it is best to create an interval scale with between four and seven points. The reason for this is that when wider scales are used, individual respondents will vary considerably in the extent to which they make use of all the points on the scale. This tends to increase measurement error and therefore lowers the reliability of the scale. At the other extreme, if one creates an interval scale with only two or three choices, many respondents will feel limited in their ability to express their opinions. The "true-false" and "yes-no" scales are examples of this problem.

Ratio Scale A ratio scale is similar to an interval scale but has the additional property of a true zero point. Many physical measures are made on ratio scales. Some examples are height, weight, sound intensity, and earth quake severity. An example of a physical measure that is not on a ratio scale is temperature measured on the Fahrenheit scale. Note that a temperature of zero does not represent a true zero point. We can have temperatures below zero on the Fahrenheit scale. Since the development of the Fahrenheit scale, scientists have learned more about the phenomenon of temperature and have created a newer scale capable of measuring absolute zero. The theoretical lower limit of temperature is -459.67 degrees F.

While the distinction between interval and ratio scales is not a crucial one in behavioral research, it is important to understand that the kinds of comparisons made with ratio scales are not possible with interval scales. For example, while it makes good sense to talk about an earthquake as being twice as severe as another, it makes much less sense to describe a person as being twice as intelligent as another. Intelligence is a psychological constuct, or variable, measured on an interval scale. A common intelligence scale is one which represents an average score as 100. Greater or lesser degrees of intelligence range upward and downward, respectively, from that midpoint. But there is no true zero point on the IQ scale. From a measurement perspective, IQ is much like temperature on the Fahrenheit Scale. It is simply not correct to say that an individual with an IQ of 150 is twice as smart as one with an IQ of 75. It is equally incorrect to say that a temperature of 100 degrees is twice as hot as one of 50 degrees.

Other variables which qualify as ratio variables are those which are based on frequency counts. Both marital status and race are considered to be measured on nominal scales. However, for certain purposes the individual categories of these variables may be thought of as ratio variables. It is perfectly reasonable to say that we have half as many "singles" as "marrieds" in a sample, or that we have twice as many Whites as Asians. In other words, meaningful ratios can be formed among the categories of a nominal variable, even though the variables themselves cannot be compared one with the other in a numerical fashion.

CHAPTER FOUR

THE INTERMEDIATE STEPS

The previous chapter dealt with a number of research steps involving the conceptualization and planning of a study. This chapter will continue the planning phase in the form of further design considerations, steps 6 through 8. It is important to note that the first 8 of the 10 steps involve very little physical involvement of the researcher. They are primarily thinking, planning, and designing--the cerebral part of research. If the cerebral part constitutes 80%, it must be extremely important to good research. It is not until Step 9, data collection, that the researcher actually makes contact with his subjects. This step also requires some considerable planning in order to determine from whom and how much data to collect.

Further Design Considerations: Steps 6-8

Step 6: State the hypothesis or hypotheses.

Although most research studies begin with a rather indeterminate situation, a vaguely stated problem or question, at some point the indeterminacy must be removed. This is the role of the hypothesis. The hypothesis is the linchpin of science. Without it there could be no behavioral science as we know it. A hypothesis is a carefully-stated conjectural statement about the presumed relation between two or more variables. There are two types of hypotheses: the relational hypothesis and the differential hypothesis. It is common to use relational hypotheses in correlational research and differential hypotheses in causal-comparative and experimental research. All investigations with the exception of a purely descriptive one must have at least one hypothesis. Hypotheses for our research types B, C, and D are given below:

B. There will be a positive and significant correlation between a student's knowledge of grammar as measured by the Usage subtest of the California Achievement Test (Jr. High Level) and his writing ability as measured by the total number of mechanical errors in an essay about *The Adventures of Tom Sawyer*.

C. Graduate students with high ratings in counseling fieldwork will have significantly higher scores on the enterprising scale of the Vocational Preference Inventory than will students with low fieldwork ratings.

D. Graduate students in educational psychology class 6020, Research Methods, who take weekly quizzes that count toward their course grades will score significantly higher on the final exam than either (1) a comparison class of students who do not take weekly quizzes or (2) another comparison class who take weekly quizzes which do not count toward their course grades.

Returning to the definition of the hypothesis, a hypothesis must specify a relationship between two or more variables. What are the relationships expressed in the above hypotheses, especially hypotheses C and D? Because these are stated as differential hypotheses, the relationships are not so clear as in hypothesis B. Hypothesis C is really calling for a test of the possible relationship between counselor effectiveness and the enterprising personality type. Hypothesis D describes a potential relationship between the use of weekly quizzes and student achievement. Because all hypotheses should express a testable relationship, the researcher should always ask the question: What is the relationship I am testing?

A final word on hypotheses: While it is possible to do desriptive research and avoid the use of hypotheses, it is very difficult to do so. For example, suppose you are interested in empirically determining several characteristics of a group of students--their ages, marital status, income levels, work status, etc. After collecting and analyzing the data for these variables, you begin to wonder if the results hold true for all types of students. For example, do males and females have similar employment, income and marital status? Are the educational backgrounds and sources of financial support the same in all ethnic groups? What is the relationship between gender and age in my sample? These are all questions which can easily be turned into testable hypotheses. The alert researcher will anticipate such questions in a descriptive study and incorporate hypotheses and tests for them in his research plan. In effect, the researcher incorporates some of the characteristics of correlational and causal-comparative research in his otherwise descriptive study. In summary, it is hard to imagine any good research which does not make use of hypotheses.

Step 7: Determine the need for a control group.

This step is really a corollary of Step 3. It is part of the process of determining the type of research being conducted. It is included here as a separate step in order to emphasized this connection. It is also included in order to repond to one of the most often-asked questions of student researchers: "Do I have to have a control group?"

Let us consider for a moment what a control group is and how it functions. The main purpose of a control group is to allow us to compare our target group with another group to find out if there are significant differences between them. If the two groups are identical except for the presence or absence of a treatment variable, then we can have great faith that any difference we find between them is due to, or caused by, the treatment.

A general rule for the use of a control group is as follows: If you have research questions of type A or B, then you don't need a control group. That is, if you are conducting either descriptive or correlational research, a control group is not required. If you have research questions of type C or D, then you must have at least one comparison group. That is, if you are conducting either causal-comparative or experimental research, you need some form of a control group. The type of control group one has will vary. In a causal-comparative study such as our comparison of two groups of counselors, one that has maximal characteristics of effectiveness and one that does not, the use of a *comparison group* allows us to determine possible causes of counseling success. But the use of such a comparison group does not rule out or control for the presence of extraneous variables that may also contribute to differences between the groups. In true experimental research where subjects are assigned to treatment groups at random, we can theoretically rule out and thus control the effects of all extraneous variables. Therefore, while both types of research, causal-comparative and experimental, use comparison groups, only in experimental research does one receive the full benefits of a true control group.

Step 8: Determine the appropriate statistical tests.

If one is conducting purely descriptive research, then only *descriptive statistics* are required. These are statistics which summarize data by providing information concerning the central tendency and variation (dispersion) of subjects' responses. Examples are shown below:

1. Measures of central tendency: mean, median, mode.
2. Measures of dispersion: range, standard deviation.
3. Graphics: histogram (bar graph), frequency polygon.

Research types B, C, and D require some type of *inferential statistic*. Inferential statistics, as opposed to descriptive statistics, are procedures for conducting tests of hypotheses. The results of such tests tell us whether our hypotheses are tenable or not. Furthermore, inferential statistics are designed to allow us to make inferences about a larger population than the sample of subjects we use in our study. Professional pollsters use inferential statistics when they compare blacks and whites or democrats and republicans on political issues. They draw inferences about the entire U.S. electorate from samples of 1500, or fewer, in some cases.

Figure 4.1 is an aid in selecting appropriate statistics for different types of research investigations. It concisely

FIGURE 4.1
Appropriate Statistics for Different Types of Research and Different Levels of Measurement

Type of Measurement	*Type of Research* *Correlational*	*Causal-Comparative or Experimental*
Nominal	Phi coefficient Contingency coef.	Chi square test Difference between proportions
Ordinal	Spearman r Biserial r Point-biserial r	Sign test Median test U-test
- - - - - - - - -	- - - - - - - - -	- - - - - - - - -
Interval or Ratio	Pearson r Multiple R Canonical R Factor Analysis	t-test Analysis of variance Discriminant Analysis Analysis of Covariance

summarizes much of the previous material in this chapter by showing the relationships among research type, measurement scale, type of hypothesis, and appropriate inferential statistics.

Figure 4.1 is an augmentation of Steven's original 1946 table which showed the relationship of scale type to empirical operation and permissible statistics (as cited in Dillon and Goldstein, 1984, p. 3). A number of multivariate statistics not present in Steven's original chart have been added here. Another addition is the horizontal broken line between the top and bottom halves of the figure. This line divides two general classes of statistics from one another, parametric and non-parametric statistics. *Parametric statistics*, the ones below the broken line, are designed for "metric" variables, those for which equal or nearly equal units of measurement have been used. *Nonparametric statistics*, the ones shown above the broken line, are used with variables that are measured less precisely, i.e., on nominal or ordinal scales. Because parametric statistics have greater power, a greater ability to detect differences between groups and relationships between variables, this book will emphasize their use over non-parametric statistics. It is this author's view that many variables can be measured with sufficient accuracy to merit the use of parametric statistics. Siegel's (1956) book remains a good resource for those who need detailed information on nonparametric statistics.

Most students are not expected to know or understand all of the statistical tests shown in Figure 4.1. The remainder of this book will explore and clarify the use of several of these. For those with a stronger background in measurement and statistics, it should be noted that, as in most fields, there is a difference of opinion among research methodologists concerning the proper relationship of measurement and statistics. This appears to be due to the fact that different methodologists and practitioners subscribe to different theories of measurement. Mitchell (1986) describes three separate theories: representational, operational, and classical. It is the representational theory which specifies the relationships shown in Figure 4.1.

Data Collection

Step 9: Collect the data.

In the previous section it was stated that inferential statistics allow a researcher to draw inferences about a larger population than just the subjects used in a given investigation. This statement is true only under certain conditions of sampling. *Sampling* refers to the collection of data in such a way as to represent a larger group, often called a "population" or "universe." The crucial question, and one of the most often-asked questions of student researchers is, *How big does my sample have to be?* This is a very important question. but unfortunately, one for which there is not a simple answer. The answer is that it depends on the nature of your investigation.

In order to shed light on the question of sample size, let us begin by exploring some aspects of the theory of sampling. There are two general types of samples: probability samples and nonprobability samples. Probability samples are the only ones which "guarantee" a representative match between sample and population. *Probability samples* include random, stratified, cluster, and systematic samples. A *random sample* is one in which every member of a population has an equal chance of being included in the research sample. There are several ways of selecting subjects for a random sample. A simple method is to use a table of random numbers. Another method, perhaps even easier, is the use of a computer program to generate random numbers within the exact limits of one's known population. That is, if a researcher is working with a population of 5000 individuals and desires a sample of 100, he can instruct a computer program to generate 100 numbers with values between 1 and 5000. This method assumes that a numbered list of population members exists. Although computer programs do not create truly random numbers, but rather "pseudo random" numbers, they are considered to be quite appropriate for research purposes. Another even simpler method which is possible with smaller populations is to write the names of population members on 3 X 5 cards, shuffle the deck, and draw out the number required. You can even draw them out of a hat if you wish. The point is that the construction of a random sample from a population does not need to be a complicated process. More important than this process is the care given to defining one's population. The reason for this should be obvious. A random sample from an ill-defined population will only represent the ill-defined population.

In some situations it is advantageous to use a form of random sampling called stratified sampling. *Stratified sampling* is random selection from within certain identified "strata" of the population--sex, age, political party, etc. The random samples are selected in proportion to their occurrence in the general population. This form of probability sampling is quite useful in survey research where it is important that minority groups receive proper representation. Stratified sampling can also be used primarily for reducing errors in prediction (cf. Selkirk, 1978, pp. 22-24). The basic procedure for stratified sampling is to first determine the percentage of persons within a population who fall into certain categories. These might include age groups, those above age 65, for example, ethnic groups, consumer categories, any conceivable subgroup in a population. Once these percentages are determined, the researcher randomly draws enough members of each category to reconstitute the proportions on a smaller scale, whatever size sample he determines is adequate.

A type of probability sampling which is conceptually similar to stratified sampling is cluster sampling. *Cluster sampling* is random sampling from hierarchical units in a population. For example, a researcher investigating reading disability might identify school districts within a state by size: large innercity, medium suburban, and small rural districts. He would then randomly select schools and then children from these clusters. The difference between cluster and stratified sampling is that in cluster sampling no attempt is made to make the clusters proportional to their actual size in the population. In fact, the clusters are made of equal size for the purpose of comparing them statistically. Cluster sampling is therefore used when the overriding concern is to compare subgroups rather than to accurately represent the overall population. The main advantage of cluster sampling is that fewer cases need be used than in random or stratified sampling. Thus, it is more economical.

Systematic sampling is a type of probability sampling in which the researcher simply takes every *nth* case from a list of all possible cases in the population. If the population consists of 5000 individuals and the researcher wants a sample of 100, he would sample every 50th person from the list. It is good practice to determine the initial sampling position randomly rather than starting with the first person on the list. Systematic sampling is simple but effective. The only drawback to its use stems from problems arising from the original list used to create the sample.

As Selkirk (1978) points out, "If 90 children are listed in alphabetical order and then placed in three classes in rotation, and you also in turn select every third child for a sample of 30, you could unwittingly select one class as your sample..."(p. 17). If your intent were to sample a cross-section of children to represent the instructional effects of three teachers, then of course, the above sample would be biased. Prior to using systematic sampling, the researcher should ascertain that a pre-constructed list of subjects is free of any potential bias.

While probability sampling is much preferred to nonprobability sampling, the fact is that much research in the behavioral sciences uses nonprobability sampling techniques (Cozby, 1985). One nonprobability technique that is usually more representative of a population than some others is purposive sampling. *Purposive sampling* is the use of a subset of the population to represent the entire population. For example, until the presidential election of 1980, the state of New Mexico had always mirrored the entire United States in its choice of the winning candidate. An aware researcher could make use of this knowledge by sampling voting behavior from New Mexico to represent the entire country.

Quota sampling is a type of nonprobability sampling similar to stratified sampling, except that the percentages to be in each group are selected in a non-random way. For example, in another hypothetical study of voting behavior, a researcher might identify a particular census tract within a voting precinct. He might then choose a starting point, a particular city block, and interview the first ten individuals who are at home and willing to give him their time. He would then move to the next block and continue interviewing, moving from block to block until he completed, say, 100 interviews, his quota. Usually, in quota sampling, as in stratified sampling, an attempt is made to include a certain number of individuals in each important subcategory. The difference is that the researcher is willing to accept the first X number of individuals who are available, rather than selecting them at random.

Probably the most common type of sampling in behavioral research is what Cozby (1985) refers to as *haphazard sampling*. There is no fancy definition of haphazard sampling, or what I prefer to call *sampling by opportunity*. It is simply a "take 'em where you find 'em" method of obtaining subjects. It may seem ironic, but a large proportion of studies in psychology use available college students as subjects. On many campuses psychology majors are required to enroll in a class in which they receive credit by acting as subjects in a certain number of research investigations. These students form the semester's "subject pool." Their reactions to a multitude of stimuli are recorded, analyzed, and often generalized, rightly or wrongly, to the population at large.

Why do researchers utilize sampling procedures which they often know to be faulty? A primary reason is economics. It can be very expensive in both money and time to create a random sample of any large population. Secondly, researchers are often more interested in exploring relationships among variables than in generalizing precisely to a given population. If a relationship is first discovered among college sophomores and there is reason to doubt its existence among senior citizens, then a study can be conducted in that specific population. One of the most important reasons for replicating past research is to verify the existence of phenomena in new populations.

While the above argument has some merit, the problem of establishing a reasonable sampling procedure remains. The fact is that sampling is often a function of the exigencies of the research situation. Heavily funded research will usually require precise sampling. Doctoral research usually requires larger samples than master's theses. Despite these differences, there are some general rules for collecting data which apply to most situations. First of all, as Selkirk (1978) points out, samples of fewer than 30 subjects are troublesome, especially when using parametric statistics. The optimal situation, then, is to have no comparison groups of fewer than 30 cases. At the other end of the spectrum, it has been shown that highly accurate results can be obtained by using as few as 200 random cases to estimate a population as large as 100,000 (cf. Slonin, 1967, p. 74). Selkirk is even more liberal in this regard:

> Samples of size fewer than 30 are often statistically awkward, needing special formulae, but with samples of a good size (perhaps 100?), the labour of collecting extra data is rarely worth the reward in increased accuracy of result in any but the largest scale research (Selkirk, 1978, p. 22).

Perhaps it would be instructive to see how data collection was performed in the research examples previously discussed. In the first study, which began as a description of a student body and ended in a comparison of graduates versus dropouts, the researchers (Hanley and Traynor, 1976) used systematic sampling. In cooperation with the campus admissions office they constructed a list of all students who had been enrolled in the Cal State, Hayward, counseling major during a five-year period. Since theirs was a mail-out survey, they had to consider the possiblity that some students might not respond to the questionnaire. Other students undoubtedly had moved from the area and could not be traced.

The problem of non-response in survey research is another tricky aspect of sampling. What is a decent response rate?--75%?, 60%?, 40%? How does one know if the subjects who responded are like the ones who didn't respond? There are no easy answers to these questions. The only thing that can be stated with certainty is that the higher the response rate, the more likely it is that the sample accurately represents the population. Sometimes researchers will compare the responses of individuals who responded early vs. those of the later respondents. A difference would suggest that non-respondents might display even greater differences. But this is mostly guesswork. There is simply no substitute for a 100% reponse rate. Anything less opens the possibility of bias in the sample. Despite this problem survey research remains the most economical, and sometimes the only, way to learn much about a large population.

In the present example, the researchers aimed for final samples of approximately 100 graduates and dropouts, respectively. They sent out questionnaires to every other person on their list of enrolled students. The list included 209 graduates and 148 non-persisters (a combination of what Hanley termed "droputs" and "stopouts"). Three successive mailings of the 100-item questionnaire were made over a two-month period. The final sample included 114 graduates and 70 non-persisters, 51.5% of the original random sample of 50%. The response rate for graduates was slightly higher than for non-persisters--54 to 47 per cent.

Sampling procedures for the other three research studies were much simpler. They all involved the use of samples of opportunity. In my own study on grammar and writing ability, I simply used all of the students in three junior high English classes I was teaching at the time. Calcagno's (1975) study of counseling effectiveness used all student interns enrolled at that time. Davis' (1972) investigation of the effect of weekly quizzes used all students in three of my research methods classes held in the spring and fall quarters of 1971. While these three studies can all be criticized because their samples did not represent a larger, well-defined population, they were all considered of value and approved by thesis committees.

At the present time it is even more difficult for graduate students to obtain representative research samples due to more stringent ethical considerations involving research on human subjects. The student researcher should be aware of the need for Institutional Review Board (IRB) approval of his or her research plan prior to the collection of data. A primary source for information on this topic is *Ethical Principles in the Conduct of Research with Human Participants* (APA, 1982). Cozby (1985) also has an excellent chapter on ethical concerns in his book, *Methods in Behavioral Research.*

CHAPTER FIVE

THE FINAL STEP

Step 10: Analyze the data and draw conclusions.

Apart from the first creative step of conceptualizing a research problem, Step 10 is probably the most important of the ten steps. Much of the remainder of this book will dwell on this last step in the research process. A separate chapter will be devoted to the special statistical procedures associated with each of the four types of research. This chapter will provide a brief summary of the results of the four research studies we have been following. Some tables will be presented and mention will be made of statistics used, but no explanation for their use will be given at this time. Detailed explanations will be provided in the later chapters.

Study No. 1: Master's Degree Graduates vs. Dropouts

In the first study (Hanley & Traynor, 1975), each researcher began by describing her population--graduate or dropout. For example, Table 5.1 illustrates categories of employment among counseling graduates. Fifty-six percent of the graduates held direct counseling jobs, 14% had jobs involving some counseling, and 22% had jobs unrelated to the counseling field. Eight percent of the graduates were unemployed. It is interesting that this employment distribution is not too far from the ideal career goal shown in Table 5.2.

After describing each of the samples, the researchers pooled their data for the purpose of making comparisons. Two of these are shown in tables 5.3 and 5.4. One aspect of the survey was an evaluation of the counseling program by each of the groups. Table 5.3 provides a comparison of graduates and dropouts on their response to a question which summarized their feelings about enrolling in the program. It is not surprising that graduates rated their decision as significantly more positive than the dropouts ($t=3.46$, $p<.001$). Another comparison is shown in Table 5.4. This comparison utilized the chi square statistic rather than the t-test. It also showed a significant difference between the groups in terms of their motivation for entering the counseling degree program (chi square=18.95, $p<.001$). While both groups were attracted to the "people orientation" of counseling, it appears that graduates were more interested in those aspects which focused on self-understanding while dropouts were drawn more by the prospects of a job.

TABLE 5.1
Counseling Graduates' Employment

Job Description	Code	Number	Percent
Direct Counseling	1	61	56
Counseling in conjunction with other job responsibilities	2	15	14
Unrelated to counseling field	3	24	22
Unemployed	4	9	8

- -

TABLE 5.2
Graduate's Ultimate Employment Goal

Job Description	Code	Number	Percent
Direct Counseling	1	51	50
Counseling with other job responsibilities	2	21	20
Unrelated to counseling	3	13	13
Don't know	4	16	16

- -

Because of the length of the questionnaire, there were many more interesting comparisons made between graduates and dropouts. However, the purpose here is not to relate all such comparisons. Let us conclude this study with a brief verbal summary from Traynor's thesis:

> No significant differences were found between graduates and dropouts on undergraduate GPA, verbal GRE scores, or grades in four core course areas. Academic aptitude, by these measures at least, did not differentiate graduates from dropouts.

TABLE 5.3
Percentage of Graduates and Dropouts According to Evaluation of Decision to Choose Counseling Program

		Graduates	Dropouts	Level of Significance
Looking back, how do you now rate your decision to choose the counseling program at Cal State?		N=113	N=70	
good decision	5	41	29	
	4	41	30	
	3	13	21	
	2	3	9	
poor decision	1	2	11	
mean		4.17	3.56	t=3.46***
S.D.		.89	1.30	p<.001

TABLE 5.4
Percentage of Graduates and Dropouts According to Original Reason for Attraction to Counseling

	Graduates	Dropouts	Level of Significance
What originally attracted you to the field of counseling?	N=106	N=68	
People-oriented reasons	26	41	
Job-related reasons	13	37	
Self-understanding	10	3	
Natural orientating	13	6	
Need for counseling	11	6	Chi square
Personal experience	27	7	=27.01*** p<.001

The graduates were motivated more strongly than the dropouts to complete the program. Such motivation was reflected by formations of particular research interests before entry, projections of shorter completion time (six or fewer quarters), selection of the doctorate rather than the master's as the final academic goal, and original attraction to the field because of personal experience or people-oriented reasons rather than job-related reasons.

Among personality factors, only the Holland (1973) adjective "ambitious" distinguished between graduates and dropouts, with more graduates saying "ambitious" was "like me" than did dropouts.

Among personal background factors, those that contributed to successful completion were unchanged marital status, and status as an otherwise unemployed full-time student rather than as a full-time employee but part-time student (Traynor, 1976, pp. iii-iv).

A final procedure used in this study was to construct a multiple regression equation containing those variables which differentiated the groups. The equation was used to classify students and resulted in identifying graduates with 31% more accuracy than chance. Dropouts were identified with 34% greater accuracy than chance prediction.

Study No. 2: Knowledge of Grammar and Writing Ability

The second study (Whalen, 1969) involved a comparison of students' writing ability and their knowledge of the English curriculum as measured by a standardized test of capitalization, punctuation, spelling, and language usage. The intent was to determine if a relationship existed between errors made in writing and those on the test. Previous research had shown a positive but rather low correlation between grammar and composition skills (see Table 5.5).

A relatively simple procedure would have been to total the composition and test errors for each student and then correlate the pairs of scores across all 77 students using the Pearson correlation method. However, this method would have masked some of the interesting interrelationships among the total of 26 variables involved--21 error types from the composition and 5 subtest scores from the English test.

A statistical procedure designed for this purpose is canonical correlation. In canonical correlation, all of the

---

TABLE 5.5
Correlation of Grammar and Composition

Date	Researcher	Correlation
1906	Hoyt	.30
1922	Asker	.37
1926	Segel	.48
1963	O'Donnell	.42

TABLE 5.6
Canonical Analysis of Selected Variables

Pearson Correlation Matrix

		Language Test Variables			
		cap.	punct.	spell.	gram.
	cap.	.30	.42	.47	.42
Compo-	punct.	.22	.70	.46	.66
sition	spell.	.28	.71	.70	.69
Variables	gram.	-.05	-.01	.11	.06

Canonical Correlation and Selected Weights

Correlation	Language Test Variables	Composition Variables
.91	-.53 punct. .43 usage -.67 gram.	-.43 punct. -.62 spell.

variables are first intercorrelated and then mathematical weights, or coefficients, are derived in such a way as to best express the overall relationship between the two sets of variables. Table 5.6 shows partial results of this data analysis. The top part of the table shows the simple coefficients of correlation between the common variables from the composition and language test. The most important coefficients are in the diagonal of the matrix. Note that the relationships between the test and composition for punctuation and spelling were quite strong, r=.70 for each one. On the other hand, the correlations for capitalization and grammar as measured by errors in the composition and errors on the test are quite low. The main reason for this lack of "fit" was that students actually made relatively few errors in grammar and capitalization in their writing. As a matter of fact, grammatical errors constituted less than six per cent of all the errors students made in their writing. The most common errors were for spelling and punctuation. Note, however, that grammatical knowledge as measured by the language test (the right-most column of coefficients) was strongly related to writing proficiency in capitalization, punctuation, and spelling (r=.42, .66, and .69, respectively). The bottom half of Table 5.6 shows the results of the canonical analysis and provides additional insight into the relationship between composition and test. We see that the overall relationship between the two was a startling .91. This means that a student's test performance would predict his writing ability with great accuracy, and vice versa. In other words, there was a highly significant relationship between these students' total language knowledge and their ability to write technically competent compositions.

One of the by-products of this and other research was the beginning of greater interest in the importance of student writing skills during the 1970's. The quality of high school and college students' writing became a subject of considerable concern. By 1980, the California State University System required each campus to carry out its own testing of students' writing as a condition of graduation. Even graduate students, if they had not already done so, were required to pass a writing examination before they could be advanced to candidacy for the master's degree. Writing classes were created by departments of English and other departments to assist students in the improvement of writing skills. Through research on cognitive processes, much has been learned in the past decade about the process and teaching of writing (cf. Hayes & Flower, 1986).

Study No. 3: Characteristics of Effective Counselors

The third study (Calcagno, 1975) sought to draw a connection between effective counseling and various personal characteristics of counselors, including their verbal ability as measured by the Graduate Record Exam (GRE), their Holland personality type (Holland, 1973), and their vocational interests as measured by the Strong Vocational Interest Blank (SVIB). Although this study was conceived of as a causal-comparative one, the data analysis utilized Pearson correlations to evaluate the significance of relationships between personal charateristics and counseling effectiveness. Originally, the reseacher had planned to divide the counselors into two extreme groups on the effectiveness rating. However, because the potential sample of 93 shrank to 51 completed ratings, a decision was made to use all the subjects and correlate their scores. Also, due to an uneven split between females (33) and males (18), much less confidence was placed in results for the men. For this reason, only the female results are reported here.

Table 5.7 summarizes some of the stronger relationships found in this study. In terms of the various SVIB scales, female counseling interns had moderately high positive correlations for the composite effectiveness measure with Life Insurance Sales, Speech Pathologist, and Housewife. The SVIB Housewife scale also correlated significantly with the personal characteristics of empathy and tolerance of ambiguity. In addition, the Speech Pathologist Scale had significant positive correlations with empathy and the ability to listen. The female subjects showed moderately high negative correlations for the SVIB scales of Physical Therapist, Dental Assistant, Telephone Operator, and Instrument Assembler. The scales of Telephone Operator and Instrument Assembler both had negative correlations with empathy, and Physical Therapist correlated negatively with self-confidence.

TABLE 5.7
Intercorrelation of SVIB, Holland, and GRE Scores With a Composite Measure of Counseling Effectiveness

Variable Name	r	alpha
SVIB Life Insurance Sales	.44	.01
SVIB Physical Therapy	-.46	.01
SVIB Housewife	.46	.01
GRE Verbal	.45	.01
Holland Enerprising	.37	.05

The GRE Verbal scale correlated significantly with the composite measure and also with the individual components of empathy, tolerance of ambiguity, and ability to listen. That is, counselors who received higher effectiveness ratings had significantly higher GRE Verbal scores than those who received lower ratings. Finally, of the six Holland personality types, Artistic, Social, Investigative, Conventional, Enterprising, and Realistic, only the Enterprising scale was linked to counselor effectiveness. Subjects with higher Enterprising scores were rated significantly higher in effectiveness.

While logically, one might have expected SVIB scales such as Psychologist and Counselor to correlate with the counselor characteristics, this trend was generally not found. An exception was a moderately high correlation between empathy and the SVIB Social Worker scale. It is interesting that while most subjects were either primarily Artistic or Social in terms of Holland's personality types, the tertiary type Enterprising nevertheless predicted a significant degree of counselor effectiveness. Perhaps this characteristic is related to the SVIB Life Insurance scale, as well. The faculty raters seem to have been impressed with a salesperson quality in counselors. Professional counselors are sometimes surprised at these results. The degree to which these results may be generalized beyond the Cal State, Hayward, campus is an open question for further research.

Study No. 4: Use of Weekly Quizzes in Graduate Instruction

The fourth study (Davis, 1972) compared the use of weekly quizzes in three different research methods classes. Table 5.8 displays average scores for the classes at the top, and the results of an analysis of variance at the bottom of the table. In the 50-item final examination, Group I, the class that received weekly quizzes that counted, had a somewhat higher mean than Group II (quizzes that didn't count) or Group III (no weekly quizzes). However, the analysis of variance (ANOVA) between the classes indicated that this 3-point difference was not beyond chance at the .05 level of significance. In other words, such a difference

TABLE 5.8
Means, Standard Deviations, and ANOVA Results for Three Experimental Classes

	Group I	Group II	Group III
N	23	17	21
M	36.9	33.8	33.9
SD	5.4	6.3	6.5

ANOVA Summary

Source	DF	SS	MS	F
Between Groups	2	126.9	63.4	1.64 (NS)
Within Groups	58	2246.0	38.7	
Total	60	2372.9		

could happen by chance alone more than five per cent of the time. This level of chance variation was considered too great by the researcher. He concluded that no significant difference existed, and, therefore, weekly quizzes did not cause additional learning to occur. One might think the researcher was unduly conservative in using the five per cent level of significance here, but indeed, the .05 level is the most common level of significance (alpha level) used in behavioral research.

The reader may wonder how the course instructor, this author, reacted to these results. Naturally, he was chagrined. However, true to his pact, he stopped giving further weekly quizzes.

Another aspect of this study which convinced me of its validity, at least in my own teaching, was a comparison of the subjective reactions of the students. The students in each class were asked to respond to a standard end-of-course faculty evaluation form. The form contained 18 items rated on a 5-point scale such as Preparation for Class Meetings, Interest and Enthusiasm in his Subject, Ability to Arouse Interest of Students, Organization of Course, etc. In a somewhat more complicated analysis of variance between the classes, it was shown that students did not perceive the instructor differently despite the presence or absence of weekly quizzes. Thus, it appeared that these graduate students were mature enough to keep up their weekly reading assignments without the threat of a quiz. And even without a weekly quiz, their perceptions of the instructor's preparation and organization, among other things, were not altered positively or negatively. The experiment demonstrated to my satisfaction that it was relatively safe to set aside the weekly quizzes.

CHAPTER SIX

THE ELECTRONIC COMPUTER

The purpose of this chapter is to acquaint the reader with an indispensable tool for conducting behavioral research, the modern electronic computer. Although it might seem more appropriate to discuss this topic later in the book, it is the author's belief that much anguish can be avoided by novice researchers if they learn the rudiments of computer usage early in the research process, certainly before the collection of data. To avoid the computer or to rely on a "statistical consultant" to handle one's data analysis problems in the final stage of a research project is often a shocking experience for the naive researcher. Many statistical consultants or "computer experts" are not very knowledgable about research methodology. Being unfamiliar with behavioral research makes it difficult for them to understand and communicate with researchers. For this reason, these consultants will often translate research hypotheses into a form which they can more easily fit into a computational procedure familiar to themselves. The output of such a process often does not fit the original questions of the investigation. For this reason it is essential that researchers become more familiar with the use of computers and the software that is available to program them. As Kerlinger has stated: "The behaviorial scientist...has to know enough of statistical analysis and computer technology to be able to use technicians as resources rather than as preceptors" (Kerlinger, 1986, p. 635).

One of the roadblocks to computer usage for many individuals is an unfamiliarity with, and even a fear of, computers. Such fear, or at least discomfort, is quite natural. We do not often feel very comfortable with another human being we have just met until we learn something about their past history and current activities. We often want to know what they "do" and how they go about doing it. We want to know "what makes them tick." This chapter and the next will attempt to make the reader more comfortable with computers by providing information on their history and design features, the languages used to communicate with them, and the computer software packages available for statistical analysis.

A Brief History of Computers

In their book on methods in educational research, Ary, Jacobs, and Razavieh (1979) make this observation about the use of computers in data processing:

> The most important event in the history of research has been the invention of the computer. This phenomenon has changed the scope of research and has made it possible to conduct research studies that one would not otherwise think of undertaking. Because computers make it possible to analyze large quantities of data quickly and efficiently, researchers are able to design studies without concern for the number of variables or the complexity of the analysis that may be required. Before the days of computers, researchers avoided studies involving several variables and large numbers of subjects because of the time and labor involved in tabulating and analyzing the data. Sophisticated statistical tests and multivariate analysis were not often undertaken. The computer can process large amounts of data and perform complex statistical analyses with phenomenal speed and accuracy (Ary et al., 1979, p. 339).

There is no doubt about the tremendous impact of computers in behavioral research and in many other aspects of modern life. Most of us by now are aware that computers are used by the airlines to make flight reservations, by police departments to track criminals, by the banks to compute our credit ratings. We are aware that computers are all around us--in cars, microwave ovens, wrist watches, VCR's. We may be less aware that computers are prevalent in education, in psychological testing and clinical practice, in biofeedback techniques for stress reduction, in preparation of manuscripts and books, and in scientific instrumentation and experimental manipulations (Cozby, 1984). But how did all this come about? *Time Magazine*'s Machine of the Year for 1982 did not spring from the head of Zeus. Let us explore some of the history of the development of the modern electronic computer.

Early European Contributions

It is possible to trace the development of computers back to the the Chinese abacus of 2500 B.C. or even further back to the Babylonians of 3000 B.C. who made marks on dust-covered tablets instead of using their fingers to count. However, we'll leave that investigation to students of ancient history.

Let's move forward to the 17th century and explore the creation of one of the very first mechanical computers. In 1642, Blaise Pascal invented a mechanical adding and subtracting machine. He was motivated in this effort by the fact that his father was a hardworking French tax collector who spent many hours laboring over hand calculations. The 19-year-old Pascal wanted to help reduce his father's load. Unfortunately, the local French clerks viewed the machine as a threat to their jobs, and it never caught on. This disappointment did not prevent Pascal from going on to achieve great accomplishments in the field of mathematics. He has been honored by having a contemporary computer language named for him--Pascal, the language of choice in many departments of computer science in American universities.

Toward the end of the 17th century, in 1694, Gottfried Leibnitz, a German mathematician, improved on Pascal's machine by adding multiplication and division to its functions. "It is unworthy of excellent men to lose hours like slaves in the labor of calculations," said Leibnitz (in *Time*, 1983, p. 30). However, his caculator was not 100% dependable. It made a few mistakes now and then.

In the year 1801, Joseph Marie Jacquard, another Frenchman, perfected a punch-card machine to weave designs in cloth. In Lyon, France, he was physically attacked and his machine destroyed. Again, the reason was fear of job loss by local workers. Later, through Napolean's support, Jacquard rebuilt his machine and turned Lyons into one of the most prosperous textile towns of its time.

Across the English Channel and a generation later, Charles Babbage, the father of the modern computer, developed the Difference Engine in 1822. Charles Babbage, described by *Time* (1983) as "an irascible 19th century English mathematician," was also the father of the speedometer, the cowcatcher, and the first reliable life expectancy tables.

Because Babbage was greatly dissatisfied with the mathematical and statistical tables of his time, he set out to design a machine which would produce accurate tables. Thus was born his Difference Engine, an intricate system of gears and cogs, for which only a model could be built. It was impossible for the craftsmen of his day to machine the precise parts required for the computer. This was a great disappointment for Babbage, and he almost gave up at this point. But later he regained hope and designed an even more complex machine called the Analytical Engine. It is this machine which is considered the true forerunner of the modern computer. It had all the essentials of a contemporary computer: a logic center which manipulated data according to rules, a memory, which Babbage called the "store," a control unit for carrying out instructions, and input and output channels. Most importantly, the Analytical Engine was programmable. Its operating procedures could be changed to suit its purpose.

It is probably fair to say that Charles Babbage became obsessed with designing his Analytical Engine. Perhaps he was the world's first computer "nerd." The machine, for which he completed more and more sketches, became hopelessly complicated.

In time, the British government cut off his research funds. No one seemed to understand what Babbage was doing except Ada, the Countess of Lovelace. The beautiful daughter of Lord Byron, a gifted mathematician in her own right, became Baggage's confidante and advocate. She encouraged him to continue his work. Together, she and Charles used their wits to concoct a betting system for recouping money at the race track. Despite this collaboration of two great minds, they lost several thousand pounds.

The Analytical Engine, which Charles Babbage spent the last 40 years of his life perfecting, was never built. It would have been as big as a football field and would have needed half a dozen locomotives to power it. One of the design feature of this computer was the use of the punched card to enter data, an idea Babbage got from Jacquard. In a rather poetic description, Ada described the process this way: "The Analytical Engine weaves algebraical patterns just as the Jacquard loom weaves flowers and leaves" (*Time*, 1983, p.30).

American Contributions

About 15 years after the death of Babbage (1872), a young American engineer put the punched card to use once again. Herman Hollerith was hired by the U.S. Census Bureau to devise a faster method of conducting the census. The 1880 census had taken seven and a half years to complete, at a time when the U.S. population numbered 50 million. The population was increasing rapidly, to 63 million by 1890, and there was concern about the ability to finish a tabulation by the year 1900.

Herman Hollerith designed a punch-card machine to code and sort census data. His new system cut the time to two and a half years of data processing for the 1990 census. Later, Hollerith left government employ and formed his own company, The Tabulating Machine Company, which later became IBM. The so-called IBM card, which is fast becoming extinct, is properly termed a Hollerith card, after its inventor.

It was not until the late 1930's and early 1940's, the World War II years, that considerable progress was made in the design and construction of real computers. Spurred on by competition and fear of Hitler's Germany, the U.S. developed a series of computers beginning in 1944. The first successful, general purpose, electro-mechanical, digital computer was the Mark I Computer. It was used to solve math and logic problems by engineers, physicists, and mathematicians at Harvard University, where the machine is now on display as an historical relic. The computer word "bug" was coined at Harvard when a program went awry because a moth flew into the machine. This was the first occasion on which a computer program had to be "debugged."

The following year, 1945, marked the introduction of the first completely electronic computer. ENIAC, which stood for Electrical Numerical Integrator and Calculator, was installed at Aberdeen Proving Grounds, Maryland. It was first used to make calculations for weather reports used to aid U.S. shipping in the North Atlantic. Later it was used to calculate artillery firing tables. This machine was designed by two professors from the University of Pennsylvania, who went on to form a company later acquired by Sperry Rand.

The interesting thing about ENIAC was its size. It had 18,000 vacuum tubes and weighed 30 tons. It required an enormous amount of electricity to power the computer, much in the form of air conditioning to cool the vacuum tubes. Even so, the computer was not very reliable. A service technician used roller skates to move about the large room and replace burned-out vacuum tubes on the average of one every seven minutes.

ENIAC's capabilities were impressive for her day. (The time has come to refer to computers as we do ships and nations--with the female pronoun). She could store twenty 10-digit numbers in memory at a time, and she could multiply, divide, and take the square root. At an original construction cost of $487,000, ENIAC could do in one day what formerly took 300 days by hand . Though ENIAC's capabilities were impressive at the time, they do not begin to compare with the performance of a modern desk computer which weighs only a few pounds and costs less than a thousand dollars. It has been estimated that if the automobile business had developed like the computer business since 1945, a Rolls-Royce would now cost $2.75 and run 3 million miles on a gallon of gas!

Another computer which debuted in 1945 was EDVAC, Electronic Discrete Variable Automatic Computer. Also designed by a University of Pennsylvania professor, J. von Neumann, EDVAC was the first computer to incorporate two important features of modern computers--use of the binary number system, and internal programming. These have become known as the "von Neumann Concept." Professor von Neumann discovered that a computer runs more efficiently when decimal numbers are converted to binary number, ones and zeroes, inside the machine. He also realized that computers would be much more convenient and versatile if one could change programs by simply entering new instructions via numeric codes rather than having to physically rewire the machine. The first internal program was written by von Neumann himself, a sorting routine which rearranged numbers in ascending order.

Perhaps the most spectacular computer of the early days was UNIVAC, Universal Automatic Calculator, produced by Sperry Rand in 1950. It was UNIVAC which predicted Eisenhower's presidential election victory of 1952 and for which the term "electronic brain" was coined. The American people were not yet accustomed to reliable election predictions, even a day after the polls closed.

Modern Developments

Many important events took place during this fertile period in the development of computers, but only a few will be enumerated here. The invention of the transistor in 1947 by William Shockley of Stanford University began the miniaturization of computers and other electrical appliances. In 1959, Texas Instruments and Fairchild Semiconductor simultaneously developed the integrated circuit, the first computer "chip." By 1970, laboratories were producing "large-scale integration" (LSI)--thousands of integrated circuits crammed onto a single quarter inch square of silicon. Thus was born Silicon Valley in Northern California, where Wozniac and Jobs revolutionized computing with their Apple II microcomputer in the late 1970's. By 1980 it was possible to fit 100,000 integrated circuits onto a single chip and, consequently, to produce a personal computer more powerful than ENIAC. By 1985, very large scale integration (VLSI) was in place, producing chips with more detail than a road map of a large metropolitan area.

Is there any end to the rapid improvements in cost, speed, size, and memory capacity of computers? No one knows for sure, but it appears that continual progress will be made. In only the past five years most small computers have more than doubled in capacity and yet cost half as much as their predecessors. One thing is certain: Computers will not go away. It is for this reason that Cozby (1984) has said: "These developments have made it almost a necessity for students of the social and behavioral sciences to acquire computer literacy. Computer literacy demands that you become familiar with how computers operate and how they are programmed and, most important, that you *use* a computer" (p. 2). Let us now explore how computers operate.

Computer Design and Operation

All computers can be reduced to four functions. Whatever their size, computers use an input device such as a keyboard for getting instructions or data into the machine; a central processing unit (CPU), the brains of the machine, for deciding what to do with the input; memory cells to store information and the results of arithmetic and logical operations on that information; and an output device such as a video screen or printer for transmitting the results of a program to the user. A program is simply a list of instructions which either resides in the machine permanently or is input by a programmer and stored in memory temporarily. Another name for a program or a collection of programs is "software" or a "software package." We will look at some statistical software packages in the next chapter. But first, let us explore some other characteristics of computer operation.

Binary Number System

One of the important charateristics of digital computers is that they use binary numbers rather than decimal numbers. This is because it is most efficient to represent bits of information in the form of on-off switches. It is sometimes helpful to think of a computer's memory as a vast bank of lightbulbs, long rows of lightbulbs, each of which can be turned on or off at will by a human programmer. The computer word "bit" actually means *bi*nary digi*t*. A "byte" is a collection of bits (lightbulbs), usually eight bits per byte, although large computers often have 16 or 32 bits to a byte. Thirty-two bit computers are much faster than 8-bit computers because they can move larger chunks of information in the same amount of time. The Apple Macintosh is a 32-bit computer, whereas the Commodore 64 is an 8-bit computer. The size of most computers is measured in terms of the number of bytes of available memory. Thus, a 640K computer has 640 kilo-bytes or 640,000 bytes of memory.

The number of bytes in a computer's memory is not too relevant to us unless we understand what kind of information resides in a byte of memory. Recall that a byte is a collection of bits and that each bit represents a binary digit. Early computer architects decided to represent common bits of information such as the letters of the alphabet, punctuation marks, and single-digit numbers in 8-bit coded form. Thus, the letter "E" is 10001011 in binary form (with even parity). The punctuation mark "," is represented as 01011001. Think of these as rows of eight lightbulbs in which the "1's" represent bulbs turned on). Thus, each character, whether it be a numerical digit or letter of the alphabet, occupies one byte of memory. Knowing this relationship, it is possible, for example, to calculate the number of pages of text one could type into a computer before exceeding its capacity, or the maximum size statistical program that could be run on a given computer.

Computer Languages

Computer languages are another important outgrowth of the binary system of representation in computers. The first computer language was "machine language," the only language a computer directly understands. Because there are 256 different 8-bit combinations, it was possible for early programmers to use some of the leftover combinations not used for the alphabet and other special characters to represent standard computer commands. A simple machine language program is shown below:

10110110 (Get a number from memory.)

```
01101101  (Get another number from memory.)
11110101  (Add the two numbers together.)
00110110  (Place the total into memory.)
```

Note the use of 8-bit codes. These codes are interpreted by the central processing unit and acted upon accordingly. The CPU knows where in memory to find each number and where to place the resultant sum.

As you might guess, programming in machine language was and still is a very exacting process, quite prone to error. One reversal of a 1 or 0 spells doom to a program. Many people believed there had to be an easier way. This led to the development of a higher level language called "assembly language." In assembly language, mnemonics are used instead of 8-bit codes. A similar program is shown below:

```
LD A, 1     (Load a number from memory.)
LD B, 100   (Load another number from memory.)
ADD         (Add the two numbers together.)
LD C, 00F   (Place the total in a new memory location.)
```

Because the CPU, called a microprocessor in personal computers, cannot really "understand" the above instructions, another program called an assembler had to be written first to interpret these mnemonics and translate them into machine language. In modern microcomputers, such a program is stored in ROM (read-only memory) for use by those who wish to communicate in assembly language.

As computer languages grew in number, even higher level languages were developed which more closely approximate our natural English language. Some of the more commonly used languages are BASIC, FORTRAN, COBOL, Pascal, and PL/1. The name BASIC, like most other computer languages, is an acronym. It stands for Beginners All-purpose Instruction Code. Wadsworth (1977) observed the great popularity of BASIC in the middle 1970's. A decade later it was still the most prominent language among users of small computers. FORTRAN (Formula Translation), a language developed primarily for mathematical and statistical work, is used largely by academics and applied scientists. COBOL (Common Business-Oriented Language) is used almost exclusively on large computer systems in the business world for such applications as financial analysis and inventory control. Pascal, named after the French mathematician, is a more recent language which is thought to possess many of the advantages of the former languages but fewer of their limitations. Programs written in Pascal are more easily understood by other programmers because of Pascal's more structured style. Another language which represented an earlier attempt to improve and standardize computer communication is PL/1 (Programming Language One). PL/1 was created by IBM with the hope that it would unify the industry and become the standard computer language. This attempt failed and many new languages have been developed since PL/1 appeared in the 1960's. An example of a BASIC program is shown below:

```
10 PRINT "THIS PROGRAM WILL MULTIPLY TWO NUMBERS."
20 PRINT "WHAT IS THE FIRST NUMBER?"
30 INPUT A
40 PRINT "WHAT IS THE SECOND NUMBER?"
50 INPUT B
60 C=A*B
70 PRINT "THE ANSWER IS..."
80 PRINT C
```

The use of higher level languages, and ultimately English, depends to a considerable degree on the speed and size of computers. Because such languages require rather large translation programs to convert commands to machine language, computers must have relative large memories to hold the main program, the interpreter program, and all relevant data at one time. What is more important, a computer must be able to make the conversion from high level language to machine language very quickly. Otherwise, a user would have to sit and wait a long time before his commands were acted upon. With large modern computers, referred to as "mainframes," it is possible through time-sharing for dozens of users to type instructions to a computer simultaneously and each receive "immediate" responses. It is because of the these capabilities and also limitations of computers that most usage of statistical packages such as SPSS is still confined to large computer systems using time-shared terminals. More about this later.

Should students of the behavioral sciences learn a programming language? Experts are not in agreement on this question. Perhaps an analogy can be drawn here between computers and cars. Many older drivers would claim they learned to drive an automobile quite well without driver education. Many of these same individuals, however, want their children or grandchildren to take such a class. Many competent researchers are not computer programmers. But those who are usually make a strong case for such knowledge. According to Kerlinger (1986):

> One thing is certain: researchers who learn a little FORTRAN or BASIC and who put two or three programs through a machine complex successfully will never again be the same. They have participated in one of the most interesting and exciting adventures they will ever experience. The main problem will then be to maintain the balance and discretion to keep the machine where it belongs: in the background and not the foreground of research activity (Kerlinger, 1986, p. 635).

This chapter has presented background information on an important research tool and ubiquitous artifact of modern civilization. The purpose was to foster a greater sense of appreciation for this powerful, yet obedient friend of the behavioral researcher. To this history and theory of the computer the following chapters will add more practical knowledge of how to use computer software for research data analysis.

CHAPTER SEVEN

USING STATISTICAL PACKAGES

It was not until the mid-1960's that statistical programs were made available for common use by researchers. One of the first of these was the *Scientific Subroutine Package* published by IBM. This was a book of printed programs which the researcher had to keypunch onto Hollerith cards, for input along with his research data. The card deck, sometimes several hundred cards, weighing several pounds, had to be submitted to a central computing facility to be run on a mainframe computer. Each "run" would require two or three hours to process, sometimes more if the computer "went down." Many American campuses experienced this kind of computer usage until the mid-1970's.

Gradually, with the greater availability of external memory devices such as magnetic tapes and disks, it became possible to store statistical programs at the computer center. As computer terminals (remote keyboard entry stations) became more common, it was possible for several individuals to make use of "canned" programs simultaneously. This environment was more conducive to data analysis than ever before. However, it lacked the quality control necessary for scientific research. Many computer installations were using statistical programs created at the local site, sometimes for special purposes, and sometimes not totally accurate. Research results were published which weren't completely correct, due to computing inaccuracies. There was a need for better, more powerful and reliable programs which could be shared nationally by academic, governmental, and private agencies. Such programs were developed at major universities and later published and disseminated widely during the 1970's. They have been refined and augmented since that time and are now widely available at most large computer installations. Let us explore four of these packages briefly before settling on one for further use.

Mainframe Packages

One of the first statistical packages, BMDP (Biomedical Programs) was developed by W.J. Dixon and his colleagues at the Health Sciences Computing Facility at UCLA. This package now contains over 40 programs in such categories as data description, frequency tables, linear and nonlinear regression, analysis of variance, nonparametric statistics, cluster analysis, multivariate analysis, and time-series analysis. This package is used widely at American universities by students and professors in a variety of disciplines. It is particularly useful for a type of analysis of variance (ANOVA) known as repeated-measures designs. BMDP is somewhat more difficult to use than some other packages and has not been disseminated widely beyond academe. In some ways it is more a collection of separate programs than a truly integrated package.

SPSS (Statistical Package for the Social Sciences) was developed at Stanford University starting in 1965. Frustrated at having to use a library of single-purpose programs written in many different languages with little documentation, a group of political science professors, with the help of computer scientists and statisticians, began to design an integrated system of computer programs. Their goal was to create a set of programs that was not only correct and efficient but which reflected the particular needs of empirical social researchers, including students who had no experience with computers. In 1971, the project was moved to the National Opinion Research Center at the University of Chicago, which still serves as an important development center for SPSS (Nie, et al., 1975). A 1986 version of SPSS contained 46 programs quite similar to BMDP. SPSS is somewhat easier to learn than BMDP and has greater flexibility in labeling variables and tailoring printed output.

A relatively new package of statistical programs is SAS, the Statistical Analysis System. SAS (pronounced "sass") is syntactically similar to SPSS and also has useful features of data treatment, clarity of output, and some business applications. It will perform the various data definition, modification, and statistical analysis procedures available in the other packages. However, because SAS is a newer system than the others, it is not available on as many computer systems as SPSS and BMDP (Cozby, 1984). SAS appears to be roughly equivalent to SPSS in ease of use.

By far the easiest-to-use of the four packages is Minitab, developed by T.A. Ryan and his associates at Penn State University. The Minitab package uses a series of 3- and 4-letter commands to call up computing routines such as *stan*dard deviation, *corr*elation, *twos*ample t-test, and *one*way analysis of variance. Many other programs are also available, including regression analysis and several different nonparametric tests. Minitab also has the ability to create various types of distributions from which cases may be sampled, a feature useful in learning about statistical probability (Cozby, 1984). It should be noted that statistical packages are a bit like word processing programs. They all share the basic goal of data reduction; however, some are a little more comprehensive than others. You often pay for the greater coverage by more complex and complicated language commands. In general, mainframe packages are more difficult to learn than microcomputer programs. But in the end, you are able to conduct a greater variety of analyses.

Microcomputer Packages

A most recent development in statistical software has been the creation of program packages for micro- or personal computers. Several different packages are available for the Apple and IBM computer lines. Fewer programs are available for other brands, and they are usually not as sophisticated. Is it wise to use a small computer package for research purposes? Perhaps, if it fits your needs.

The attractiveness of small computer packages is that they are fairly easy to learn and use. Some of them are inexpensive enough for individual purchase and use with a home computer. However, there are several drawbacks to using packages designed for microcomputers. First, although most packages now have provisions for creating and saving data files, they often have restrictions on the size of samples and the number of variables that can be analyzed at one time. Secondly, while data entry is often aided by menu-driven prompts, it is often more time-consuming than on a large computer. More importantly, data files are not usually transferable from one package to another. Thus, if a package does not contain a program you need, you would have to reenter all your data for analysis by a second program package. Sometimes, a great deal of reentering of data is necessary, even within a single package, because of memory restrictions or the inablity to join files together. Finally, most small computer packages are not as robust as those on mainframes. They cannot perform the variety of analyses nor can they always cope with common problems such as missing data or unequal cell sizes in analysis of variance.

Despite some of the problems noted above, it would appear that increased use of microcomputers for data analysis is a reasonable prediction. As small computers grow in number and in size and speed, more sophisticated programs will be written for them. It is probably only a matter of time before mainframe packages become widely available for microcomputers. Two such packages, SPSS and SAS, are already available for installation on IBM PC's and compatibles. However, they require machines with approximately 500K of memory and a 10 megabyte hard disk. While such hardware configurations are well within the reach of many home users, the price of $750 for a single copy of SPSS/PC makes it an unlikely purchase for most individuals.

For many of the reasons stated above, it seems best for most student researchers to invest time in learning how to use a mainframe statistical package. Because some of the packages, such as SPSS and SAS, are widely used in business and industry as well as in research, the effort to master a package will enhance one's knowledge of statistics and computers while also creating marketable skills.

For several reasons, not the least of which is its wide availability, this book will focus on the use of SPSS, the Statistical Package for the Social Sciences, for data analysis in the remaining chapters. The chances are very good that your computer center has SPSS installed. But if not, many of the principles of data entry, file construction, and program development discussed here will help you to more easily learn another system.

Computer Files

A concept that is very useful when working with any computer is the file. A *computer file* is simply a collection of instructions or data which fit together and are stored in a single location. Most of us are familiar with office files--sheets of paper concerning a particular subject, which are often stored in a manila file folder. A computer file amounts to the same thing, except that the contents of the file are stored electronically in a computer's memory or on a peripheral medium, such as a disk or tape.

In data analysis, it is common to construct and work with different types of files. A typical approach is to start by constructing a *data file*. This is an arrangement of numerical and sometimes verbal data according to some pre-arranged structure. Once the researcher has created and stored a data file, he proceeds to build a second file called a program or *command file*. In SPSS, the command file contains the list of SPSS commands which instruct the system how to process the data file. Sometimes it is convenient to create a third file called an SPSS system file. An *SPSS system file* is an elaborate form of a "raw" data file in which additional information concerning variable names and locations is stored along with the data.

Constructing a Data File

A task that is common to all statistical packages is the construction of a data file. One of the benefits of mainframe packages is that data files constructed for one package are readily used by other packages. Let us see how to build a data file. In Appendix A of this book is a questionnaire on personal happiness. The author has used this questionnaire for a number of years to collect data from students and other subjects for both research and pedagogical purposes. The first five items of the happiness questionnaire are shown in Figure 7.1. Although I have collected data on more than 400 subjects, let us consider the construction of a data file containing the data for only 10 individuals on questions 1 through 5.

FIGURE 7.1
Items from Happiness Questionnaire

1. In general, how happy or unhappy have you been over the last six months?
   1. Very happy
   2. Moderately happy
   3. Slightly happy
   4. Slightly unhappy
   5. Moderately unhappy
   6. Very unhappy

2. Does your level of happiness change or remain fairly constant?
   1. It remains stable.
   2. It rarely changes.
   3. It changes infrequently.
   4. It sometimes changes.
   5. It changes often.
   6. It changes very often.

3. If you suddenly inherited a large fortune, would you continue in your present work (including student)?
   1. Definitely yes
   2. Probably yes
   3. Perhaps yes
   4. Perhaps not
   5. Probably not
   6. Definitely not

4. How confident are you that your guiding values are right for you and will last?
   1. Very confident
   2. Considerably confident
   3. Somewhat confident
   4. Not very confident
   5. I'm questioning my values constantly.
   6. I don't really have any constant guiding values.

5. How optimistic or pessimistic about your life would you say you are?
   1. Very optimistic
   2. Moderately optimistic
   3. Slightly optimistic
   4. Slightly pessimistic
   5. Moderately pessimistic
   6. Very pessimistic

- -

A general principle for data files is the use of a row-by-column matrix in which the rows represent persons, also referred to as subjects or cases, and the columns represent variables. Such a configuration generates a rectangular matrix as shown in Figure 7.2. There are several rules of thumb that apply to data files, only some of which are illustrated in Figure 7.2.

FIGURE 7.2
Sample Data File

		Questions (Variables)					
		1	2	3	4	5	
	Subjects						
	036	1	3	2	2	4	
	062	2		2	1	5	
	081	2	2	1	3	2	
	087	2	2	4	2	2	
	204	2	4	3	2	5	
Rows	232	2	5	2	1	2	
	246	3	2	1	1	2	
	278	3	5	5	4	4	
	293	4	4	5	5	4	
	305	5	3	6	3	3	
	1-3	5	7	9	11	13	 80

C o l u m n s

Thumb Rules for Data Files

1. Whenever possible, use numbers rather than alphabetic letters to represent responses. Although it is possible in SPSS and other packages to use alphabetic characters as data points, it is simpler to use numbers.

2. Do not use commas with large numbers. For example, if you are entering a subject's annual income, enter "25000" rather than "25,000". Also, do not use other special characters such as the dollar sign. The computer will only become confused with "$25,000" as a data entry.

3. Make provisions for missing data. Note that in Figure 7.2 there is a missing data point for subject 062. This subject did not respond to question 2. Perhaps he or she could not decide on an answer to the question. Perhaps it was an inadvertent omission. Sometimes a subject will refuse to answer a question on privacy grounds. These are all common reasons for missing data in survey studies using questionnaires. A simple remedy for missing data is to leave a blank space in the data file, as has been done here. SPSS will recognize a blank as missing data and ignore it. In research using personal interviews, where the researcher is often aware of a subject's reason for omitting a response, different numbers can be used to represent the reasons. For

example, we could use the numbers 7, 8, and 9 to signify the reasons stated earlier, since these numbers cannot possibly represent true responses to the questions. It is a good idea to avoid the use of the number 0 for missing data. This is because with ratio variables such as income, the number 0 might be confused with an actual income level. In such a case, use a blank to represent missing data and 0 for no actual income.

4. When entering numbers with decimal values, it is not necessary to include the decimal point. For example, if you are entering a grade-point average of 2.62, you may enter this as "262" and later instruct SPSS to insert the decimal point electronically for all computations. This saves time in file construction. However, if you prefer to include the decimal point, you may do so with no harm.

5. While it is possible to use free-form data input in some versions of SPSS, it is usually best to use formatted input of the type shown in Figure 7.2. Formatted data is that which specifies a particular column number for each variable. For example, in the happiness data each subject's response for variable 3 is in column 9, and this is uniform throughout the data file.

6. When convenient, leave one blank space between variables. It is much easier to proof read a data file if there are spaces between the entries. If one has a great many single digit variables, as in the happiness questionnaire, it is sometimes easier and faster to omit blanks between the numbers. Another reason for omitting the blanks is to avoid using a second data line, or "record." In most applications there are a maximum of 80 columns for data entry per record. If one has 80 single digit variables, as in the happiness questionnaire, it is more convenient to string them together on a single line than to create two records for each subject.

7. Whenever possible, enter a subject identification number at the beginning of that subject's row of data. This practice aids in checking printed data files against the original data source for accuracy. It also helps in restoring "scrambled" data files or in sorting subjects into some logical order. In experimental or causal-comparative research it is a common practice to include a group designation within the ID number. For example, an experimental subject might be coded "1" and a control subject "2." Thus, the 10th subjects from each of these groups would have ID numbers of "110" and "210," repectively. In studies providing subject anonymity, true ID numbers are not possible. That is, ID numbers should not appear on data collection forms which subjects will fill out, lest they become unduly concerned about their loss of privacy. Sequence numbers can be added to the data documents later and included in the computer records.

Entering Data into the Computer

Now that we have created the data file on paper, we need to transfer it to the computer. This can be done in the original way with punched cards, or it can be accomplished by typing the data from a terminal keyboard. For most students it will be the latter. The first thing you must usually do is obtain an *account number*. This is a number which certifies you as a bona fide user and which is sometimes used for billing purposes. You might receive an individual or class account number. You may also need to use a *password*. This is a word or number, perhaps of your own choosing, which further provides security for your account. After all, you won't want someone else "snooping" in your "file space." Computer thievery, including plagiarism, can be a real problem. You should protect yourself accordingly through the judicious use of your account number and password.

The next thing you will need to find out is how to "log in" to your computer. *Logging in* is the process of introducing yourself to the computer and receiving a welcome as a proper user. Each computer system has a somewhat different procedure. Your instructor can probably tell you the right keys to press. The computer will prompt you to enter your account number and password. Once you have been given access to the system, the computer will wait for further instructions from you. Typically, at this point you will give a command to enter an Editor subsystem. An *Editor* is simply a program which allows you to type verbal or numeric data and arrange the screen as you wish. There are two types of editors. A *full screen editor* is much like a word processor on a small computer. It allows you to move the blinking cursor all around the screen and make as many changes as you like. A *line editor* allows you to change only one line at a time. The reason for your using an editor is not that you want to change anything as yet, but that you want to create a data file. The editor is your vehicle for accomplishing that. If you are a perfect typist and enter the data correctly the first time, you won't have to use the correcting features of the editor. You will simply save your file for further use with SPSS. However, it is likely from time to time that you will make an error in entering a number. You should spend some time becoming familiar with the way your editor works, so that you can correct such errors when they occur. Most editors are not difficult to use. They have commands such as (I)nsert, (D)elete, (M)odify, and (S)ave. The time it takes you to master this system will be well spent. You might also find the editor useful for typing class papers.

This chapter has presented information on the development and characteristics of statistical program packages for both mainframe and microcomputers. The concept of the computer file was explored, and specific rules for the construction of data files were presented. Finally, some rules for entering data into a computer were described. The next chapter will provide very specific information on the use of SPSS for data analysis.

CHAPTER EIGHT

USING THE STATISTICAL PACKAGE FOR THE SOCIAL SCIENCES

There are actually several different versions of SPSS*, the Statistical Package for the Social Sciences. There is the original SPSS Batch system, designed for punched cards. There is an on-line, or conversational version, called SCSS, for use with terminals. Another more recent and enhanced version is SPSS-X. And finally, there is SPSS/PC+ for use on personal computers. There are slight differences between these versions that affect program creation. This chapter will present information on writing programs for both SPSS and SPSS-X, the two major "dialects" of SPSS. The example programs and associated output were obtained from SPSS Release 9 and SPSS-X Release 2 from Northwestern University, for implementation on the California State University CDC Cyber 170/180 computer, with NOS operating system. The programs should run with little or no modification on most other computer systems.

Creating an SPSS Program File

There are two essential components of any SPSS program. These are data definition statements and task definition statements. A *data definition statement* consists of one or more lines which instruct SPSS in the arrangement of your data file--the number and names of the variables and their column locations. A *task definition statement* consists of one or more lines that tell SPSS which of several possible statistical subprograms you want to use in your data analysis. Perhaps you would like to generate frequency distributions and also calculate some Pearson correlations between selected variables. There are separate subprograms which can perform these tasks.

Data Definition Statements

One of the features of SPSS on-line is the use of program line numbers. Many programming languages use line numbers at the left side of each line so that reference can be made to various parts of the program. Sometimes when one attempts to "execute" an SPSS program, it will not run because of the presence of an error. SPSS will provide a diagnostic error message by referring to a line number where the error was encountered. The researcher can then quickly focus on that line to make a correction in spelling or syntax, so that the program will run correctly the next time. It is customary to begin a program using the number 5 as the first

* SPSS is a trademark of SPSS, Inc., of Chicago, IL, for its proprietary computer software

line number. Subsequent lines are incremented by 5 so that a series of lines will be 5, 10, 15, 20, etc. Line numbers are skipped so that additional lines may be inserted later, if necessary. Most SPSS statements contain both a primary command and a secondary specification. The primary commands are represented by the whole numbers above. Secondary statements are given decimal values, e.g., 5.005, which identify the statement as part of the primary command statement on line 5. SPSS refers to all lines beginning with the same whole number as a "block." Diagnostic error messages always refer to blocks of lines where an error is suspected of occurring. All of this explanation becomes much simpler if we view an actual data specification statement:

```
5.    DATA LIST
5.005 FIXED(1)/1 V1 TO V5 4-13
```

These two lines are simply a short-hand way of describing how we constructed the data file discussed earlier in the chapter. Line 5 contains the primary command indicating that what follows, Line 5.005, will contain specific information about the organization of the data file. The keyword FIXED indicates that our data file has a fixed, or formatted, structure. The number 1 in parentheses after FIXED indicates one record per case, that is, only one line of data for each subject in our sample. Note that one or more blanks may appear on either side of the parentheses, or between the parentheses and the number, although none is required. Such blank spaces are optional and are normally used to improve readability. In our present situation, in which we have only one record per case, we could actually omit "(1)" from the specification, and SPSS would assume only one record per case. The remaining part of the statement provides more information about the variables we want SPSS to analyze and their location in the file. The number 1 which appears after the slash mark indicates that the list of variables which follows is part of the first data record. This is actually redundant information because we have already said we only have one record per case. However, the structure of SPSS syntax requires that we "retell" our story, by placing a "1" after the slash mark.

A useful device in SPSS language is the use of the "TO convention," which allows one to specify a whole list of variables: V1, V2, V3, V4, and V5. These variables correspond to subjects' responses to the first five questionnaire items. If you prefer, you may use the term ITEM instead of V to name the variables. SPSS will understand both terms equally well. The final part of the data specification statement indicates the location of the five variables. Recall that we actually used two columns per variable, in order to leave a space between numbers. Because of this, we must instruct SPSS to begin reading our data in column 4 and continue reading through column 13. Notice that, although we typed ID numbers for each subject, we do not include these as variables in the analysis and we instruct SPSS to skip over columns 1-3 and begin reading in column 4. Let's summarize what we've covered thus far by looking at several different versions of the same data definition statement all of which are correct:

```
5.005 FIXED(1)/1 V1 TO V5 4-13
5.005 FIXED   /1 V1 TO V5 4-13
5.005 FIXED/   1  V1 TO V5   4-13
5.005 FIXED / 1  V1 V2 V3 V4 V5  4-13
5.5   FIXED / 1  V1,V2,V3,V4,V5   4-13
5.1   FIXED / 1  V1 5, V2 7, V3 9, V4 11, V5 13
5.6   FIXED / 1  ITEM1 TO ITEM5  4-13
```

Several things are apparent in the above equally good statements. The first is that "(1)" after the keyword FIXED may be omitted, since there is only one record per case. Secondly, spacing is usually flexible in SPSS language. However, you should be aware that spaces are used as breaks, or delimiters, between terms. Thus, it is necessary to have a space between a variable name and other terms. The spaces you see in the first example above are absolutely required. If you omit any one of them, SPSS will give you a diagnostic error message referring to block 5 when you attempt to run the program. Lines 5.5 and 5.1 show that you may use commas as delimiters in place of, or in addition to, blank spaces. SPSS does have a degree of human-like flexibility. But there may be times when you will wish it had more. You can see also by these same two examples that it is possible to list each of the variable names separately rather than using the TO convention. Furthermore, you may indicate after each variable name the exact column location for that variable, rather than making a collective statement at the end. This is shown in line 5.1. Finally, it is not necessary when typing your program to use decimal values beginning with ".005." The only thing you must do is use a decimal value higher than 5.0. However, if you later instruct SPSS to list your program, the line numbers will automatically be reset. This will become clearer as you gain experience in writing programs.

Another part of data definition involves a specification concerning missing values. Although a *missing values statement* is not a required part of an SPSS program, it is often a necessary evil with much behavioral research data. If our sample data file did not have a missing data point for subject 062, we could omit the statement below:

```
10.     MISSING VALUES
10.005 ALL (BLANK)
```

There are other ways of writing statement 10.005, just as there were for statement 5.005 above. Notice, for example, that I have declared blank spaces as equivalent to missing data for *all* variables. Actually, for our specific data it was not necessary for me to do this, since the missing data point involved only variable 2. Thus, the following statement would work as well in this case:

```
10.    MISSING VALUES
10.5   V2 (BLANK)
```

It should be obvious to you why the first statement above is preferable, even though the second will work in this one situation. There is a missing values statement, however, that is better than either of the two shown so far. Consider for a moment the possibility of miskeyed data. Suppose while you are entering data on many individuals for a large number of variables, your hand slips every once in a while and you type an incorrect number. Even after listing the file on the computer screen, you don't find all your errors and correct them. (A better way is to print out the file on paper and scan it with the aid of a ruler.) Consider the possible mistakes you could make. There are actually nine single digit numbers you could type in place of the correct one. Some of those possible mistakes would be more obvious than others. If you typed a 7, 8, 9, or 0, it would automatically be wrong, since those are invalid responses to any of the five questions. Thus, a better missing values statement would be the one below:

```
10.    MISSING VALUES
10.005 ALL (0,7 THRU 9)
```

Statement 10.005 will act as an effective screen for many typing errors you might miss when you check your data file. The process of data cleansing is very important in behavioral research. But wait! What happened to BLANK and where did THRU come from? SPSS, like other programming languages, treats blanks and zeros in the same way, unless instructed differently. That is, SPSS interprets a blank space as a zero for computational purposes. Since we do not have any true zeros in our data set, the missing values statement above will perform just as the previous one. It will screen out blanks as data, by considering them as zeros. The THRU term above is another of the useful keywords in SPSS. Unfortunately, it can be easily confused with TO. Although both terms mean the same thing, TO is used to specify series of variables, while THRU is used strictly with numbers. If you want to avoid this confusion, simply specify (0,7,8,9) and avoid THRU.

Task Definition Statements

The second part of an SPSS program or command file requires that you specify the use of one or more statistical tasks. Figure

8.1 gives a partial list of the many statistical programs in the SPSS package (Nie, et al., 1975).

- -

FIGURE 8.1
Statistical Subprograms in SPSS

Program Name	Description
FREQENCIES	One-way frequency distributions with descriptive statistics
CROSSTABS	Two-way to N-way cross-tabulation tables and related statistics
BREAKDOWN	Description and comparison of sub-populations
T-TEST	Test of mean differences between two groups or variables
PEARSON CORR	Bivariate correlation analysis
SCATTERGRAM	Scatter diagram of data points and simple regression
NEW REGRESSION*	Bivariate and multiple regression and correlation
ONEWAY	One-way analysis of variance with a priori and post hoc tests
ANOVA	N-way analysis of variance and covariance
RELIABILITY*	Analysis of additive scales and repeated measures ANOVA
DISCRIMINANT	Comparison of multiple groups on nominal dependent variable
FACTOR	Reduction of multiple variables and rotation of factor matrix

* Hull, C. & Nie, N., SPSS Update 7-9: New Procedures and Facilities for Releases 7-9, 1981.

- -

For the present time, let us be satisfied with a frequency distribution of the five variables in our data set. That is, we want to know the levels of happiness, etc., of all the individuals in our sample--how many were extremely happy, very happy, and so on. In addition, we would like to get some summary descriptive statistics, such as the mean and standard deviation for each item. These might be useful in interpreting and comparing items. The SPSS subprogram which performs these calculations is called FREQUENCIES. We must therefore write a task definition statement which calls for this subprogram to operate on our data file. A valid statement is shown below:

```
15.    FREQUENCIES
15.005 GENERAL=ALL
```

As you might deduce, this task definition statement requests that SPSS conduct a series of frequency analyses on all variables. The keyword GENERAL refers to a type of analysis which can be performed on both integers (whole numbers) and decimal numbers. Always use the GENERAL mode of analysis. Naturally, the task definition statement can be adjusted so that only specific variables are included. If we wanted frequency distributions only for questions 1 and 5, we could use the statement below:

```
15.    FREQUENCIES
15.005 GENERAL = V1, V5
```

Any variables listed to the right of the equals sign will be included in the analysis. Subprogram FREQUENCIES will only provide frequency counts unless given further instructions. This subprogram is like most others in the package. There are associated options and additional statistics which can be requested. A list of selected Options and Statistics for FREQUENCIES is provided in FIGURE 8.2. We will select Option 8, a histogram, and all available statistics as follows:

```
20.    OPTIONS
20.005 8
25.    STATISTICS
25.005 ALL
```

As usual, different options and statistics may be specified by using different numbers in statements 20.005 and 25.005. Just remember to separate your choices with blanks or commas. For example, if you wanted to print the output in condensed format in addition to getting a histogram, you would specify:

```
20.    OPTIONS
20.005 5,8
```

These statements constitute the entire SPSS program. As you can see, an SPSS program is not overly complicated. The most important command for you to master is the DATA LIST statement. Because our sample data file contains only 1-digit variables and is therefore simpler than most, you will need to practice constructing DATA LIST statements involving a greater variety of data types. Figure 8.3, adapted from the *SPSS Primer* (Klecka, 1975), provides a very realistic example of a data file with a variety of variables. Notice that this example file has three records per case, shown in column 1 of the table. The next two columns show the locations and names of the variables. Column 4 indicates the number of implied decimal digits for each variable. For example, variables ITEM1, ITEM2, ITEM3, and ITEM4

FIGURE 8.2
Selected OPTIONS and STATISTICS for Subprogram FREQUENCIES

Selected OPTIONS:

1. Causes the missing value indicators to be ignored.
3. Causes all output to be printed on an eight and one-half by eleven inch space.
5. Causes the frequency tables for all requested output to be printed in condensed format.
8. Causes a histogram to be printed for each variable.

STATISTICS:

1.	Mean	7.	Kurtosis
2.	Standard error	8.	Skewness
3.	Median	9.	Range
4.	Mode	10.	Minimum
5.	Standard deviation	11.	Maximum
6.	Variance		

- -

have two decimal digits. From the second column of the table you can see that these variables occupy three columns each. Therefore, the last two columns of each variable will be regarded as decimal numbers to the right of an implied decimal point, one that has not been physically typed in the file. These might be numbers like gradepoint averages--2.35, 3.66, 1.95, etc. The last column of Figure 8.3 gives information on missing values used with each variable. Note the variety of possibilities.

At the bottom of Figure 8.3 is a DATA LIST statement which correctly specifies all of the variables in the sample file. Notice the "(3)" after FIXED. This indicates 3 records per case. The information for each record is preceded with a "/", followed by the record number. The implied decimal digits for the ITEM variables are coded as "(2)" following the columns designation. This DATA LIST statement is so long that it requires continuation statements after 5.005. These have been numbered 5.010 through 5.020. SPSS understands that these lines constitute one long data specification. When using continuation lines, it is important not to split variable names between lines. Most versions of SPSS allow a maximum of 72 characters per line including blanks. If a variable name will not fit completely on a line, terminate the line and begin the complete name on the next line. You should study Figure 8.3 at length, until you are familiar with all facets of the DATA LIST command. This example contains all the variations you will need for most behavioral research data.

*FIGURE 8.3**
DATA LIST Specification for 15 Variables

Record	Column(s)	Variable Name	Number of Implied Decimal Digits	Missing Value(s)
1	26	EYECOLOR	0	0,8,9
	27	BALDNESS	0	0,8,9
	28	ANEMIA	0	0,8,9
2	5-7	ITEM1	2	9.99
	8-10	ITEM2	2	9.99
	11-13	ITEM3	2	0
	14-16	ITEM4	2	0
	57	HAYFEVER	0	0,8,9
	63	ALGYCATS	0	0,8,9
	64	ALGYDOGS	0	0,8,9
3	30-31	SCALE15	0	0,-1
	32-33	SCALE16	0	0,8,9
	34-35	SCALE17	0	0
	48-49	HRTBEAT	0	None
	69-71	BLDPRESS	0	0

```
5.     DATA LIST
5.005 FIXED(3)/1 EYECOLOR BALDNESS ANEMIA 26-28/ 2 ITEM1 TO
5.010 ITEM4 5-16 (2), HAYFEVER 57, ALGYCATS 63,
5.015 ALGYDOGS 64/ 3 SCALE15, SCALE16, SCALE17  30-35,
5.020 HRTBEAT 48-49, BLDPRESS 69-71
```

- -

* adapted from Klecka, et al. (1975), SPSS Primer

Accessing SPSS

Figure 8.4 shows the process of accessing SPSS once you have logged in to the computer. The first step is to type SPSSONL. This system command calls up the SPSS on-line package and reads it into memory from disk storage. The computer then asks you three questions: Do you want to USE AN SPSS STSTEM FILE THIS RUN? Your answer, typed from the keyboard, would be NO. Next: Do you want to USE A RAW DATA FILE THIS RUN? Your answer is YES. Third, ENTER FILE NAME. The name of the file is SAMDAT7 (SAMple DATa file for chapter 7), which you would type in from the keyboard.

At this point the system places you in what is called AUTO-MODE. Once you are in AUTO-MODE, you may do one of two things. You may actually type your SPSS program from the keyboard, or you may READ a program which has been previously created and saved either in AUTOMODE or in an editor. In this

FIGURE 8.4
Using SPSS Online

```
 SPSS/ONLINE 9.0

 USE AN SPSS SYSTEM FILE THIS RUN
? NO
 USE A RAW DATA FILE THIS RUN
? YES
 ENTER FILE NAME
? SAMDAT7
 AUTO-MODE
? READ,SCOM71
? L
   5.     DATA LIST
   5.005 FIXED(1)/1 V1 TO V5  4-13
  10.     MISSING VALUES
  10.005 ALL (BLANK)
  15.     FREQUENCIES
  15.005 GENERAL=ALL
  20.     OPTIONS
  20.005 8
  25.     STATISTICS
  25.005 ALL
? E
```

---

case, a previously stored program was brought into SPSS by the command, READ,SCOM71. SCOM71 is the name of the SPSS command file which contained the program we just constructed in this chapter. The program is listed in its entirety in Figure 8.4

If you choose to write your SPSS program in AUTO-MODE, you need to be aware of a few simple procedures. Program lines may be corrected by simply retyping a new line. The new version will replace the old. A program may be listed on the screen at any time, by typing LIST or L. Unwanted lines may be deleted by Typing D, followed by the line number. Typing D,5 would delete line 5. Typing D,5,25 would delete lines 5 through 25. If you want to insert a line in the program, simply type it at the bottom of the screen, with the proper line number. It will be automatically inserted when the program is executed. To run a program, type the command EXECUTE or E. To save an SPSS command file, type WRITE, followed by your file name. Upon leaving SPSS with an END command, it is necessary to save your program permanently by typing SAVE,(filename). Although these procedures may vary somewhat from one computer system to another, this description should be helpful in running an SPSS program on your computer.

SPSS Printed Output

Referring back to the happiness survey data, Figure 8.5 is the actual output from SPSS FREQUENCIES for V2. Recall that V2 was the question about the stability of one's happiness: Does your level of happiness change or remain fairly constant? Figure 8.5 shows that our sample of ten individuals ranged from 2 through 5 on the 6-point response scale. This is shown in the column headed CODE. The numbers to the right under the heading ABSOLUTE FREQ indicate how many individuals responded. Here we see that three individuals felt their level of happiness "rarely changes." Two felt "it changes infrequently," two more thought "it sometimes changes," and another two determined that "it changes often." There was one non-respondent in the group, shown next to BLANK on the printout. The column entitled RELATIVE FREQ gives the percentages of group membership for each of the scale points. Thirty percent of the sample said their happiness level "rarely changes," etc. The next column to the right, entitled ADJUSTED FREQ provides percentages after excluding the missing respondent from consideration. Both of these sets of percentages are often useful in describing research data. Finally, the column headed CUM FREQ provides a summation of the adjusted frequencies. With these percentages it is possible to quickly see, for example, that more than half of the individuals who reponded felt their levels of happiness changed infrequently or less often.

It should be noted here that these percentages are not meant to describe the actual sample of 402 individuals from which these ten were selected. Some actual output from the larger sample will be given in the remaining chapters to illustrate various types of data analysis.

The next part of the SPSS FREQUENCIES output was provided by the OPTIONS 8 command in our program. Here we see a histogram, a sideways bargraph. This provides us with a quick visual image of the distribution and is often more satisfying than the numerical data above or below it. Notice that the horizontal baseline of this bar chart represents frequencies of occurrence in our sample of respondents. The code numbers for various points on the scale are on the vertical axis. The numbers in parentheses to the right of the "bars" are the actual number of respondents at each point on the scale.

Finally, at the very bottom of the printout there are the summary descriptive statistics. We will discuss the exact meaning of these statistics in the next chapter on descriptive research. Recall that we called for these statistics in the STATISTICS ALL statement. While these statistics may not seem impressive to you,since they were calculated on only ten cases, try to imagine how long it would take you to compute them for 400 cases, even using a hand calculator. And then increase the number of variables from

FIGURE 8.5
Printed Output from SPSS FREQUENCIES

CATEGORY LABEL	CODE	ABSOLUTE FREQ	RELATIVE FREQ (PCT)	ADJUSTED FREQ (PCT)	CUM FREQ (PCT)
	2.	3	30.0	33.3	33.3
	3.	2	20.0	22.2	55.6
	4.	2	20.0	22.2	77.8
	5.	2	20.0	22.2	100.0
	BLANK	1	10.0	MISSING	
	TOTAL	10	100.0	100.0	

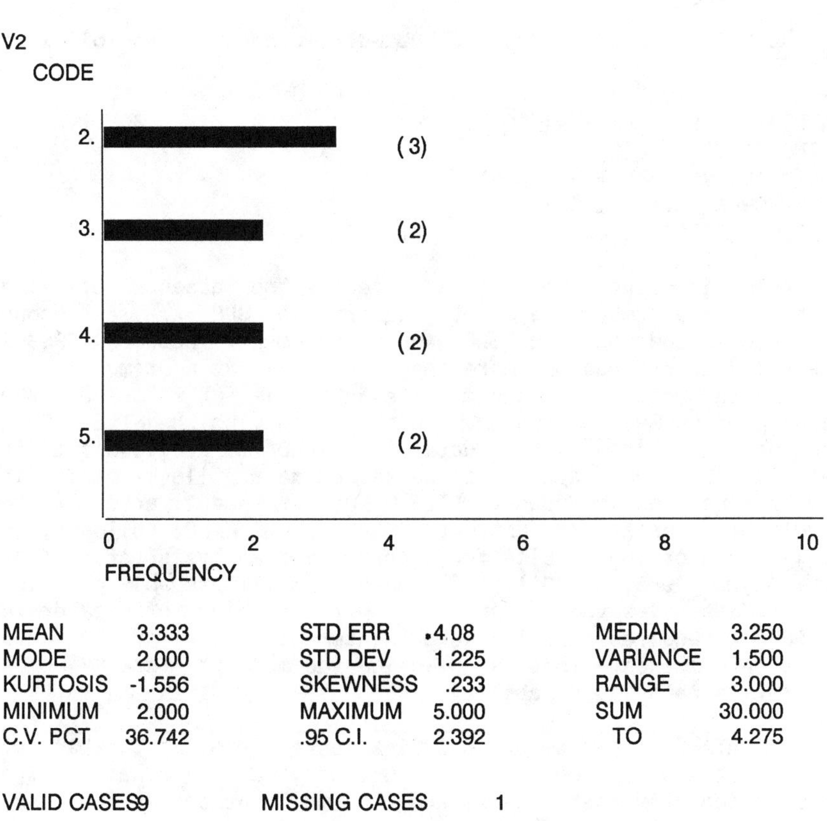

MEAN	3.333	STD ERR	.408	MEDIAN	3.250
MODE	2.000	STD DEV	1.225	VARIANCE	1.500
KURTOSIS	-1.556	SKEWNESS	.233	RANGE	3.000
MINIMUM	2.000	MAXIMUM	5.000	SUM	30.000
C.V. PCT	36.742	.95 C.I.	2.392	TO	4.275

VALID CASES 9 MISSING CASES 1

five to 80 as on the actual happiness questionnaire. Do you see the tremendous power of SPSS? With only a minor change to the DATA LIST statement we can use our present program to analyze the full data set of 80 variables and 402 cases.

SPSS-X

SPSS-X is a newer, enhanced version of SPSS. In general, its syntax is somewhat more flexible than SPSS. However, the differences are minor, and users of SPSS should have little difficulty in making the transition to SPSS-X. The main differences between the two systems are: (1) SPSS-X is capable of processing multiple data files, (2) there are some additional statistical programs available in SPSS-X, and (3) some improvements were made to the printed output of earlier programs. It is likely that the two packages will coexist for several years. But, eventually, SPSS-X will supersede and replace SPSS. Additional computer memory requirements for SPSS-X may delay this process for a while at some locations.

The SPSS-X version of our FREQUENCIES program is as follows:

```
FILE HANDLE SAMDAT7
DATA LIST FILE=SAMDAT7/V1 TO V5  4-13
MISSING VALUES ALL(0)
FREQUENCIES VARIABLES=V1 TO V5
     BARCHART/STATISTICS ALL/
     PERCENTILES 25 50 75
```

The first difference you notice here is the absence of line numbers. Line numbers are not required in SPSS-X. A second difference is the use of a FILE HANDLE statement. Because SPSS-X is capable of processing more than one file at a time, it is necessary to declare the name of the data file (or files) at the beginning of an SPSS-X program. This is done with the FILE HANDLE statement. The name of the data file, SAMDAT7, follows and is separated by a blank space. If a second data file is used, it would be specified in another FILE HANDLE statement, after which it would be necessary to instruct SPSS-X to GET FILE, followed by the file name of your choice for a particular analysis (cf. *SPSS-X User's Guide*, 1986, p. 305). Although you will probably not use multiple data files very often, the important thing to remember is that SPSS-X requires a FILE HANDLE statement as part of the data definition commands. This is the price you must pay for SPSS-X's greater file handling capability.

The DATA LIST statement in SPSS-X is very similar to that of SPSS, with the exception that you must provide a file name. The specification of variable names and column locations is the same as in SPSS. Most SPSS-X subprograms operate with OPTIONS and

FIGURE 8.6
Printed Output from SPSS-X FREQUENCIES

V2

VALUE LABEL	VALUE	FREQUENCY	PERCENT	VALID PERCENT	CUM PERCENT
	2	3	30.0	33.3	33.3
	3	2	20.0	22.2	55.6
	4	2	20.0	22.2	77.8
	5	2	20.0	22.2	100.0
	*	1	10.0	MISSING	
	TOTAL	10	100.0	100.0	

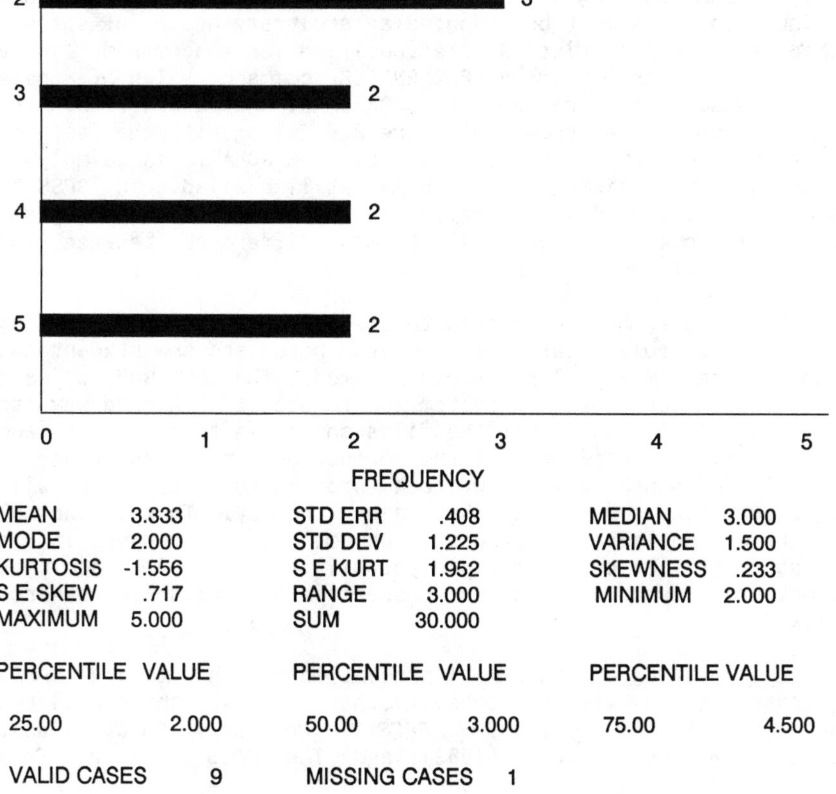

MEAN	3.333	STD ERR	.408	MEDIAN	3.000
MODE	2.000	STD DEV	1.225	VARIANCE	1.500
KURTOSIS	-1.556	S E KURT	1.952	SKEWNESS	.233
S E SKEW	.717	RANGE	3.000	MINIMUM	2.000
MAXIMUM	5.000	SUM	30.000		

PERCENTILE	VALUE	PERCENTILE	VALUE	PERCENTILE	VALUE
25.00	2.000	50.00	3.000	75.00	4.500

VALID CASES 9 MISSING CASES 1

11 MAR 87 SPSS-X RELEASE 2.0 FROM NORTHWESTERN UNIVERSITY
CALIFORNIA STATE UNIVERSITY CYBER 170/180 NOS 2.4.3

STATISTICS as in SPSS. However, the FREQUENCIES subprogram is different. As explained in the *SPSS-X User's Guide*:

> The FREQUENCIES procedure operates via subcommands. Each subcommand begins with a subcommand keyword, followed by an optional equals sign and subcommand specifications. Subcommands can be names in any order and are separated by a slash....The only required subcommand is VARIABLES, which specifies the variables being analyzed. All other subcommands are optional (*SPSS-X User's Guide*, 1986, p. 316).

The SPSS-X FREQUENCIES program has a wide assortment of new options and statistics, some of which are illustrated in our program here. Notice that the final two lines of the program are indented. This is because they are continuation lines. In SPSS-X primary commands begin at the far left margin, and all continuation lines must be indented an arbitrary number of spaces. Both options and statistics are specified as subcommands in a continuation of the primary FREQUENCIES command. Two of these were included in the program here, BARCHART and PERCENTILES, the results of which are shown in Figure 8.6 along with the rest of the printed output. As you can see, BARCHART is simply a variation of the histogram, which is still available in SPSS-X. PERCENTILES is a useful enhancement to the FREQUENCIES subprogram. All in all, however, there are not many differences between the two versions of SPSS.

This chapter has instructed the reader in data analysis using SPSS. Considerable material was covered here, and the student new to this process may feel a bit overwhelmed. The best way to learn SPSS or any other computer system is to use it. A good way to start would be to construct the files shown in this chapter and run the programs until you get the correct output. Then create a data file of your own and write a program for it. You will undoubtedly make some mistakes along the way. This is normal and part of the learning process. Do not give up because it is hard at first. Be persistent and you will master SPSS. Once that has occurred, you will be in possession of valuable research skills.

The remaining chapters will present more on how to use SPSS. For those who may wish to consult other sources, there are two excellent books by Norusis: *SPSS Introductory Guide, Basic Statistics and Operations* (1982); and *The SPSS Guide to Data Analysis* (1986).

CHAPTER NINE

DESCRIPTIVE METHODS

In this section of the book each chapter will begin with a prototypic study. The example investigation will be followed by a section describing appropriate statistics for the particular method under discussion. The final section of each chapter will illustrate how to perform the statistical tests using SPSS with data from the happiness questionnaire.

From Chapter Two you will recall that descriptive research was defined as that which attempts to answer the question: What is the status of X? The emphasis in descriptive research is on determining the existence of a phenonemon and its degree of severity. Less concern is given to discovering why the condition exists or how one might predict its occurrence.

Research Example: An Analysis of the Motivational Factors Influencing Mature Women to Enter Graduate Studies Programs

At a time when large numbers of "older" women were returning to college and university campuses, DeLong (1975) was curious about their reasons for entering graduate programs. She developed a long and creative list of research questions which can best be stated in her words:

> ...Several questions occur in this context. Do the reasons given for returning to school vary with age, income, and marital status? Which significant others are most influential in the decision to return? What are the goals after obtaining the degree? Do they vary with age, income, and marital status? How many of these women see themselves as independent, confident of their abilities, and competitive? For how many has entering a graduate studies program resulted in increased self esteem? Are enjoyment of reading and boredom of housework typically associated with married women who enter graduate programs? For married women, what are the effects of their being students upon their families? Is the family an important source of encouragement? Does the family resent the time required for study? Are family members becoming more independent and self-reliant? If necessary, would family obligations take priority over studies?

...Do these factors vary according to major? How satisfied are students with their graduate studies? Does the degree of satisfaction vary with major? Is there a relationship between how challenging graduate school is for the subject and her degree of satisfaction with the graduate program? Has academic counseling influenced the decision to enter graduate school? if so, what implications for counseling might be drawn from the data?

Finally, is it possible to draw a profile of the typical female graduate student over twenty-five on the basis of the information provided? What are her income, marital status, age, goals, number of children, degree of life satisfaction, and view of herself? (pp. 1-2).

DeLong selected her subjects for this investigation from a population of 494 females aged 25 or older who were attending graduate programs at California State University, Hayward, in the winter of 1975. Using stratified random sampling, she selected 200 subjects from five curriculum areas: humanities and fine arts, science and mathematics, business and public administration, educational psychology, and teacher education. The researcher developed a Graduate Women's Questionnaire (see Appendix B), which she pilot tested, revised, and mailed out to the 200 sample subjects. Usable responses were received from 140 subjects, a response rate of 70 per cent.

Because of the complexity of this study, only a few of the highlights are summarized here. Of initial interest is the composition of the sample. Nearly two-thirds of the subjects were between the ages of 25 and 34. Only nine percent were over 45. Marital status was as follows: 22% single, 6% separated, 15% divorced, 1% widowed, and 54% married. Seven percent were only children and 45% were first-born. More than half the women had children, the most frequently reported number being two. The mean age of the subjects was 33, their husbands 37. The average number of years married was eleven. Fifty percent of the sample had 1975 annual incomes of $15,000 or more.

The central outcome of the study as reported by DeLong was as follows:

Primary among the motivational factors for all groups in the decision to enter graduate school was the desire for personal fulfillment, rated important or very important by 85 percent of the sample. Preparation for a challenging career ranked second in importance (75 percent), followed by the need to enhance feelings of self-worth (61 percent). Only 39 percent of the subjects rated raising their economic

> level important or very important. The need to alleviate boredom was least important as a motivating factor.
>
> Data were analyzed by grouping the subjects by age, income, and marital status, as well as academic major. No significant differences in the factors influencing the decision to enter graduate school occurred among either age or academic major groups when analysis of variance procedures were applied. Significant differences among income groups and marital status categories were found. Specifically, those subjects with incomes of $25,000 or more were less motivated by economic need. Women who are separated or divorced were found to be more likely to have economic-related motivations than those in other marital categories (pp. ii-iii).

While group comparisons did not reveal many differences between students in different majors, some interesting associations were found within majors. For example, among educational psychology students, older women were significantly less motivated by income or the prospect of a challenging career. Among business majors, affluent women were less motivated by the need to raise their economic level than was the case in other academic groups. Older humanities and education students had a greater need to alleviate boredom, although their absolute need levels were relatively low.

The final question on the Graduate Women's Questionnaire is subjective. Each subject was asked to complete the statement, "I would describe myself as the kind of person who...." Although data derived from such a question can not usually be analyzed statistically, it often provides the researcher with needed insight into the personalities of subjects, and it adds a human touch to the research report. These subjects' responses were wide-ranging. Some examples: "When I entered school I was both excited about my "new life" and afraid...Today I am far less unsure, more assertive, and welcome all experience." Several spoke of testing their capabilities, their potentials, wanting "to achieve academically and professionally to the utmost of my potential." The relationship between career and self-concept was mentioned by some subjects, wanting "to experience success in a career in order to feel like I am a successful person." The search for self and the development of individuality were other themes expressed. In summarizing these verbal data, DeLong commented:

> In the process of examining each of the responses, looking for commonalities and differences, a feeling of admiration developed for so many of these women who are involved in the process of becoming. Their sense

of purpose, commitment to achievement, and candidness regarding their doubts and difficulties are noteworthy (p. 44).

In the concluding paragraphs of her thesis, DeLong states, "A follow-up study perhaps ten years hence on the results and effects of each subject's graduate studies might prove worthwhile." Indeed, such a study would be of great interest. So too would a replication of DeLong's original study on the graduate women of today. How universal are women's motivations for attending graduate school? How much of what was reported here was colored by the women's movement? Would the same quest for personal growth and disdain of economic gain apply today? A replication of this study would be a worthwhile endeavor toward answering these questions.

Statistics for Descriptive Research

There are two general groups of statistics used commonly in descriptive research. These are measures of central tendency and measures of dispersion. In addition, a knowledge of standard scores based on the normal distribution is essential in understanding and describing various types of data distributions.

Measures of Central Tendency

There are three measures of central tendency commonly used in all forms of research. These are the *mean*, *median*, and *mode*. Of these three, the mean, symbolized *M*, is by far the most common. The mean is simply the arithmetic average of all the scores in a distribution. The formula for calculating the mean is as follows:

$$M = Sum(X) / N$$

where M equals the mean, Sum signifies adding up all scores, X is the symbol for a score, and N equals the total number of scores or responses in a distribution. The slash mark is used to indicate the operation of dividing Sum(X) by N.

A variation of this formula is as follows:

$$M = Sum(fX) / N$$

where f stands for frequency. This formula is used when the data have been grouped into categories as in an SPSS printout. Turn back to Figure 8.6 in the previous chapter and note that the scores or *values* for Item 2 on the happiness questionnaire are coupled with the *frequency* of their occurrence. With data grouped in this way it is easier to apply the second formula above to calculate the mean. One simply multiplies the frequency by the score (value), sums these products, and then divides by the number of values (N).

While it is of some interest to understand how the mean is computed, you will almost never have to carry out a calculation if you use SPSS. This is also true of the other statistics shown in Figure 8.6. The *median* (*Mdn*) is defined as the midpoint of a distribution. It is that point which divides the top and bottom halves. The easiest way to determine the median is to count up from the bottom (or down from the top) of a distribution until you find the middle person. In Figure 8.6, since there are only nine valid scores in the distribution, the fifth score from the bottom (or top) represents the median. Thus, the median equals 3. You will notice at the bottom of Figure 8.6 that the 50th percentile also equals 3. The percentile scale is divided into 100 units which designate points below which a certain percentage of the scores in a distribution occur. Thus, the 50th percentile is equivalent to the median. The *mode* is defined simply as the most frequent score in a distribution. In Figure 8.6 you see that the scale value of 2 occurred most frequently. Therefore the mode is 2.

The important thing about measures of central tendency is to know when to use them. Most of the time, when distributions are relatively balanced, a researcher will simply report the mean as a single measure of the "average." We often talk about the "average person," or the "average score" on a test. What we need to be aware of is that the term average can mean either the mean, median, or mode. And in certain situations, the mean is not the best average to use. For example, if we were to collect data from the IRS on personal income in the U.S., we would find that the distribution is not balanced. There are some people, though not many, who are multi-millionaires. Their incomes, when added to the much lower incomes of most individuals, would tend to inflate the mean, to pull it upward toward these very high incomes. In such a distribution, the mean would no longer be the best measure of "average income" because the mean would be much higher than the 50th percentile. With such a *skewed* distribution as this, it is best to use the median as the measure of central tendency, or at least to report both the mean and the median. They could be several thousand dollars apart. Although the *mode* is used less often than the mean or median as a measure of central tendency, it is appropriately used with nominal data. For example, if one were describing the distibution of religions in the U.S., it would be correct to say that the modal religion is Protestant.

Another statistic shown at the bottom of Figure 8.6 is related to the measures of central tendency discussed above. The standard error (*STD ERR*) shown on the SPSS-X printout refers to the *standard error of the mean*. This is a measure of the confidence we have in a sample mean, based on the size of sample from which it was computed. The standard error represents the amount of fluctuation which might be expected in another sample of equal size from the same population. If we were to extract another sample of 10 individuals from the population of 400 respondents to the happiness questionnaire, we could expect the new mean to be within plus or minus .408 of the mean of 3.33 calculated on the present sample of 10 individuals. That is, we could expect such a deviation approximately two-thirds of the time. On about one-third of the occasions the mean would fall outside of this range of plus or minus .408. We will explore the standard error statistic in greater detail in a later chapter.

Measures of Dispersion

There are two measures of dispersion or variability most commonly used in behavioral research. These are the *standard deviation* and the *variance*. Let us consider the latter statistic first. The formula for computing the variance is as follows:

V = Sum((X - M)**2) / N - 1

where V represents the variance, and the quantity (X-M) is a deviation score derived by subtracting the mean from each raw score. This deviation score, the difference between a given score and the sample mean, is then squared, denoted by the double asterisk and 2. This notation, **, means to raise the preceding quantity to the power of 2, in other words, to square it. The squared deviation scores are then summed and finally divided by N-1, the number of scores (or individuals) minus one.

It is not crucial that you memorize the above formula. What is important is that you understand the concept of variance, that it represents a kind of collective deviation from the sample mean. It is the extent to which individuals in a distribution depart from the average score. The greater the variance, the more dispersion around the mean. If all individuals have the same score, there would be no variance. Everyone would be "average."

The *standard deviation* (*SD*) is used more often than the variance in descriptive research to signify the degree of dispersion in a distribution. It is simply the square root of the variance:

SD = Sqrt(V)

The standard deviation has special properties which can be related to the normal distribution, a topic we will take up in the next section. The standard deviation can be interpreted in much the same way as the standard error. At the bottom of Figure 8.6 we see that SD=1.225. This means that approximtely two-thirds of the responses to Item 2 fell within plus or minus 1.225 of the mean of 3.333. In the context of a 6-point scale with only 10 respondents this is not a very meaningful statistic. However, the standard deviation is extremely useful when interpreting large distributions from many educational and psychological tests. *Skewness* and *kurtosis* are sometimes referred to as the 3rd and 4th "moments" of a distribution (the mean and standard deviation are the first two moments). *Skewness* is a measure of balance or symmetry. A skewness value of 0 indicates a perfectly balanced distribution in which the mean, median, and mode are identical. A positive skewness value indicates a distribution with a "tail" on the positive or high end of the distribution. The previous example of personal income is an example of a positively skewed distribution. The distribution shown in Figure 8.6 is also positively skewed, very slightly. Note the skewness coeficient of .233. This is due to the piling up of individuals at the low end of the scale. A negative skewness value would obviously represent a reversed situation with a tail to the left and piling up on the right.

Kurtosis is also a measure of the shape of a distribution. Positive values signify a peaked curve, whereas negative values denote a flat distribution. Our SPSS-X printout has a fairly substantial negative value due to the relative flatness of the distribution. Both skewness and kurtosis are informative statistics, but they are seldom reported in the research literature.

Some other statistics shown in the SPSS-X printout are related to the measures of dispersion above. The *minimum* and *maximum* simply refer to the highest and lowest scores in the distribution. Together, they represent the range of scores, a crude measure of dispersion. The *sum* represents Sum(X) in the formulas above.

Standard Scores and the Normal Distribution

Jensen (1981) has noted that the bell-shaped, or "normal distribution," is characteristic of many physical and psychological properties such as height, blood pressure, strength of grip, reaction time, etc. Many intellectual and personality test also produce normal distributions. Because of this phenomenon, it was useful for researchers to develop standard measurement scales which can be meaningfully applied to different distributions. Figure 9.1 shows a normal curve and several of the standard scores associated with it.

We have already discussed some of the information in Figure 9.1. Notice the percent of cases under portions of the normal curve. Somewhat over 68% of all cases are found between the mean and the 1st standard deviation in both directions. Do you now understand why we say that approximately two-thirds of all scores

FIGURE 9.1
The Normal Curve and Standard Scores

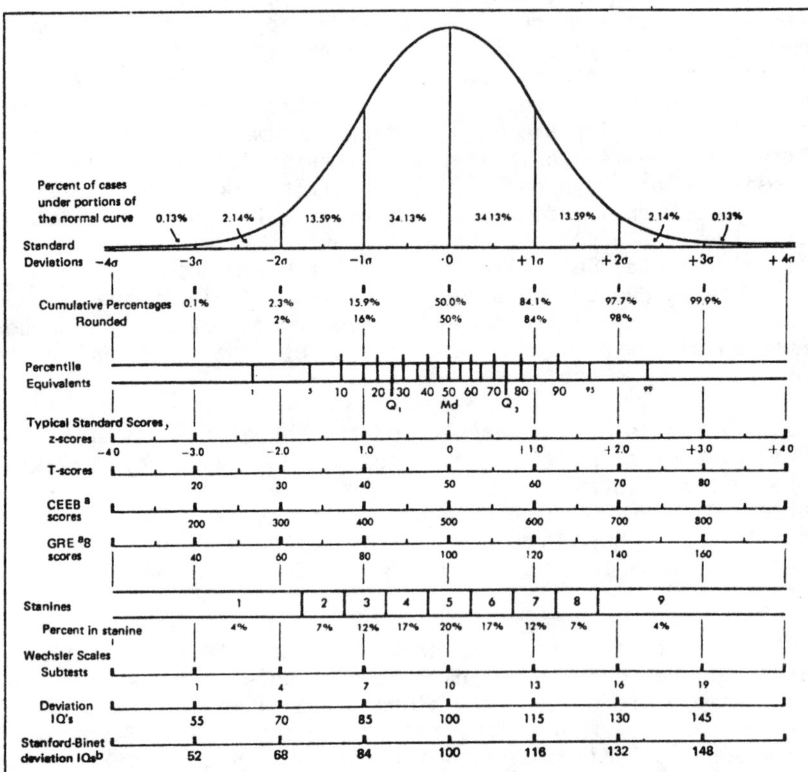

THE NORMAL CURVE, PERCENTILES AND STANDARD SCORES

Distribution of scores of many standardized educational and psychological tests approximate the form of the NORMAL CURVE shown at the top of this chart. Below it are shown some of the systems that have been developed to facilitate the interpretation of scores by converting them into numbers which indicate the examinee's relative status in a group.

The zero (0) at the center of the baseline shows the location of the mean (average) raw score on a test, and the symbol σ (sigma) marks off the scale of raw scores in STANDARD DEVIATION units.

Cumulative percentages are the basis of the PERCENTILE EQUIVALENT scale.

Several systems are based on the standard deviation unit. Among these STANDARD SCORE scales, the z-score, the T-score and the stanine are general systems which have been applied to a variety of tests. The others are special variants used in connection with tests of the College Entrance Examination Board, the Graduate Records Examination, and other intelligence and ability scales.

Tables of NORMS, whether in percentile or standard score form, have meaning only with reference to a specified test applied to a specified population. The chart does not permit one to conclude, for instance, that a percentile rank of 84 on one test necessarily is equivalent to a z-score of +1.0 on another; this is true only when each test yields essentially a normal distribution of scores and when both scales are based on identical or very similar groups of people.

Most of the scales on this chart are discussed in greater detail in Test Service Bulletin No. 48, copies of which are available on request from the Psychological Corporation, 304 East 45th St., New York, N.Y. 10017.

[a] Score points (norms) on the scales refer to university students and not to general populations.

[b] Standard-score "IQ's" with σ = 16 are also used on several other current intelligence tests, e.g., California Test of Mental Maturity, Kuhlmann-Anderson Intelligence Test, and Lorge Thorndike Intelligence Test.

Types of standard-score scales. The figure is adapted from Test Service Bulletin No. 48, The Psychological Corporation, New York, by permission of The Psychological Corporation.

are plus or minus one SD from the mean? If we move out to the 2nd SD, we can say that approximately 96% of all cases will occur within this region of the distribution. And if we move out to the 3rd SD we see that virtually 100% of the cases are represented. The normal curve is a very powerful model of human characteristics. If we know, for example, that the Wechsler Adult Intelligence Test has a mean of 100 and a SD of 15, we can quickly understand how rare an IQ of 150 is. Or if we know that the mean height of American males is five feet nine inches and the SD is three inches, we can begin to realized how difficult it is for a man of six feet six to find clothes and shoes to fit him.

Two points need to be made concerning the scales shown in Figure 9.1. First, there are some scales which cannot be used appropriately for statistical analysis. These include percentiles, deciles, and stanines. Because these scales do not have equal intervals between numerical points, they cannot be used for many computational purposes. Therefore, if you have data in these scale units, you must first transform them to an equal interval scale such as the z-score scale. Secondly, some data in raw score form will generate misleading results when analyzed statistically if it is not first transformed. Let us explore the process of creating a z-score from a distribution of raw scores. The formula for the z-score is given below:

$$z = (X - M) / SD$$

where z represents a score in standard deviation units, X is a raw score, M is the mean of the raw score distribution, and SD is the standard deviation of the raw scores. What this formula tells us is that if we first calculate the mean and SD of any set of scores, we can transform them to z-scores very simply by using the above formula. Let us see why this is sometimes important by looking at an example from education:

Suppose a teacher has given three tests during the term. The tests are all combinations of multiple choice, true-false, and fill-in responses. Each test represents six weeks work and the teacher feels the tests should be weighted equally toward a final grade. He grades each test in terms of answers correct. He adds the scores from the three tests to determine total points and final grade. Table 9.1 illustrates this process for three students, John, Mary, and Joe.

Let us calculate a z-score for John on the first test:

$$z = (X - M) / SD$$
$$z = (45 - 35) / 10$$
$$z = 10 / 10 = 1$$

TABLE 9.1
Using Standard Scores:
The z-score

	Test 1		Test 2		Test 3			
	M=35		M=65		M=50			
	SD=10		SD=20		SD= 5			
	Scores		Scores		Scores		Totals	
	Raw	z	Raw	z	Raw	z	Raw	z
Students								
John	45	+1	45	-1	50	0	140	0
Mary	55	+2	25	-2	55	+1	135	+1
Joe	35	0	30	-1.75	65	+3	130	+1.25

For Mary on the second test:

$$z = (25 - 65) / 20$$
$$z = -40 / 20 = -2$$

The numbers in Table 9.1 are arranged so that you should be able to calculate z-scores without benefit of the formula. Try it until you are sure you understand the concept of the z-score. Notice that when raw scores are added up for the three students, John would receive the highest grade and Joe the lowest. But when z-scores are used the reverse is true. Joe is now slightly above Mary, and John has the lowest score. What has happened here?

Because the three test score distributions are not equal in their variances, the points assigned to students have different meanings. That is, a difference of 10 points on Test 1 is not the same as a difference of 10 points on tests 2 and 3. John's score of 45 on Test 1 is actually better than his score of 50 on Test 3, and much better than his score of 45 on Test 2. But when we add these raw scores together we treat the numbers as if they have equivalent value. They don't, and therefore we must transform them to a standard scale which gives them equal status, the z-score scale.

The moral of this story is not that you have been cheated all through school. Many teachers in the above situation would first convert individual test scores into letter grades before "adding them up." A letter grade is just another type of standard score. So this procedure is correct. Some teachers, though, keep a running count of points accumulated. These teachers, the ones who think they are being the most precise, are indeed guilty of the raw score fallacy shown above. The chances are that their errors balanced out for you over the years. Your personality has not been totally warped.

Fortunately, all research data need not be transformed prior to analysis. In fact, most analyses are conducted on raw data. The above example, however, should convince you that whenever you must combine variables together in summative fashion, you should be aware of the distortion that can occur, and strongly consider using the z-score transformation. An example of data transformation from the happiness questionnaire will be presented in the next section to show you how to perform the transformation using SPSS.

SPSS and the Happiness Questionnaire

It is possible to ask innumerable research questions of a descriptive nature concerning the data on personal happiness (see Appendix A for the complete questionnaire). Let us consider a few of these here, and see how we would go about answering them with SPSS:

1. What is the overall level of happiness of the student subjects?

2. What is the sample profile in terms of age, gender, and marital status?

3. What do the students consider most important to their happiness (Items 1-22)?

4. How do single men and women compare with married men and women in their choices?

5. How do the sample students compare with a more general sample of readers of Psychology Today?

6. How do males compare with females in the extent to which they possess four psychological attitudes essential to happiness?

Several of the questions above are variations of a more general question: How did the sample subjects respond to questionnaire items 1 through 80? The answers to this question can be achieved by a single SPSS program. Look back to Figure 8.4 in the previous chapter to refresh your memory of the FREQUENCIES program. The program from Chapter 8 can be expanded very easily to provide frequency distributions for items 1-80 of the questionnaire. Here is the SPSS version:

```
 5.     DATA LIST
 5.005 FIXED(1)/1 V1 TO V80 1-80
10.     MISSING VALUES
10.005 V1 TO V46 (0, 7 THRU 9)/ V47 (0, 5 THRU 9)/
```

```
10.006 V48 (0, 3 THRU 9)/ V49 TO V80 (0, 7 THRU 9)
15.    FREQUENCIES
15.005 GENERAL=ALL
20.    OPTIONS
20.005 8
25.    STATISTICS
25.005 ALL
```

The SPSS-X version looks like this:

```
FILE HANDLE HAPPY
DATA LIST FILE=HAPPY/ V1 TO V80 1-80
MISSING VALUES V1 TO V46 (0, 7 THRU 9)/ V47 (0, 5 THRU 9)/
     V48 (0, 3 THRU 9)/ V49 TO V80 (0, 7 THRU 9)
FREQUENCIES VARIABLES=ALL/ BARCHART/ STATISTICS ALL
```

This is an extremely powerful program which produces output like that shown in Figure 9.2 for all 80 items on the questionnaire. Figure 9.2 shows output from the SPSS program for question 1 on general happiness. As is evident from the histogram, general happiness is characterized by a positively skewed distribution with a mean of 2.317 and a median of 2.061. More than 85% of the sample indicated they were at least slightly happy. The modal response of "moderately happy" captured 57% of the students. The least frequent response was "very unhappy." Only three percent chose this extreme vs. 18% who selected "very happy" at the other end of the scale.

While the output from this program is extremely informative, it can be made even more so by two addititions to the program. They are the VAR LABELS and VALUE LABELS statements. These are optional statements which produce descriptive labels on the computer output. Consider Item 49, which asks the subjects, "What is your age?" He or she responds to one of six categories. The variable name, AGE, as well as the specific age categories can be designated in the SPSS program as follows:

```
7.    VAR LABELS
7.005 V49 AGE
8.    VALUE LABELS
8.005 V49 (1) 25 OR LESS (2) 26-30 (3) 31-35
8.006 (4) 36-40 (5) 41-45 (6) OVER 45
```

The above statements are numbered 7 and 8. Thus they come between the DATA LIST statement and the MISSING VALUES statement in the previous program. Notice that VAR LABELS provides an overall name for a variable while VALUE LABELS gives names to the categories of measurement for a variable. The effect of these statements is shown in Figure 9.3. Because this student sample is a mixture of undergraduate and graduate students, a wide range of

FIGURE 9.2
SPSS FREQUENCIES Output for Item 1
General Happiness

CATEGORY LABEL	CODE	ABSOLUTE FREQ	RELATIVE FREQ (PCT)	ADJUSTED FREQ (PCT)	CUM FREQ (PCT)
	1.	72	17.9	18.0	18.0
	2.	229	57.0	57.1	75.1
	3.	43	10.7	10.7	85.8
	4.	27	6.7	6.7	92.5
	5.	18	4.5	4.5	97.0
	6.	12	3.0	3.0	100.0
	BLANK	1	.2	MISSING	
	TOTAL	402	100.0	100.0	

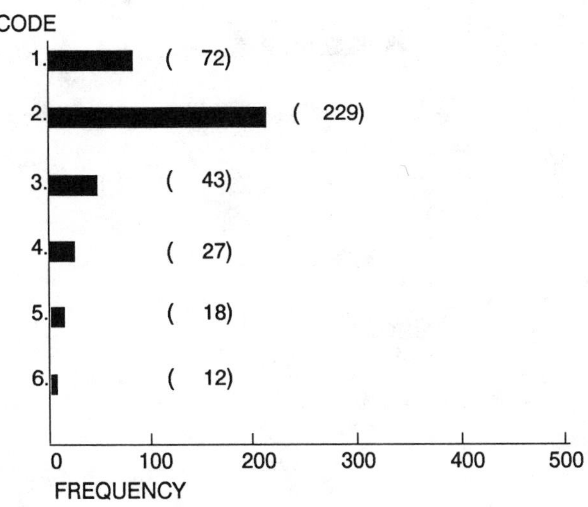

MEAN	2.317	STD ERR	.058	MEDIAN	2.061
MODE	2.000	STD DEV	1.158	VARIANCE	1.342
KURTOSIS	2.032	SKEWNESS	1.484	RANGE	5.000
MINIMUM	1.000	MAXIMUM	6.000	SUM	929.000
C.V. PCT	50.003	.95 C.I.	2.203	TO	2.430

VALID CASES 401 MISSING CASES 1

FIGURE 9.3
SPSS FREQUENCIES Output for Item 49
Age

CATEGORY LABEL	CODE	ABSOLUTE FREQ	RELATIVE FREQ (PCT)	ADJUSTED FREQ (PCT)	CUM FREQ (PCT)
25 or less	1.	87	21.6	21.7	21.7
26-30	2.	107	26.6	26.7	48.4
31-35	3.	84	20.9	20.9	69.3
36-40	4.	59	14.7	14.7	84.0
41-45	5.	33	8.2	8.2	92.3
Over 45	6.	31	7.7	7.7	100.0
	BLANK	1	.2	MISSING	
	TOTAL	402	100.0	100.0	

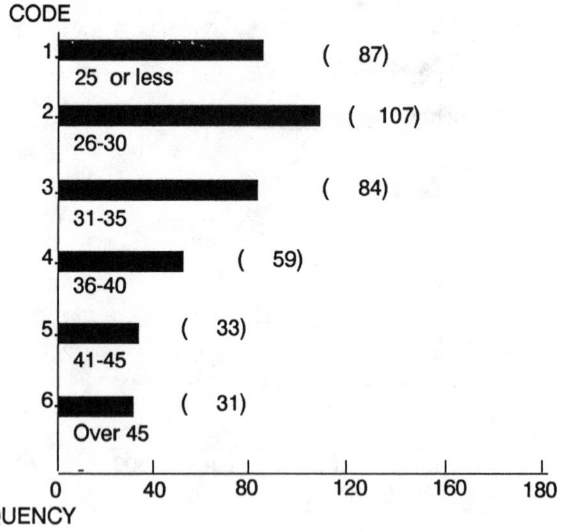

CODE
1. 25 or less (87)
2. 26-30 (107)
3. 31-35 (84)
4. 36-40 (59)
5. 41-45 (33)
6. Over 45 (31)

0 40 80 120 160 180
FREQUENCY

MEAN	2.843	STD ERR	.076	MEDIAN	2.577
MODE	2.000	STD DEV	1.513	VARIANCE	2.288
KURTOSIS	-.619	SKEWNESS	.574	RANGE	5.000
MINIMUM	1.000	MAXIMUM	6.000	SUM	1140.000
C.V. PCT	53.204	.95 C.I.	2.694	TO	2.991

VALID CASES 401 MISSING CASES 1

age categories is represented. Though 48% of the students are 30 years of age or less, 16% of them are over the age of 40.

SPSS-X provides somewhat more ease and flexibility in labeling variables. All labels are enclosed in single quotation marks as shown below:

```
VARIABLE LABELS
    V49 'AGE'
VALUE LABELS
    V41 1 '25 OR LESS'
        2 '26-30'
        3 '31-35'
        4 '36-40'
        5 '41-45'
        6 'OVER 45'
```

These statements would also be placed between the DATA LIST and MISSING VALUES statements in the previous SPSS-X program. Although it is not necessary to go to a new line after each label, the readability of the program is enhanced by doing so. Additional variable and value labels can be added below the present ones. A longer program with multiple VAR and VALUE LABELS is shown at the end of the chapter.

Comparisons in Descriptive Research

A common feature of descriptive research is the need to make a comparison of one's data with a previous study. The happiness questionnaire used in this book was adapted from one originally used by Shaver and Freedman (1975). These two professors organized a graduate seminar, inviting their students to study a subject they considered important. The group settled on happiness, and designed a questionnaire that appeared in the October, 1975, issue of *Psychology Today*. After collecting data from approximately 52,000 PT readers, the authors published their findings in the August, 1976, issue of the same publication.

Because many sections of the two questionnaires are quite similar (the main differences are in the scaling and number of items), it is possible to compare some of the results between Shaver and Freedman's extensive sample of PT readers and Whalen's sample of 400 students. In doing so, it is important to note that while both samples are similar in their common interest in psychology, they are different in many other ways. Apart from the obvious difference between university students and a more general population, the most important difference between the two samples is that Shaver and Freedman's subjects all responded to their questionnaire during a limited period of time in the Fall of 1975. Whalen's sample is composed of subjects who responded to the questionnaire across an entire decade between 1976 and 1986.

Some of the differences in attitudes between the groups are undoubtedly due to general social influences specific to the time of data collection.

One of the outcomes reported in the 1976 article by Shaver and Freedman concerned 16 "pillars of happiness." Their subjects were asked to rate the importance of 16 factors to their general happiness. The researchers summarized these ratings and then ranked the factors from one to sixteen. The results of this analysis are displayed in Table 9.2. As you can see, the results are reported separately for each of four groups categorized by marital status and gender. Table 9.2 shows, for example, that both single men and women ranked "friends and social life" as the most important of the 16 pillars of happiness while married men and women gave this factor only a medium rating of 8th and 7.5, respectively (the married women's rating for this item was tied with "job or primary activity").

*TABLE 9.2**
The 16 Pillars of Happiness:
The importance of each of the following items to general happiness, ranked in order.
Shaver & Freedman (1976)
(N=52,000)

	Single Men	Single Women	Married Men	Married Women
Friends and social life	1	1	8	7.5
Job or primary activity	2	3	4	7.5
Being in love	3	2	2	1
Recognition, success	4	4	7	5.5
Sex life	5	6	6	4
Personal growth	6	5	1	5.5
Financial situation	7	9	10	13
House or apartment	8	10.5	11	14
Body and attractiveness	9.5	8	16	16
Health & physical cond.	9.5	7	13	9
City you live in	11	13	14	11
Religion	12	10.5	12	12
Exercise, recreation	13	12	15	15
Being a parent	--	--	9	10
Marriage	--	--	3	2
Partner's happiness	--	--	5	3

In contrast to the results of Shaver and Freedman, those for this author's research are shown in Table 9.3. These data are also reported by marital status and gender. Before discussing how to derive such summary results using SPSS, let us explore some of the similarities and differences between the two samples. The students differed from the Psychology Today readers most strongly on the importance of personal growth, recognition and success, and health and physical condition. Three of the four student subgroups ranked personal growth as the most important ingredient to overall happiness. Only one of the PT groups ranked personal growth so highly. While recognition and success was ranked between 4th and 7th by PT readers, it received relatively weak rankings of 11th to 13th by the students. Finally, the students placed much greater importance on health and physical condition than did the PT subjects. Student rankings for this item ranged between 2nd and 3rd, while PT subgroups varied between 7th and 13th.

TABLE 9.3
The 16 Pillars of Happiness
Whalen, (1987)
(N=402)

	Single Men	Single Women	Married Men	Married Women
Friends and social life	7	6	14	8
Job or primary activity	4	2	5	5
Being in love	5	9	6	7
Recognition, success	11	13	12	13
Sex life	8	12	9	11
Personal growth	1	1	2	1
Financial situation	13	10	10	12
House or apartment	12	7	8	10
Body & attractiveness	10	8	13	9
Health & physical cond.	2	3	3	2
City you live in	15	15	15	15
Religion	16	16	16	16
Exercise, recreation	9	11	7	14
Being a parent	14	14	11	6
Marriage	6	5	4	3
Partner's happiness	3	4	1	4

Some of the differences between subgroups within the student sample are of interest. For example, there appears to be great similarity between single men and women students in their perceptions. They disagree substantially on only three items: being in love and sex life, which are both more important to men; and house or apartment, which is more important to the single women. There is less agreement between the married men and women students. Married women place more importance on friends and social life, their body and attractiveness, and being a parent. Married men value exercise and recreation, and their partner's happiness. Somewhat surprisingly, married male students ranked their partner's happiness higher than any other factor, while married female students ranked this item only 4th.

There is actually considerable overall agreement among the various student groups. They all ranked personal growth first except married men who ranked it 2nd. They all ranked religion last. In between there was considerable agreement on the importance of health, primary job, partner's happiness, and marriage. It is interesting to note that in Shaver and Freedman's study, they did not collect data on the importance of marriage and a partner's happiness from single persons, apparently assuming these were not relevant. The student data in Table 9.3 show that these happiness factors were almost as important for unmarried students as they were for the married ones.

A few final observations: though "being in love" received uniformly high rankings among PT subgroups, it was ranked much less importantly by the students and highest by single male students (5th vs. 9th for single females). The importance of one's sex life was rated higher by men than women students, but received only medium rankings by all groups. Relatively low scores were assigned to one's financial situation, attractiveness, exercise, and being a parent, except for married women. Although these student data are vastly smaller than the PT reader data (400 vs. 52,000 observations), in some ways they may be more representative because they have stood the test of a decade of shifting social attitudes and values concerning the many issues involved in personal happiness.

Making Comparisons with SPSS

In the previous comparison of students with readers of Psychology Today, it was necessary to break the sample into four subgroups by gender and marital status. Usually, this is a straightforward process. But in the present case it was a bit more involved. Notice that Item 50 from the happiness questionnaire places students into six categories of living status. The question reads as follows:

50. What is your current living status?
    1. With your husband or wife
    2. Cohabiting on a long term basis.
    3. Cohabiting on a "temporary" basis.
    4. With one or more persons with whom you have a personal but "non-love relationship(s).
    5. With one or more persons with whom you have a relatively impersonal relationship(s).
    6. Alone.

This is not a typical question on marital status. The problem is to reconstitute the six categories above into two--married and single. Fortunately, SPSS has provided for this need with the RECODE statement. We can collapse the six categories into two as follows:

```
12.     RECODE
12.005 V50 (1=1) (2 THRU 6=2)
```

The comparable statement for SPSS-X is this:

```
RECODE V50 (1=1) (2 THRU 6=2)
```

As you can see by the line numbers in the SPSS program, the RECODE statement is inserted ahead of the FREQUENCIES procedure statement. Thus when a frequency distribution for Item 50 is carried out, it is done on the newly scaled item, one which now has a 2-point scale rather than the original 6-point scale. The results of this analysis indicated a fairly even split; 45% of the students were married. The gender split was not so well balanced. Females constituted 75% of the sample.

Now, let's recap the task before us. We want to determine the extent to which four subgroups attribute their happiness to 16 "pillars" of happiness. The pillars of happiness refer to items 7-22 on the questionnaire, questions which deal with issues such as recognition and success, being a parent, your financial situation, being in love, and so on. Which of these issues is considered more or less important by single vs. married men and women? And furthermore, how do the 1 to 16 rankings for the student subgroups compare to those of the PT reader sample.

One might suppose that this task could be accomplished by using the FREQUENCIES program once again. By generating separate distributions for the four subgroups, one could arrange the item means from high to low and rank the 16 pillars in terms of average values given by the members of each separate subgroup. Indeed, this can be done. But it is not the most efficient way to solve the problem. There is a statistical procedure in SPSS called *BREAKDOWN* which will calculate means and standard deviations of variables by sample subgroup. The proper statement is given below:

```
30.     BREAKDOWN
30.005 TABLES=V7 TO V22 BY V48 BY V50
```

The comparable SPSS-X statement is:

```
BREAKDOWN V7 TO V22 BY V48 BY V50
```

FIGURE 9.4
SPSS BREAKDOWN Output for Item 17
The Importance of One's Sex Life to Happiness

CRITERION VARIABLE V17 SEX LIFE

BROKEN DOWN BY V48 GENDER

BY V50 MARITAL STATUS

VARIABLE	CODE	MEAN	STD. DEV.	N	VALUE LABEL
FOR ENTIRE POPULATION		4.659	1.005	393	
V48	1.	4.609	1.048	294	FEMALE
V50	1.	4.657	1.051	140	MARRIED
V50	2.	4.565	1.047	154	SINGLE
V48	2.	4.808	.853	99	MALE
V50	1.	4.553	.891	38	MARRIED
V50	2.	4.967	.795	61	SINGLE

TOTAL CASES = 402

MISSING CASES = 9 OR 2.2 PCT

The first thing to note about this specification is that it has been added to the present program after the FREQUENCIES procedure. This means it is possible to run a single SPSS program which can accomplish more than one analysis of the data. In fact there is no limit to the number of statistical procedures which can be specified in a single program. Concerning the BREAKDOWN procedure specifically, it is important to understand the exact meaning of the statement above. We are telling SPSS to calculate means and standard deviations for items 7 through 22 first by males and females separately (V48) and then, within each gender group, for singles and marrieds separately. We would not accomplish quite the same thing by reversing V48 and V50 in the above statement. Nor would we accomplish the same thing if we substituted a comma for the final BY. Such a statement would be interpreted by SPSS as two separate one-way breakdowns, first by gender (V48) and then separately by marital status (V50). The specification statement above is termed a *two-way breakdown* because the sample is first divided into males and females and then further subdivided by marital status. Perhaps this can be best understood by viewing some output from this analysis. Figure 9.4 shows the results for Item 17, the importance of one's sex life to happiness. The overall sample mean, termed "entire population" on the printout, is 4.659. Thus the average student rates his or her sex life between "moderate" and "considerable" on the 6-point scale, a little closer to "considerable." The mean for all females is 4.609 vs. a mean of 4.808 for all males. A slight difference exists between married and single females, 4.657 vs. 4.565, respectively. A greater difference exists between married and single men, 4.553 vs. 4.967. And, whereas married women consider their sex lives more important to their happiness than do single women, the opposite is true among married and single men.

Now, how does one take the kind information shown in Figure 9.4 for each of the pillars of happiness and convert it into the results shown in Table 9.3? The answer is: by hand. Yes, despite the miracle of SPSS, there is no program available which will extract the 16 X 4 = 48 means and arrange them in descending order so that rankings may be assigned. Aren't you glad there is still some work left for the researcher to do?

Transforming Data to Standard Scores

The last question posed at the beginning of this section concerned the extent to which men and women students might differ in their possession of four psychological attitudes identified as essential to happiness by Shaver and Freedman (1976). In the words of Shaver and Freedman:

> Four psychological attitudes are especially essential to happiness:

--Emotional security: disagreeing with the statement "good things can't last."
--Lack of cynicism: disagreeing with statements that reflect a cynical or Machiavellian view of human nature, such as expressed by P.T. Barnum's "there's a sucker born every minute."
--The beliefs that life has meaning, that one's guiding values are right.
--Feelings of control over the good things that happen, as opposed to feeling that one is the pawn of events (Shaver and Freedman, 1976, p. 75).

These four attitudes about life correspond very well with items 63, 62, 4, and 58, respectively, on the happiness questionaire. If these four characteristics are especially important to personal happiness then it follows that their sum total ought to be quite indicative of an individual's state of mental health. How can we derive such an index of well-being from responses to the four questionnaire items? The answer is by using standard scores. This process is analogous to adding up the points on different tests to determine a student's grade. Recall that the formula for a z-score is:

$$z = (X - M) / SD$$

We must first use the FREQUENCIES program to determine the mean and standard deviations of the four questionnaire items. Having done this we then compose a second SPSS program which uses a COMPUTE statement to create new standardized variables from the original four items. The SPSS COMPUTE statements are as follows:

```
13.     COMPUTE
13.005 Z63=(V63-3.940)/1.524
14.     COMPUTE
14.005 Z62=(V62-3.871)/1.560
15.     COMPUTE
15.005 Z4=(V4-1.743)/0.941
16.     COMPUTE
16.005 Z58=(V58-2.418)/0.981
```

The numeric values in the COMPUTE specifications represent the means and standard deviations of the respective items, which we derived from the output of a previous FREQUENCIES program.

Following these statements is one that sums the four items into a factor score which may then be used as a variable for statistical analysis. A useful procedure for comparing males and females on this interval variable is the BREAKDOWN program. Thus we need two more statements to complete our program:

```
17.     COMPUTE
```

```
17.005 FACTOR=Z63+Z62+Z4+Z58
18.    BREAKDOWN
18.005 TABLES=FACTOR BY V48
```

This program will compute means and standard deviations for females and males separately for the composite well-being variable, FACTOR. (Note: we could have given FACTOR any other name such as COMPOSIT or SUMTOTAL.) With the addition of a STATISTICS 1 statement this program will also conduct an analysis of variance to determine if the difference between the sexes is significant. Such an analysis was conducted by the author. It revealed a very slight but insignificant difference in favor of the males on this composite indicator of happiness. We will explore the method of analysis of variance in considerable detail in a future chapter. This chapter concludes with sample computer programs for SPSS and SPSS-X shown in figures 9.5 and 9.6.

FIGURE 9.5
Sample SPSS Program

```
L
EDIT
DATA LIST
FIXED(1)/1 V1 TO V80 1-80
VAR LABELS
V1 GENERAL HAPPINESS/V48 GENDER/V49 AGE/V50 MARITAL STATUS/
V7 RECOGNITION,SUCCESS/V8 BEING A PARENT/
V9 FINANCIAL SITUATION/V10 HEALTH & PHYSICAL CONDITION/
V11 HOUSE OR APARTMENT/V12 JOB OR PRIMARY ACTIVITY/
V13 PERSONAL GROWTH/V14 EXERCISE.RECREATION/V15 RELIGION/
V16 BEING IN LOVE/V17 SEX LIFE/V18 MARRIAGE/
V19 PARTNER'S HAPPINESS/V20 FRIENDS AND SOCIAL LIFE/
V21 BODY & ATTRACTIVENESS/V22 CITY YOU LIVE IN
VALUE LABELS
V1 (1)VERY HAPPY (2)MODERATELY HAPPY (3)SLIGHTLY HAPPY
(4)SLIGHTLY UNHAPPY (5)MODERATELY UNHAPPY (6)VERY UNHAPPY
/V48 (1)FEMALE (2)MALE/V49 (1) 25 OR LESS (2) 26-30
(3)31-35 (4)36-40 (5)41-45 (6)OVER 45/
V50 (1)MARRIED (2)SINGLE/V7 TO V22 (1)OF NO IMPORTANCE
(2)OF VERY LITTLE IMPORTANCE (3)OF SLIGHT IMPORTANCE
(4)OF MODERATE IMPORTANCE (5)OF CONSIDERABLE IMPORTANCE
MISSING VALUES
V1 TO V46 (0, 7 THRU 9)/ V47 (O, 5 THRU 9)/
V48 (0, 3 THRU 9)/ V49 TO V80 (0, 7 THRU 9)
RECODE
V50 (1=1) (2 THRU 6=2)
FREQUENCIES
GENERAL=V1, V48, V49, V50, V7 TO V22, V41, V42
OPTIONS
8
STATISTICS
ALL
BREAKDOWN
TABLES=V7 TO V22 BY V48 BY V50
CROSSTABS
TABLES=V41, V42 BY V48
STATISTICS
1
? D,1
? E
ENTERING SPSS.
            127700B -- MAXIMUM CM AVAILABLE FOR THIS RUN


CPU TIME REQUIRED            .501 SECONDS
```

FIGURE 9.6
Sample SPSS-X Program

```
1      0        FILE HANDLE HAPPY
2      0        DATA LIST FILE=HAPPY/ V1 TO V80 1-80
3      0        VARIABLE LABELS
4      0        V41            'SEX LIFE SATISFACTION'
5      0        V42            'NO. OF SEX PARTNERS'
6      0        V48            ' GENDER'

109 APR 87   SPSS-X RELEASE 2.0 FROM NORTHWESTERN UNIVERSITY
             CALIFORNIA STATE UNIVERSITY    CYBER 170/180    NOS 2,4,3

7      0        VALUE LABELS
8      0        V41            1 'VERY SATISFIED
9      0                       2 'MODERATELY SATISFIED'
10     0                       3 'SLIGHTLY SATISFIED'
11     0                       4 'SLIGHTLY DISSATISFIED'
12     0                       5 'MODERATELY DISSATISFIED'
>WARNING 4490 LINE 11, COLUMN 8, TEXT: SLIGHTLY DISSATISFIED
>A LABEL APPEARING ON THE VALUE LABELS COMMAND EXCEEDS 20 CHARACTERS
IN LENGTH
>THE LABEL WILL BE TRUNCATED TO 20 CHARACTERS

13     0                       6 'VERY DISSATISFIED'

>WARNING 4490 LINE 12, COLUMN 8, TEXT: MODERATELY DISSATISFIED
>A LABEL APPEARING ON THE VALUE LABELS COMMAND EXCEEDS 20 CHARACTERS
IN LENGTH
>THE LABEL WILL BE TRUNCATED TO 20 CHARACTERS
14     0        V42            1 'NONE'
15     0                       2 'ONE'
16     0                       3 'TWO TO FIVE'
17     0                       4 'SIX TO TEN'
18     0                       5 'ELEVEN TO 20'
19     0                       6 'MORE THAN 20'
20     0        V48            1 'FEMALE'
21     0                       2 'MALE'
22     0        SET WIDTH=80
23     MISSING VALUES V1 TO V46 (0, 7 THRU 9)/ V47 (0, 5 THRU 9)/
24                  V48 (0, 3 THRU 9)/ V49 TO V80 (0, 7 THRU 9)
25     RECODE V50 (1=1) (2 THRU 6=2)
26     CROSSTABS TABLES=V41, V42 BY V48
27     OPTIONS 14
28     STATISTICS 1
```

CHAPTER TEN

CORRELATIONAL METHODS

This chapter begins with a prototypic correlational study. The example investigation is followed by a section describing various statistics associated with the correlational method. The final section provides illustrations of the statistical tests using SPSS with data from the happiness questionnaire.

From Chapter Two you will recall that correlational research is concerned with discovering and measuring the degree of relationship between two or more variables. Such research is often conducted for the purpose of making predictions. Correlational research can also be useful in exploratory studies which prepare the way for more precise experimentation to follow.

Research Example: A Study of Possible Indicators of Emotional Problems in Adolescents

This study by Mathon (1986) was an outgrowth of a larger evaluation and student follow-up study conducted by Frey (1984). Frey was commissioned by a high school district in Contra Costa County, California, to conduct a study of students' perceptions of their counseling and guidance program, their courses of study, and the administration of their school. The evaluation also involved the collection of data concerning students' social and psychological development, and their academic and career goals.

A questionnaire was developed and administered to students at the end of their senior year in 1984. Three hundred forty-two students were randomly selectd from 1,268 seniors in four district high schools. The high schools are located in an upper-middle-class, relatively homogeneous, predominantly white suburb in the San Francisco Bay Area.

When the results of the descriptive evaluation were reviewed by school officials, several teachers and administrators were concerned about student responses to one questionnaire item which asked students on a 5-point scale how long they thought they would live. It was noted that 43 students (12.6%) responded that they would die at a very young or relatively young age. Faculty reactions ranged from alarm to disbelief. Some teachers thought such responses were indicative of unhealthy emotional states, possibly associated with suicidal ideas on the part of the "die-young" group. Others were inclined to discount these responses, believing they were the product of "goof-offs" who were simply trying to unduly alarm the faculty. Furthermore, they felt that these 43 questionnaires were probably invalid and should be excluded from the data analysis.

Thus, a need for further investigation was evident. An analysis of the data was undertaken by Mathan to determine if students' responses to the die-young question were related to other social, emotional, and scholastic responses indicative of poor mental health. As such, this study served as a kind of validation of the larger evaluation as well as exploring important mental health issues of its own. The study's purpose was stated by Mathen as follows:

> This study was designed to examine the relationship between an adolescent's subjective indication that he/she will die young and various psychological, behavioral, attitudinal, and demographic characteristics of the emotionally at-risk adolescent. It was expected that the die-young group of subjects would exhibit in their responses characteristics similar to those that have been found in previous studies of adolescents with emotional and social problems (Mathan, 1986, p.35).

The following hypotheses were tested:

1. There is a significant relationship between the die-young item (#55) and other selected psychological and behavioral self-measures from the questionnaire.

2. There is a significant multiple correlation between the die-young variable and a set of variables made up of both psychological and demographic variables.

3. There is a significant canonical correlation between the set of psychological variables and a set of school-related variables, including both performance and attitude variables.

The questionnaire items selected for analysis were from several categories including stress and coping, self-perceptions, health, feelings about high school, academic skills and achievement, independent living, personal enrichment, vocational development, and use of guidance services. The items represented about 43% of the total items on the questionnaire.

The tests of hypothesis 1 indicated that 41 of the 86 items chosen from the entire inventory were significantly correlated to the die-young item. In particular, the variables that showed the highest correlations were degree of depression, use of street drugs, use of tobacco, use of alcohol and cigarettes to relieve stress, inadequate sleep, and lack of optimism about the future.

In an effort to determine the specific cluster of psychological variables most highly related to the die-young response, Mathan selected items from three scales: health, self-perception, and stress and coping. She regressed the die-young variable onto this set of predictors in a stepwise multiple regression. The most potent predictors were depression, use of tobacco, lack of optimism, a liking for unpredictability, and use of street drugs. These along with four other variables accounted for 27% of the variance in students' die-young (or old) responses.

The last hypothesis addressed the relationship between a set of school-related attitudes and behaviors and a set of psychological and social attitudes and behaviors. A significant canonical correlation of .68 was obtained. Among the important school-related variables were: the extent to which outside events positively affected school work, feelings about high school, the degree to which students felt liked by teachers, satisfaction with academic skills, and a variety of academic test results. Important contributors in the second set were non-use of street drugs, satisfaction in pleasing parents, social relationships seen as helpful and supportive, and life as pleasurable.

From her analysis of the high school data, Mathan drew these conclusions:

> From the responses in the areas mentioned above a profile develops of the adolescent at-risk for social/emotional problems....the adolescents who felt they would die young reported a higher degree of depression and nervousness, and a lower degree of pleasure in life. All these factors indicate possibilities of depression, alienation, and suicidal ideation....it tends to paint a picture of a pattern or syndrome of attitudes and behaviors that fits the emotionally and socially at-risk adolescent....Although the magnitude of the relationship is probably not strong enough to bring accurate prediction at the individual level, the intent was to uncover a pattern of related variables associated with responses on the die-young question. This was accomplished.
>
> The results of this investigation suggest that there are factors which may be used to identify the emotionally distressed adolescent from his/her peers. It is particularly important, at a time when emotional and social problems among adolescents seem to be increasing, that schools play an active role in prevention and indentification. Programs in the schools that are designed to increase self-esteem, strengthen coping abilites, social skills, and

interrelationships with peers and teachers would be beneficial. The development of identification methods and effective programs to assist adolescents with emotional and social problems is an obvious and important area for further research (Mathan, 1986, pp. 66-67).

Statistics for Correlational Research

The name Sir Francis Galton is sometimes associated with the method of correlation because of studies he conducted in England in the latter part of the 19th century. In one investigation, Galton was able to show a positive correlation in heights between fathers and sons. He also noticed, however, that although tall fathers tended to produce relatively tall sons, the sons were somewhat shorter than the fathers. He referred to this phenomenon as a "regression." This was but one of his many studies in the field of human heredity. In another investigation, Galton sought to determine a possible relationship between prayer and the longevity of monarchs. He wondered if the many prayers offered for the long life of kings and queens had any effect. He discovered that British monarchs did not live significantly longer than the general population.

It remained for one of Galton's students, Karl Pearson, to work out the precise mathematical formulas which could describe the kinds of relationships Galton investigated. Pearson, who became a professor of mathematics at the University of London, is generally recognized as the founder of the science of statistics. His book, Grammar of Science (1892), was one of the first textbooks on the scientific method. We shall begin this section by exploring Pearson's "product-moment" coefficient of correlation, the most ubiquitous statistic of association used in behavioral research.

The Pearson r

While there are several different ways of formulating the Pearson r (the r stands for Galton's *regression* effect), a conceptually elegant formula is this:

$$r = \text{Sum}(\ z(X)\ z(Y)\ ) \ /\ (\ N - 1\ )$$

where z(X) signifies a standard score for an X variable, pronounced "z of X;" and z(Y) is a standard score for a Y variable, pronounced "z of Y;" and N is the number of subjects in the sample. The formula indicates that z-scores should first be computed for all subjects on each variable, then a cross product is derived by multiplying z(X) by z(Y) for each subject. The N cross products are summed for all subjects, and that total is divided by the mumber of subjects minus one. This formula produces a standard coefficient of correlation which fluctuates in value between 0 and 1 and may be either positive or negative in sign.

While you may never have to compute a Pearson r by hand, it is instructive to go through the necessary calculations. Suppose we are interested in determining the degree of relationship between items 5 and 6 on the happiness questionnaire. Item 5 asks the question: How optimistic or pessimistic about your life would you say you are? Item 6 asks: How optimistic or pessimistic are you about the future of the country? One might hypothesize a positive relationship between individuals' responses to these two questions.

To make the calculations simple, let's compute a Pearson r on data from three subjects (a feasible but unlikely endeavor). The raw responses are as follows:

Individuals	Item 5 (self)	Item 6 (country)
1.	5	3
2.	6	4
3.	4	2

Method: r = Sum(z(X) z(Y)) / (N - 1)

1. First calculate the mean for each variable. The mean of X (Item 5) equals 5. The mean of Y (Item 6) equals 3.
2. Calculate the standard deviation (SD) of each variable:

SD = SQRT (Sum((X - M)**2) /(N - 1))

Recall from the previous chapter that SD is the square root of the variance, a measure of dispersion. For the X variable:

X - M	**2	Sum	N - 1
5 - 5 = 0	0	0	2
6 - 5 = 1	1	1	
4 - 5 =-1	1	1	
		---	
		2 = Sum((X-M)**2)	

Now, if we divide the sum of the squared deviation scores by N-1, we have 2/2 = 1. The square root of 1 is 1. Therefore, the standard deviation of Item 5, the X variable, is 1.

For the Y variable:

Y - M	**2	Sum	N - 1
3 - 3 = 0	0	0	2
4 - 3 = 1	1	1	
2 - 3 =-1	1	1	
		---	
		2 = Sum((Y-M)**2)	

Now, if we divide the sum of the squared deviation scores by N-1, we have 2/2 = 1. The square root of 1 is 1. Therefore, the standard deviation of Item 6, the Y variable, is also 1.

3. Calculate z-scores for each distribution.

z = (X - M) / SD

Individuals	Item 5 (X - M)/ SD	Item 6 (Y - M)/ SD
1.	5 - 5 / 1 = 0	3 - 3 / 1 = 0
2.	6 - 5 / 1 = 1	4 - 3 / 1 = 1
3.	4 - 5 / 1 =-1	2 - 3 / 1 =-1

4. Calculate the sum of the cross products of the z-scores, Sum(z(X) z(Y)):

Individuals	Item 5 z(X)		Item 6 z(Y)		cross product (z(X)z(Y))
1.	0	*	0	=	0
2.	1	*	1	=	1
3.	-1	*	-1	=	1
					---
					2 = Sum

5. Calculate r:

r = Sum(z(X) z(Y)) / (N - 1) = 2 / 2 = 1

Does it surprise you that the coefficient of correlation is perfect, that there is a total correspondence between the two questionnaire items? How can this be when the means of the two items are so different? Don't the means have to be the same to get a Pearson r of 1.00? The answer is no for this reason: Correlation is a method which measures the congruence between individuals' *relative* positions in two distributions, X and Y. You will notice above that individuals 1, 2, and 3 hold the same relative positions in both distributions. That is, their z-scores for the two distributions are identical.

A correlation coefficient of 1.00 tells us that there is a perfect linear relationship between X and Y, that given knowledge of a person's response to one item, we can perfectly predict his response to the other item. In this case if we want to know how optimistic an individual feels toward his country, we can ask him how optimistic he is about his own future and then subtact two points. The actual happiness data do not, of course, show a perfect correlation between these items. Perfect correlations are quite rare in behavioral research. We will explore the actual relationship between these items later.

Interpreting Correlation Coefficients

Now that you are aware of the nature of a perfect relationship, an r of 1.00, what about an r of 0.00? And how about various numbers in between? Intuitively, you might guess that an r of zero represents no association whatsoever between variables. Knowledge from one variable provides us with no predictive information at all concerning the other variable. Some other typical correlation coefficients are as follows: height of identical twins, .90 to .95; height of fraternal twins, siblings, or parent and child, .50 to .60; height of grandparent and grandchild, .25 to .35; height and IQ, .10 to .20.

Although the interpretation of correlation coefficients can be tricky at times, there are a few important *rules of thumb* to follow. First, correlation does not imply causation. If a researcher discovers a relationship between watching certain television programs and violent behavior in children, it cannot be automatically assumed that TV-watching produced the violent behavior. A third variable may influence, or "cause," the other two. Secondly, inverse or negative relationships are just as important as positive ones. Sometimes a negative relationship is brought about simply by the scaling of the two variables. For example, from the happiness questionnaire the correlation between general happiness (Item 1) and time spent with one's partner (Item 69) is -.33. This apparent negative relationship is due to scaling differences in the two items. If either of the two scales were reversed, the coefficient of -.33 would become positive. Thus, happiness and time spent with one's partner is really a conceptually positive relationship.

A third, and very important, point is that the statistical significance of a coefficient must be determined in relation to its sample size. Appendix C contains a table for determining the significance of a Pearson coefficient of correlation. The reader is urged to turn to this appendix and study the table briefly. The left-most column of this table, headed "*df*," represents the degrees of freedom associated with a coefficient. What is this illusive term *degrees of freedom*? Let us digress a moment to answer this question. Assume you have three numbers: 2, 4, and

6. Their mean is 4. You are told you may change any of the numbers as long as the mean remains 4. How many numbers are you free to vary? If you change the first two numbers to 3 and 7, the remaining number is determined. It must be 2 for the mean to remain 4. If you had 30 numbers and were given the same task, you would be free to vary only 29 of them. In statistical terms you have lost one degree of freedom to the mean. Since a correlation coefficient is computed from two variables (two means), we lose two degrees of freedom. Thus, we enter the table of critical values of r at df equal to N-2.

Notice in Appendix C that the values of r listed under .10, .05, and .01 start with numbers very close to 1.00 for df=1, and fluctuate downward considerably for df=100. These r values specify the lowest correlation coefficient needed for statistical significance at each of three levels of significance--the ten percent, five percent, and one percent levels. The most commonly used level is the five percent, or .05 level of significance. This is the level at which we are willing to take five chances in 100 of being wrong when we say there is a relationship between two variables. If we enter the table for our sample calculation above, what is the value needed for significance? Remember that N=3; therefore we enter the table at df=1 (N-2 degrees of freedom). At the .05 level of significance we need a coefficient of .997 for significance. Since our coefficient was 1.000, we can say with some degree of confidence (95%) that there is indeed a significant relationship between X and Y.

Let's take another example from the happiness data, this time a real one, to illustrate another property of the table of critical values of r. The computed r between items 1 and 4 is .2307 (SPSS did the calculation). This r was computed for 401 cases. Item 1 is general happiness and Item 4 asks: How confident are you that your guiding values are right for you and will last? Question: Is there a relationship between confidence in one's guiding values and one's level of happiness? Method: enter the table for df=399 (401-2). Since the tabled degrees of freedom do not exceed 100, enter the table at 100. Note the coefficient of .195 needed for significance at the .05 level. Answer: yes, there is a significant relationship between guiding values and happiness.

There are two further points to be made about correlation coefficients. The first is that they, like other statistics, are highly sensitive to sample size. In the case of a sample of 3 we need virtually a perfect correlation to achieve significance. With a sample of 100, we need only .195 for significance at the .05 level. The reason the table stops at df=100 is that requirements for significance change very little with samples of more than 100 cases. Because of this phenomenon, it is important for you to know the sample size when you read or are told about a "significant" correlation. With a sample of 1000 cases, a researcher is almost guaranteed to find a significant relationship between any two variable he chooses. The coefficient required for significance is only .062 at the .05 level. Thus you can see that, contrary to intuition, a significant correlation from a small study might be more meaningful than one from a large-scale investigation.

Turney and Robb (1971) offer further advice about interpreting r values. They point out that r's are not interpreted as percents. An r of .88 does not imply that X and Y are correlated 88 percent of the time. Furthermore, we cannot say that an r of .88 is twice as strong as an r of .44. As a rough guide to providing qualitative descriptive terms for coefficients of correlation, Turney and Robb offer the following system:

.80 to 1.00	Very high correlation
.60 to .79	High correlation
.40 to .59	Moderate correlation
.20 to .39	Slight correlation
.01 to .19	Very slight correlation

Uses of Correlation Coefficients

Coefficients of correlation are used in many ways by researchers, but three of them are prevalent in behavioral research. Coefficients of r can be used for (1) testing hypotheses, (2) determining test reliablilty, and (3) determining test validity. Let's look at each of these uses briefly.

Much of our discussion in the preceding section pertained to hypothesis testing. However, some additional points need to be made concerning this use of r values. First, it is possible when stating a relational hypothesis to formulate two different types. These are known as one-, and two-tailed hypotheses. In a one-tailed test we specify a relationship in one direction only. That is, we specify either a positive or negative relationship, but not both. In a two-tailed test, we are looking for any relationship, either positive or negative. We do not specify the directionality of our hypotheses. One-tailed hypotheses are much more common in correlational research than two-tailed hypotheses. We usually have a strong hunch that a relationship will be either positive or negative. If we are willing to "go out on a limb" and make a directional (one-tailed) hypothesis, then we are entitled to reduce the requirement for significance. In Appendix C we would use the r values under .10 when testing a one-tailed test for significance at the .05 level. For example, with df=16 the critical value for r is .400 for a one-tailed test versus .468 for a two-tailed test.

Correlation coefficients are often used in test construction for determining test reliability and validity. A typical approach is to give a test to a sample group, score it, and then administer it again at some future date. This is the test-retest paradigm. To the extent that individuals' scores are correlated for the two time periods, we make a judgment about the stability or reliability of the test. In this situation, the usual significance test is not of concern. Reliability coefficients (r's) are interpreted in relation to the type of test under consideration. Standardized mental abilities tests often have reliabilities of about .90. Academic achievement tests usually range from .80 to .90. Good personality scales will show test-retest reliabilities in the .70's. Some are in the .60's, or even lower.

Validity coefficients are computed in exactly the same way as reliablilty coefficients, except that a second test or external performance criterion is used. For example, the SAT is given to high school juniors and later correlated with their college GPA's. The resultant correlation is referred to as a validity coefficent. As you might expect, the size of a test's validity coefficient is usually much lower than its corresponding reliability coefficient.

The criterion-related validity of educational and psychological tests has been a matter of controversy in recent years (cf. Jensen, 1981, pp. 22-34). Although the use of tests is a complex technical and social issue, part of the criticism of testing is due to a lack of understanding of validity coefficients--how they are computed and interpreted. Howell (1987) provides a hypothetical example of how a reasonably high validity coefficient can be attenuated (artificially lowered) in the normal course of correlational research. Suppose a college selects applicants on the basis of SAT scores which range from 200 to 800 scale points. The admissions officer decides to admit only those students with scores above 400. At a future time a statistical correlation is made between the students' SAT scores and their cumulative college GPA's. The resultant validity coefficient is .43. This scenario is fairly common in validation studies where tests are used for selection purposes.

The problem with this approach to test validation is that it restricts the range of the original sample to a subsample of selected applicants whose SAT scores fluctuate within a narrower band of the SAT scale. If all of the applicants had been admitted to college and a correlation were computed between their SAT and GPA scores, a higher validity of .65 would have resulted. The problem of *range restriction* is endemic to correlational research. Imagine how low a validity coefficent might be for the Graduate Record Exam when derived from a sample of Ph.D. students. Once 90% of all candidates have been screened out, and a coefficient of correlation is computed for the top 10% between their GRE and GPA scores, the apparent validity of the GRE would be quite low or nonexistent. This does not mean that the GRE is not a good predictor of successful Ph.D. students from the general population, but that its predictive power is lessened when applied to an elite group of candidates.

Another reason for criticism of testing is due to a lack of understanding of validity coefficients, even if they are corrected for attenuation. An informative way of looking at test validities is to compare the criterion performance of a group selected on the basis of test scores with the performance of a group selected at random. In relation to our college admissions example above, this would be a comparison of college GPA's for a group of students selected on the basis of their SAT scores vs. an equal number selected at random, perhaps by lottery. Jensen (1981) had this to say about a test with a validity coefficient of only .33:

> That is like 33 percent annual interest on your investment. Who would sneer at that?
>
> A one-third increase in productivity or quality of performance would hardly be regarded as a trivial gain by most employers or college faculties. But that is the gain resulting from a test with a "mediocre" validity of only .33. Yet the Ralph Nader organization, in blasting college entrance exams, likened them to a "roulette game" on the ground that their typical predictive validity coefficients are in the range of .40 to .55. With this much predictive power at his disposal, a gambler playing the roulette wheel could easily break the bank at Monte Carlo within half an hour! (Jensen, 1981, pp. 25-26)

Although Arthur Jensen's views on testing have been controversial in the fields of education and psychology, one cannot deny the considerable predictive power of tests with apparently low validities. Professionals from these fields need to be aware of the generally high technical quality of most of the instruments used in testing. They should also be aware that arguments against testing made on technical grounds are often smokescreens for social and economic motivations. It is this author's view that the use of behavioral tests is an important professional and public issue which deserves careful scrutiny and constant review. There is room for argument against testing. But the bulk of argumentation should concern social, emotional, and economic reasons, rather than technical ones. And we should all be aware that when we give up the predictive power of tests, we also give up the quality of performance which they predict.

From the discussion in this section you should now be aware that correlation coefficients have both an absolute and relative meaning. Their absolute meaning is based on the actual size of the coefficient. A coefficient of .50 is absolute with respect to its predictive power. However, the same coefficient has a relative meaning when compared to other coefficients which might be put to similar use. A reliability coefficient of .50 might be considered adequate for a personality scale, but would be entirely inadequate for a test of scholastic aptitude. In the next section we will explore how correlation coefficients are actually used to make predictions of behavior.

Regression Analysis

At the beginning of the Statistics section it was pointed out that Sir Francis Galton discovered a relationship between the heights of fathers and sons. He actually conducted his study among the landed gentry of England in the 19th century. He found that upper class men were on the average taller than the average Englishman, and that their sons were also taller on the average. There was a substantial relationship between the heights of fathers and sons, but the sons as a group were somewhat shorter than their fathers.

A great deal of research has been conducted in the past century on the heritability of human characteristics including both physical and psychological traits such as temperament and mental ability. Another British researcher, a contemporary educational psychologist, has estimated that at least 60% of the variation in IQ is hereditary (Vernon, 1979). Jensen (1981) gives a figure of .52 as the average correlation between the IQ's of parent and child. Given this information it should be possible to make a prediction of an unborn child's IQ given knowledge of the IQ of one of the parents. For the sake of simplicity let's round off the coefficient to .50 and see how we can estimate the child's IQ using regression analysis. The basic equation for a simple two-variable regression is:

$$Y' = bX + C$$

This equation can be read as follows: Y prime, an estimated value, can be best predicted by multiplying a regression weight, called a b-weight, by an actual X value and then adding to that product a constant, C. While this is not an overly complicated formula, it can be made even simpler. When used with standard scores such as the z-score, we may write the formula in this simplified manner:

$$Y' = rz(X)$$

This equation reads: Y prime ,the child's estimated IQ, can be predicted by multiplying the Pearson r by the z of X, that is, by the standard score of the parent's IQ.

You will recall that a common test of mental ability is the Stanford Binet Intelligence Test which has a mean of 100 and a standard deviation of 16 points (see Figure 9.1 in the previous chapter). Let us assume that the parent in our example is quite intelligent with an IQ of 132. That is an IQ exactly two SD's above the mean, which is equivalent to a z-score of 2. Let us now construct the prediction equation:

$$Y' = rz(X)$$
$$Y' = .5*2$$
$$Y' = 1$$

Note that Y' is in z-score units. We must transform the value of 1 back to the original Binet scale. A z-score of 1 is equal to a Binet IQ of 116. Thus our predicted IQ for the child is 116.

What has happened here? Are intelligent parents doomed to have less intelligent children? Will all children eventually be average as each succeeding generation regresses further to the mean? The answer to both questions is no. Because the correlation between parent and child is much less than perfect, our prediction is not perfect either. Although our prediction is much better than chance, there is considerable room for error. It is possible for this parent to have a child who is more intelligent than he or she. It is also possible for the parent to have a child with below-average IQ. But our best possible estimate for the child's IQ is 116. If this parent had an infinite number of children, their mean IQ would in fact be 116 and they would be distributed in a wonderful symetrical distribution about that mean.

What would the result of our prediction be if the parent's IQ were 68 instead of 132? Convert this score to a z-score and complete the calculation. Your predicted score should be 84. Thus a parent who borders on mental retardation will most likely have a child of greater mental ability. The regression effect, discovered by Galton a century ago, is real. To the extent that an imperfect correlation exists between two variables, a regression toward the mean will occur in predicting one score from another. Tall parents do indeed have tall children, but given equal care and nutrition, they will not be quite so tall as their parents on the average.

Multiple Regression and Correlation

Regression analysis can be extended to two or more predictor variables, and, although the calculations are complex, they are no problem for high speed computers. The formula for an n-variable regression is this:

$$Y' = b1X1 + b2X2 + ... + bnXn + C$$

As you can see this is just an extension of the previous equation for one predictor variable. As in simple regression, when multiple regression is performed on standardized data, the intercept constant C is not needed.
The formula is then specified as follows:

$$Y' = beta1\ X1 + beta2\ X2 + \ldots + betan\ Xn$$

The b-weights in the first equation become beta-weights in the second one. These are referred to as standard regression weights because the weights themselves have been rescaled with a common standard deviation. For this reason, beta-weights provide information about the relative strength of predictors. An example should make this clear:

Many universities make use of SAT scores for college entrance. Many others also use high school GPA's in conjunction with SAT's. They formulate a multiple regression equation which includes these two predictors of Y', college performance, which is the criterion variable. Researchers have found that for the majority of students, high school grades are a better predictor of college grades than are SAT scores. Thus, a multiple regression equation for predicting college grades might be as follows:

$$Y' = .66\ X1 + .33\ X2$$

where Y' is college GPA, X1 is high school GPA, and X2 is SAT score. In this equation, the beta-weights for X1 and X2 indicate that a student's high school grades are twice as important as his SAT score. In other words, college performance is made up of two parts high school performance and one part scholastic aptitude, or, prior performance is a better indicator of future performance than presumed ability.

Whenever a multiple regression is performed, a by-product is produced called the multiple correlation, R. The mathematical calculations for R are quite complex when several variables are involved. But for only two predictor variables, the equation is straightforward:

```
R = Sqrt((r**2y1 + r**2y2 - 2ry1ry2r12) / 1 - r**212)
```

where r**2y1 is the squared correlation between college GPA and the first predictor, high school GPA; r**2y2 is the squared correlation between the y criterion, college GPA and the second predictor, SAT score; ry1 is the simple correlation between college GPA and high school GPA, ry2 is the simple correlation between college GPA and SAT, and r**212 is the squared correlation between the two predictors, high school GPA and SAT score. All that is required to solve this equation are the intercorrelations among the three variables. A matrix of intercorrelations is first computed by SPSS and these values are then used for various calculations in multiple regression and correlation. Incidentally, the multiple correlation R for the example above is typically in the range of .50 to .60. This coefficient is interpreted in the same fashion as its cousin, r; R also fluctuates between 0 and 1, and the size of the coefficient indicates its predictive power. The only difference between R and r is that R cannot be negative. There is no such thing as an inverse multiple correlation.

Canonical Correlation

Canonical Correlation is a logical extension of multiple regression. Instead of a single criterion variable on the left side of the equation and multiple predictors on the right side, we now have multiple variables on both sides of an equation with canonical weights for all variables. Consider the previous example of predicting college performance. One might argue that success in college is more than a high grade-point average. What about participation in extra-curricular activities, athletics, student government, etc.? Many tasks, whether attending school or selling used cars, are multifaceted. Although a salesman won't hold his job with a poor sales record, neither will he hold his job if he can't get along with his boss and fellow salespersons. Canonical correlation is a method which allows us to correlate two sets of optimally-weighted variables to determine the strength of their association. A canonical coefficient is derived and interpreted in much the same way as r or R.

SPSS and the Happiness Questionnaire

It is possible to ask inumerable research questions of a correlational nature concerning the data on personal happiness. Let us consider a few of these here, and see how we would go about answering them with SPSS:

1. What are some of the more important correlates of personal happiness?

2. Are these correlates the same for men and women?

3. To what extent is childhood happiness related to present happiness? How does this relationship compare with that discovered by Shaver and Freedman (1976) for their sample of Psychology Today readers?

4. How does sexual behavior relate to overall happiness? Specifically, does satisfaction with one's sex life relate to one's general happiness? Are persons who have had many sexual

partners happier than those who have not? How do these outcomes compare with those found by Shaver and Freedman?

5. What attitudes and behaviors are related to liberal vs. conservative sexual behavior? Specifically, what is predictive of the number of sex partners an individual has had? How well can this variable be predicted?

6. Is there a significant relationship between religious beliefs and sexual attitudes and behavior?

The first question above can be answered very easily with SPSS by using the PEARSON CORR subprogram as follows:

```
15.     PEARSON CORR
15.005 V1 WITH V2 TO V80
```

This command tells SPSS to compute coefficients of correlation for V1, general happiness, with all other items on the happiness questionnaire. In SPSS-X the command is:

```
PEARSON CORR  V1 WITH V2 TO V80
```

It should be noted that the "default option" for the Pearson correlation program is for one-tailed tests of significance, since they are more common than two-tailed tests. If the user desires two-tailed tests he should specify OPTIONS 2 in the usual way. Also, it is possible to obtain a table of means and standard deviations for all of the variables by using STATISTICS 1.

The output from this program is printed in rows as follows. Only the first row of the printout is shown here:

```
        V2         V3         V4         V5         V6         V7

V1     .2826      .1034      .2307      .4316      .1225      .0127
     (  398)    (  401)    (  401)    (  401)    (  399)    (  399)
     P= .001    P= .019    P= .001    P= .001    P= .007    P= .400
```

Each bivariate relationship is denoted by three values. The top value is the Pearson coefficient. Underneath this in parentheses is the number of cases on which the calculation is based. The bottom value is the probability associated with the coefficient, i.e., the level of significance. For example, the correlation between V1 and V5, personal optimism, is .4316. This coefficient was computed on 401 individuals. Since there are 402 sample cases, one individual did not respond to either Item 1 or Item 5. This correlation is significant at or beyond the .001 level, meaning that we would take only one chance in 1000 of being wrong if we stated a relationship between optimism and happiness in a population of similar students. Note the extremely low correlation between V1 and V7, the importance attached to recognition and success. The coefficient of .0127 based on 399 cases is not significant at the .05 level. In fact, the P-value of .400 means that we would take a 40% chance of being wrong if we claimed the existence of this relationship in the general population of students.

A rather striking feature of this output is the number of high significance levels (low P-values) displayed despite the mostly weak correlations. Six of the seven coefficients are "significant" at or beyond the .05 level. This is due to the very large sample size used here. In a situation like this, it is wise to set a very conservative level of significance such as the .001 level. Another strategy is to select an arbitrary cut-off for the size of coefficients, say .30. When this is done there are only five variables substantially correlated with happiness. These are items 5, 41, 68, 69, and 75, which are optimism, sexual satisfaction, satisfaction with the pace of one's life, the amount of time spent with one's partner, and satisfaction with the overall allotment of one's time. The coefficients for these variables range from .30 to .43. Another five variables have coefficients between .25 and .30. These are items 2, 43, 59, 65, and 76, which are stability of happiness, frequency of sex, control over bad things, emotional security, and lack of desire to change lives with someone else.

Comparing Subgroups

Occasionally, one wishes to determine if a discovered relationship is the same for two or more subgroups of a sample population. For example, is the relationship between sexual satisfaction and general happiness the same for both men and women? This question is analogous to the BREAKDOWN procedure discussed in the previous chapter. Though there is no subprogram designed to break down correlations by subgroups, there is an SPSS command which can be used to accomplish this purpose. This is the SELECT IF command. The program segment below illustrates its use:

```
13.     *SELECT IF
13.005 (V48 EQ 1)
15.     PEARSON CORR
15.005 V41 WITH V1
20.     *SELECT IF
20.005 (V48 EQ 2)
25.     PEARSON CORR
25.005 V41 WITH V1
```

In statement 13 we instruct SPSS to select only the data for females by specifying V48 equal to 1. Recall that V48 is gender. The asterisk in front of the statement tells SPSS that this is a temporary condition. After SPSS selects the data for women and calculates the correlation between items 41 and 1, we then specify a second temporary SELECT IF which carries out the same procedure for men (V48 EQ 2). If an asterisk is not used with a SELECT IF command, it becomes a permanent feature of the program, and all statistical procedures which follow will be based on only the data selected.

The SPSS-X version is a bit different. It requires the use of a TEMPORARY statement prior to the SELECT IF as follows:

```
TEMPORARY
SELECT IF  (V48 EQ 1)
PEARSON CORR  V41 WITH V1
TEMPORARY
SELECT IF  (V48 EQ 2)
PEARSON CORR  V41 WITH V1
```

When this program is run, the output indicates that the coefficients for women and men are .3857 and .4160, respectively. The relationship between sexual satisfaction and general happiness is somewhat higher for men than for women. While this does not appear to be a significant difference between the groups, a method for testing the significance of the difference should be applied. Such a method, referred to as a *test for the difference between independent correlations*, is described by Bruning and Kintz (1977) as follows:

Step 1. First, change the two correlations into Fisher z-scores. This can be done by using the table in Appendix D.

Correlation of .3857 = z of .412
Correlation of .4160 = z of .442

Step 2. Subtract either z-score of Step 1 from the other.

$$.442 - .412 = .030$$

Step 3. Subtract 3 from the number of people in the group for which the first correlation was computed (296 women). (Note: the number 3 is always used.)

$$296 - 3 = 293$$

Step 4. Divide the result of Step 3 into the number 1 (ie., take the reciproical of the number). Carry the answer to four decimal places.

$$1 / 293 = .0034$$

Step 5. Subtract 3 from the number of people in the group for which the second correlation was computed (99 men in this case).

99 - 3 = 96

Step 6. Divide the result of Step 5 into the number 1 (ie., take the reciprocal of the number). Carry the answer to four decimal places.

1 / 96 = .0104

Step 7. Add the result of Step 4 to the result of Step 6.

.0034 + .0104 = .0138

Then take the square root of the sum.

Sqrt of .0138 = .1175

Step 8. Divide the result of Step 2 by the result of Step 7. This yields a z statistic.

z = .030 / .1175 = .2553

A z value of 1.96 or larger is required for significance at the .05 level. Thus the correlations for men and women are statistically equivalent. They do not differ much beyond chance fluctuations. And, therefore, in this population of students the relationship beteen sexual satisfaction and general happiness is the same for women and men.

Childhood Happiness

Research question 3 above concerned the relationship between childhood happiness and current happiness. Shaver and Freedman (1976) reported the following concerning their study of several thousand readers of *Psychology Today*:

> We asked readers a number of questions about their childhoods, to see what events in a person's background might make a happy adult....
>
> To our surprise, few childhood experiences told us with any certainty about adult happiness. People who recall their early years as being very happy are less likely to be in therapy and to have irrational fears, and more likely to believe that life is meaningful, than people who remember unhappy childhoods. But many readers came through bad early and teenage years without a mental scratch, and are

> perfectly happy as adults (Shaver and Freedman, 1976, p. 31).

Items 23 through 38 on the happiness questionnaire deal with childhood experiences and memories. Their correlations with Item 1, general happiness, were computed in our first SPSS program. While the happiness questionnaire does not probe irrational fears and therapy history, there is general agreement among the other childhood items with the results of Shaver and Freedman. Most of the correlations on these childhood items are positive but rather weak. Some exceptions to this general outcome were items 24, parents' relationship to each other; 30, mother's relationship to you; and 32, mother's expression of her emotions. These items all had positive coefficients in the range of .19 to .20 and were significant beyond the .001 level. Loving and supportive parental relationships and an open expression of emotions by one's mother were associated with greater happiness. The more direct items on childhood happiness, 34 and 36, childhood and adolescent happiness, showed even weaker positive correlations of .132 and .189, respectively. An interesting investigation would be to determine if these relationships are equivalent in older and younger subjects. One might hypothesize a stronger connection between childhood and adult happiness in younger individuals.

Sexual Behavior and Happiness

Shaver and Freedman (1976) reported these findings:

> Happiness with life, for these readers (of *Psychology Today*), is not based on having the conquests of Casanova or the seductiveness of Salome. Sexual satisfaction comes from quality, not quantity. But...in this era of sexual obsession, many readers assume that "most people of their age and sex" have had more partners and are more satisfied than they are (Shaver and Freedman, 1976, p. 31).

The student data are in agreement with that of Shaver and Freedman concerning the quantity vs. quality dimension. While sexual satisfaction is strongly related to general happiness, the number of one's sex partners, Item 42, had an insignificant correlation of .08 with happiness. The quality of one's present sexual relationship far outweighs the history of one sexual exploits. In contrast to Shaver and Freedman's readers, Whalen's students appeared to be much less envious of their peers' sexual exploits and satisfaction. Among the students there was little difference between their own behavior and that which they perceived in most people of their age and sex. And the students' satisfaction with their sex lives was generally positive.

Predicting Sexual Behavior

If one's sexual history, ie., the number of one's partners, is not related to current happiness, then what is it related to? Are there other variables on the happiness questionnaire which are predictive of one's sex history? Is it possible to accurately predict the number of one's sex partners? These questions can be probed through the use of multiple regression and correlation.

In 1981 SPSS Inc. published an update to its original manual which incorporated several revisions and refinements to its earlier programs. One of these was the NEW REGRESSION procedure used here:

```
15.     NEW REGRESSION
15.002 DESCRIPTIVES/
15.003 MISSING=PAIRWISE/
15.005 VARIABLES=V42,V15,V26,V37,V39,V44,V50,V51,V53,V57/
15.025 DEPENDENT=V42/STEPWISE
```

The SPSS-X version is quite similar:

```
REGRESSION  DESCRIPTIVES/
            MISSING=PAIRWISE/
            VARIABLES=(same list as above)/
            DEPENDENT=V42/
            METHOD=STEPWISE
```

A few comments about this regression program are in order. The DESCRIPTIVES substatement is optional. Its purpose is to call for a set of descriptive statistics including means, SD's, and an intercorrelation matrix. The MISSING command specifies pairwise vs. *listwise deletion*, the default option. What this means is that unless one specifies otherwise, cases will be eliminated from the regression if there is a missing value (response) on any one of the variables listed in the VARIABLES= statement. By specifying MISSING=PAIRWISE, all cases (subjects) are included in the regression; however, an individual is eliminated from a particular "pairwise" computation if he is missing a response to one of the two paired variables. Listwise deletion can cause a severe reduction in sample size if there is considerable missing data in one's sample. The DEPENDENT command simply specifies which variable in the list we wish to predict. This is the the criterion or dependent variable. Finally, STEPWISE indicates a type of regression in which variables are added to the equation one step at a time so that the researcher may see the effect of each new predictor on the overall regession.

It should be noted that the nine predictor variables specified in the SPSS program were selected on the basis of a previously run PEARSON CORR program which showed those variables having the highest correlations with Item 42. These correlations ranged from .20 to .55. Several variables had negative coefficients including items 15, 26, 37, 51, and 57. The negative coefficients meant that persons with many sex partners tended to be: uninterested in religion, first-borns, early daters, politically liberal, and physically attractive (at least they thought so). The variables with positive coefficients were items 39, 44, 50, and 53. These coefficients indicated that persons with many sex partners tended toward greater use of alcohol and drugs, believed others also had many sex partners, were single, and lived in a large city vs. a small city or suburb. The most potent predictor by far, r=.545, is Item 44, which asks: How many sexual partners do you think most people of your age and sex have had? It appears that the sample students believe their own behavior is appropriate and normal. Or perhaps they rationalized their behavior by projecting it on to society at large. Contrary to the PT readers of Shaver and Freedman, the students as a group do not feel they missed out on the sexual revolution. Their perception of others' behavior (V44) was within a tenth of a point of their own (V42) on the six point scale for these items.

Figure 10.1 shows the SPSS printout for Step 1 of the regression process. The first variable to enter the equation is V44 because it has the highest bivariate correlation with V42. At Step 1, stepwise multiple regression is the same as simple regression with two variables. The MULTIPLE R is the same as the Pearson r. The next statistic shown on the printout is R SQUARE, sometimes called the *coefficient of determination.* It is so-called because it represents the proportion of variance in the criterion which is "determined" by the predictor. In this case .297 or, rounded-off and transformed to a percentage, 30% of the variance in individuals' responses to Item 42, their number of sexual partners, can be accounted for by knowing their response to Item 44. In other words, the quickest way to find out the most about persons' past sex lives short of asking them directly is to ask them how many sex partners they think other people have had.

The ADJUSTED R SQUARE is a statistic which attempts to predict the shrinkage of R Square if the regression equation is actually used to predict behavior in a new group of subjects from the same population. The value of .295 is extremely close to the R Square of .297, thus little shrinkage is predicted. As the number of predictor variables in the equation increases, the amount of shrinkage forecasted by the adjusted R Square also increases. The STANDARD ERROR is another measure of the effectiveness of the prediction equation. Note that if we had no information at all about a person's sexual history, the best estimate we could make about the number of partners he has had would be the group mean, in this case 3.7 or, roughly, six to ten partners. (In this sample, this would be true regardless of the person's age, since age did not correlate with partners.) And

FIGURE 10.1
Step 1 of Multiple Regression

DEPENDENT VARIABLE V42

BEGINNING BLOCK NUMBER 1 METHOD: STEPWISE

VARIABLE(S) ENTERED ON STEP NUMBER
1 V44

MULTIPLE R	.54524
R SQUARE	.29728
ADJUSTED R SQUARE	.29549
STANDARD ERROR	1.21669

ANALYSIS OF VARIANCE

	DF	SUM OF SQUARES	MEAN SQUARE
REGRESSION	1	245.49311	245.49311
RESIDUAL	392	580.29290	1.48034

F = 165.83573 SIGNIF F = 0

VARIABLES IN THE EQUATION

VARIABLE	B	SE B	BETA	T	SIG T
V44	.82266	.06388	.54524	12.878	.0000
(Constant)	.58079	.25050		2.319	.0209

VARIABLES NOT IN THE EQUATION

VARIABLE	BETA IN	PARTIAL	MIN TOLER	T	SIG T
V15	-.15298	-.18170	.99132	-3.654	.0003
V26	-.11823	-.13912	.97299	-2.778	.0057
V37	-.12643	-.14845	.96884	-2.968	.0032
V39	.17921	.21252	.98819	4.301	.0000
V50	.13776	.16248	.97746	3.256	.0012
V51	-.15287	-.18155	.99109	-3.650	.0003
V53	.15385	.18196	.98295	3.659	.0003
V57	-.19148	-.22743	.99139	-4.618	.0000

also, our best guess, the group mean, would have as much error associated with it as the original standard deviation for Item 42, which is 1.45. The *standard error of estimate*, therefore, will fluctuate downward from the SD of the criterion variable to zero. The lower it gets, the more accurately the equation predicts.

The next part of the SPSS printout shown in Figure 10.1 gives information about an analysis of variance of the regression. This statistical method will be covered in the next chapter. The "bottom line" for the ANOVA is SIGNIF F=0, which tells us that there is zero probability that we would be wrong in stating that the regression is statistically significant. The next section of the printout gives values for the b-weight, beta-weight, and constant, along with significance tests for the weights. Note that the BETA weight of .545 is the same as the Multiple R in this two variable regression. The most important information in this section is that needed to actually construct the regression equation--the b-weight and constant, which are .82 and .58, respectively. Using these numbers we can set up the regression equation as follows:

$$Y' = bX + C$$
$$Y' = .82X + .58$$

Assume for a moment that we have an individual who has checked category 2 for Item 44. That is, he believes that most other people his age and sex have had one sexual partner. What is our prediction for the number of partners he has had?

$$Y' = .82*2 + .58$$
$$Y' = 1.64 + .58$$
$$Y' = 2.22$$

Our best prediction is 2.22 on the 6-point scale. This is rounded to 2 on the scale, which specifies one partner. Thus, a person who thinks most other individuals of his age and sex have had one partner most likely has had only one partner himself. How about an individual who checked 6 for Item 44? He believes most other people have had more than 20 sex partners.

$$Y' = .80*6 + .58$$
$$Y' = 4.92 + .58$$
$$Y' = 5.50$$

Our estimate this time is exactly between 5 and 6 on the 6-point scale. If we round upward to 6, we would predict that the subject himself has had more than 20 partners. If we round downward to 5, we would predict 11 to 20 partners. We can be pretty sure that the individual fits into one of the two categories, but we're really not sure which one. In fact, it's possible he is not in either of these categories. There is some uncertainty about our prediction.

The final part of the SPSS printout shows the variables which are still not in the regression equation, all the rest of them. This information is not pertinent until the final step. Before we get there, however, let us look at STEP 2, shown in Figure 10.2. The next variable entered into the regression is V57, attractiveness. This is the variable which together with V44 creates the highest multiple correlation with V42. Note that R increases from .545 to .578, not a great deal but enough to account for three percent more of the variance (R SQUARE=.33 vs. .30 at STEP 1). The reason that the multiple correlation R does not increase more is due to the intercorrelation of the predictors themselves. To the extent that attractive individuals make higher estimates of sex partners for their peers, the attractiveness variable overlaps with V44 as a predictor of V42. Its unique ability to predict the criterion is limited by its relationship with the first predictor. This intercorrelation problem becomes more severe as each new predictor enters the regression. Eventually, it becomes impossible for SPSS to find a new predictor which isn't in some way related to the previous ones already in the equation. It is at this point that the steps are terminated and a final equation representing the optimal prediction model is derived.

Figure 10.2 provides the information necessary to employ the second equation:

$$Y' = .80X1 + (-.29)X2 + 1.58$$

Once again, let's assume we have an individual who checked "2" for Item 44. In addition, this individual checked category 4 for Item 57. He believes most people have had one sex partner and he considers himself of average attractiveness.

$$Y' = .80*2 + (-.29)*4 + 1.58$$
$$Y' = 1.60 + (-1.16) + 1.58$$
$$Y' = 2.20$$

Our best prediction for this individual is 2, or one sex partner. Consider the second person once again. He has a score of 6 on Item 44. He also sees himself as average in attractiveness.

$$Y' = .80*6 + (-.29)*4 + 1.58$$
$$Y' = 4.80 + (-1.16) + 1.58$$
$$Y' = 5.22$$

Our best prediction is 5. Now, consider a third individual who checked "6" on Item 44 but who considers himself considerably more attractive than others (2 on Item 57).

FIGURE 10.2
Step 2 of the Multiple Regression

VARIABLE(S) ENTERED ON STEP NUMBER
2 V57

MULTIPLE R	.57761
R SQUARE	.33363
ADJUSTED R SQUARE	.33022
STANDARD ERROR	1.18632

ANALYSIS OF VARIANCE

	DF	SUM OF SQUARES	MEAN SQUARE
REGRESSION	2	275.50902	137.75451
RESIDUAL	391	550.27699	1.40736
F =	97.88164	SIGNIF F =	0.0000

VARIABLES IN THE EQUATION

VARIABLE	B	SE B	BETA	T	SIG T
V44	.79586	.06256	.52747	12.722	.0000
V57	-.28535	.06179	-.19148	-4.618	.0000
(Constant)	1.58498	.32701		4.847	.0000

VARIABLES NOT IN THE EQUATION

VARIABLE	BETA IN	PARTIAL	MIN TOLER	T	SIG T
V15	-.15411	-.18796	.98276	-3.779	.0002
V26	-.12701	-.15332	.96349	-3.064	.0023
V37	-.10813	-.12972	.95914	-2.584	.0101
V39	.16645	.20219	.98108	4.077	.0001
V50	.12813	.15497	.97054	3.098	.0021
V51	-.14649	-.17855	.98320	-3.584	.0004
V53	.14458	.17537	.97575	3.518	.0005

Y' = .80*6 + (-.29)*2 + 1.58
Y' = 4.80 + (-.58) + 1.58
Y' = 5.80

Our best prediction for the third person is 6. Notice how the attractiveness variable modifies the predictability in the above equation. You should now have a good idea of how multiple regression equations are employed. One can gain a better understanding of the accuracy of a regression equation by calculating predicted scores for all subjects and then comparing them to their actual scores. SPSS will calculate the predicted scores with this command:

```
RESIDUALS=PRED
```

Figure 10.3 shows the final step of the regression. The R is .66 and accounts for 43% of the criterion variance. The overall regression is highly significant with F=.0000. All but one of the variables entered the equation. Item 15, the importance of religion, did not increase prediction significantly. Notice under SIG T the value .2185. This value represents the level of significance of the b-weight which would have been assigned to V15 had it been in the equation. Similar values are given in the SPSS printout for the variables in the equation. Notice that all of them are less than .05. What this means is that the b-weights (and beta-weights) assigned to these variables really make a difference, whereas the b-weight assigned to V15 is really not different from zero and doesn't make a difference. Notice also that both b-weights and betas change their values from step to step. The virtue of beta-weights, but not b-weights, is that they give a sense of the relative contributions of the variables. Figure 10.3 shows that V44, the first predictor still retains the lion's share in the overall regression. It is more than twice as potent as any other single predictor.

Caveats Concerning Multiple Regression

While multiple regression is an extremely powerful tool in the researcher's workshop, it has some limitations that you should be aware of. When regression is used to build prediction models, the researcher must realize that the ordering of variables in the equation, and hence the weights assigned to the variables, is sometimes rather arbitrary. In the equation here, if V44 had not entered first, its ability to "capture" the criterion variance would be lessened, and therefore its beta-weight would be lower. Thus the relative contribution of variables is partly a function of when they enter the regression. The reordering of variables will not change the overall predictability of an equation, but it will change the relative potency of the predictors.

FIGURE 10.3
Final Step of the Multiple Regression

VARIABLE(S) ENTERED ON STEP NUMBER
8 V51

MULTIPLE R	.65881
R SQUARE	.43403
ADJUSTED R SQUARE	.42227
STANDARD ERROR	1.10179

ANALYSIS OF VARIANCE

	DF	SUM OF SQUARES	MEAN SQUARE
REGRESSION	8	358.41524	44.80190
RESIDUAL	385	467.37077	1.21395

F = 36.90589 SIGNIF F = 0

VARIABLES IN THE EQUATION

VARIABLE	B	SE B	BETA	T	SIG T
V44	.64651	.06123	.42849	10.559	.0000
V57	-.23904	.05803	-.16041	-4.119	.0000
V39	.21604	.05544	.15414	3.897	.0001
V53	.16334	.04643	.13707	3.518	.0005
V26	-.13718	.03934	-.13731	-3.487	.0005
V50	.35589	.11569	.12234	3.076	.0022
V37	-.11861	.04705	-.10062	-2.521	.0121
V51	-.15407	.06744	-.09027	-2.285	.0229
(Constant)	1.57492	.50343		3.128	.0019

VARIABLES NOT IN THE EQUATION

VARIABLE	BETA IN	PARTIAL	MIN TOLER	T	SIG T
V15	-.05113	-.06277	.85319	-1.233	.2185

FOR BLOCK NUMBER 1 PIN = .050 LIMITS REACHED.

CPU TIME REQUIRED: 10.473 SECONDS

Another characteristic of predictive research is that model-building is perhaps as much an art as a science. How does one know which variables to include in a regression? Sometimes an apparently useless variable, one with a very low correlation with the criterion, turns out to work quite well in an equation. Such variables are called *supressors*. Because of their relation to one or more other predictors, they become good predictors even though they are unrelated to the criterion.

Sometimes, though not very often, certain variables have a curvilinear component in their relationship with the criterion. Because "least squares" regression analysis, the type we have used here, is designed for linear relationships, some variables might not fit a regression for this reason. It is possible at times to improve the fit of variables by using certain kinds of transformations of the data.

Finally, consider the task of theory-building using multiple regression; for example, a theory of happiness, which this researcher has attempted to build. Even assuming all of the important variables are included on the happiness questionnaire, what is the best way to combine them together to represent happiness? And how does one sort out the individual contributions of each variable to the total. The plain fact is that the ingredients of happiness, and most other human characteristics, are quite complex. No single recipe for happiness works well for all people. Different people can be quite happy, or sad, for very different reason. Therefore, there must be innumerable regression equations which can explain happiness equally well (or poorly).

These caveats are not so much an indictment of multiple regression as they are a statement about the challenges of behavioral research in general. The beauty of multiple regression as a method is that it is a kind of microcosm of the research process. The challenge facing the researcher is to account for as much variance as possible in the criterion of his choice and in so doing to find out which variables have the greatest effect. Though multiple regression is not a perfect tool for this effort, neither is any other system of data analysis. Research is not cut-and-dried. Though the development of modern statistics has moved behavioral research out of the "dark ages" of introspective psychology, there is still much art left in the science of behavioral research.

Religion and Sex

The final question posed at the beginning of this section concerns the relationship between religious belief and sexual behavior and attitudes. Because there are several questionnaire items on religion as well as sexual attitudes and behavior, this question can best be probed through canonical correlation. The SPSS program to relate these two sets of variables is given below:

```
15.     CANCORR
15.005 VARIABLES=V15,V46,V47,V55,V17,V29,V37,V38,V41/
15.006 V42,V43,V44,V45/
15.101 RELATE=V15,V46,V47,V55 WITH V17 TO V45/
20.     OPTIONS
20.005 2
25.     STATISTICS
25.005 ALL
```

In SPSS-X the procedure for canonical correlation has been incorporated in MANOVA, multivariate analysis of variance. The SPSS-X MANOVA program corresponding to the SPSS CANCORR program is:

```
MANOVA  V15,V46,V47,V55 WITH V17,V29,V37,V38,V41 TO V45/
        DISCRIM(STAN)/
        DESIGN/
```

Output from the SPSS program is given in Figure 10.4. Notice that there are actually four different canonical correlations specified. Common practice is to use the first and most significant relationship. However, it is sometimes instructive to inspect other relationships if they are significant. The primary relationship here has a highly significant canonical coefficient of .37. The associated EIGENVALUE is .14 (rounded). An eigenvalue represents the proportion of variance shared in common by the two canonical variates, in this case about 14 percent. Its meaning is the same as that of R squared in multiple regression. The significance test for the canonical coefficient can be made with either the WILK'S LAMBDA or CHI-SQUARE statistic, both of which are shown on the printout. As usual, the important statistic is the P-value displayed at the far right. This shows that the second relationship was also significant beyond the .05 level.

The next part of the SPSS printout shown in Figure 10.4 gives the standardized canonical coefficients for the variables in each set. Coefficients for the second set (the sex variables) are given first. Because the coefficients are standardized (like beta weights in multiple regression), they provide information on the relative contributions of the variables to the overall relationship. In the primary relationship, under CANVAR 1, we see that the most important sex variable is V29, parents' attitudes toward sex. The most important religious variable in this relationship is V55, religious atmosphere in one's childhood home. Under CANVAR 2, the less significant relationship, two sex variables dominate--V42 and V43, number of sex partners and

FIGURE 10.4
SPSS Output for Canonical Correlation

NUMBER	EIGEN VALUE	CANONICAL CORRELATION	WILK S LAMBDA	CHI SQUARE	D.F.	P
1	.13731	.37056	.77817	95.30739	36	.000
2	.06247	.24994	.90203	39.18088	24	.026
3	.02948	.17168	.96213	14.66888	14	.401
4	.00865	.09298	.99135	3.29976	6	.770

COEFFICIENTS FOR CANONICAL VARIABLES OF THE SECOND SET

	CANVAR 1	CANVAR 2
V17	-.37969	.16269
V29	.77406	.24605
V37	-.17411	.26998
V38	.38058	-.05514
V41	-.16256	-.24786
V42	.22714	-.59347
V43	.09220	.66663
V44	-.00597	.07431
V45	.32179	.08523

COEFFICIENTS FOR CANONICAL VARIABLES OF THE FIRST SET

	CANVAR 1	CANVAR 2
V15	.18572	1.06419
V46	-.57552	-.02940
V47	.51719	.03361
V55	.83930	-.26804

CPU TIME REQUIRED 8.361 SECONDS

TOTAL CPU TIME USED 8.642 SECONDS
SPSS/ONLINE AUTO-MODE

frequency of intercourse. These are coupled with the dominant religion variable, V15, importance of religion to one's happiness.

Thus we see that religious belief does seem to influence sexual attitudes and behavior to a limited degree. There is a relatively stronger aspect involving one's family background, and a weaker one concerning adult behavior. Individuals who consider religion important to their happiness show some tendency to have fewer sex partners and less frequent sexual intercourse. Consider, however, that both religious and sexual behavior may be the products of an underlying personality construct which influences them and other behaviors as well. This is a classic case of the "third-variable problem" in correlational research.

CHAPTER ELEVEN

CAUSAL-COMPARATIVE METHODS

This chapter begins with a prototypic causal-comparative study. The example investigation is followed by a section describing various statistics associated with causal-comparative methodology. The final section provides illustrations of the statistical tests using SPSS with data from the happiness questionnaire.

From Chapter Two you will recall that causal-comparative research, also known as *ex post facto* research, is concerned with discovering possible causes for phenomena which have already occurred. In causal-comparative research, the "treatment" has already had its effect by the time a researcher enters the scene. In this respect it is not unlike correlational research. The difference between these two types of research is mostly in one's point of view regarding the nature of a relationship between variables. In correlational research the researcher's efforts are directed toward the discovery of a relationship, whereas in causal-comparative research, one's efforts are directed more toward bolstering support for a causal connection between variables.

Because of the emphasis on causality, it is much more important in causal-comparative research that there be a sound theoretical framework underlying the research. Causal-comparative research is much less a "fishing expedition" than correlational research. Another important difference is that in causal-comparative research, data are collected from two or more groups of subjects, and relationships between variables are deduced by making statistical comparisons between the groups. Thus, considerable use is made of the family of data analytic methods known as the analysis of variance (ANOVA).

Research Example:
A Cross-Cultural Study of Test Anxiety Among Students in Japan and America

In a master's thesis remarkable for its scope, Okamoto (1981) investigated past theories and research on anxiety before conducting her own theory-based investigation of test anxiety in Japanese high school and college students. The background information which follows was extracted from her report:

The concept of anxiety and its relationship to mental health is largely a product of 20th century thinking. Freud (1936) defined anxiety as an internal reaction to a danger signal. He distinguished between objective and neurotic anxiety. Objective anxiety was viewed as a reaction to danger from the external world. Neurotic anxiety was aroused by the danger from an individual's own internal impulses.

Other psychologists incorporated Freud's concept into their own theories of behavior. Mowrer (1939) extended Freud's danger-signal theory to the concepts of stimulus-response learning theory. Taylor (1951) conducted experimental research on anxiety in human subjects and constructed the Manifest Anxiety Scale. Although the MAS was originally constructed to measure Hull's (1943) drive-reduction learning theory, it led to a shift away from general anxiety to a study of anxiety in specific situations.

Sarason and Mandler (1952) were probably the first researchers who conducted investigations of anxiety and learning. They developed the Test Anxiety Questionnaire. Many research studies have been conducted since the TAS was developed. The majority presented evidence that test anxiety is negatively correlated to intellectual performance. For example, Sarason (1961) reported that subjects scoring high on the TAS tended to perform more poorly on both aptitude and classroom examinations than those scoring low on this scale.

Against this backdrop of theory and research on anxiety, concern was expressed by some educators and members of the public about the extent to which the American system of education produces anxiety in school children. To help answer this question, a few researchers conducted cross-cultural studies comparing American children with those in other countries. For example, Sarnoff and his associates (1958) studied anxiety among English and American children. At the time of Sarnoff's study the English school system was characterized as one in which examinations, particularly the "eleven plus" exam, had a tremendous influence on the future education and social mobility of English children. Sarnoff reasoned that English children would exhibit greater levels of test anxiety than American children. The results supported his hypothesis.

In another investigation (Suinn, 1969) designed to obtain normative data for the Suinn Test Anxiety Behavior Scale, the researcher discovered that his Hawaiian sample scored higher on this scale than a comparable sample in Colorado. Suinn speculated that the higher score for the Hawaiian sample, which was composed of a high number of Oriental students, "may be a function of the academic achievement stress of this cultural group."

Upon reviewing the English and Hawaiian investigations, Okamoto (1981) commented as follows:

> These two studies suggest the importance of

> examinations due to school systems, or in a broader sense to social structures....It may be possible to apply the implication drawn from these studies to the case of a comparative study of test anxiety between Japanese and American students, that is to say that examinations act a more important role to Japanese students than to American students because a student's academic and social future in Japan tends to be determined by a one-time-only challenge of an entrance examination (p. 5).

At the time of Okamoto's investigation there had been no direct comparative study of test anxiety between Japanese and American students reported in either Japan or America. She used her intimate knowledge of the Japanese culture and school system to formulate several hypotheses concerning differences between students in the two countries. The most important hypothesis was that Japanese high school students would exhibit significantly greater anxiety than their American counterparts, whereas Japanese college students would have significantly lower anxiety than American college students. On the basis of past research she hypothesized greater anxiety for females in both cultures.

In discussing her hypotheses, Okamoto described Japanese education as follows:

> Until 1979, each university had its own entrance examinations. Now the candidates are selected on the basis of uniform all-Japan examinations, although private universities still give their own entrance exams. Since the students desire to enter the "right" universities (or they are expected to), it is not unusual to find students who failed in entrance exams of universities in which they wanted to be enrolled, going to preparatory schools to prepare for entrance exams of the next year. Some unfortunate students spend a good number of years in preparatory schools until they are accepted by the "right" universities. It is not surprising, by now, that there are even entrance examinations to be able to enroll in the "right" preparatory schools (pp. 21-22).

Okamoto used several instruments in her study including the Test Anxiety Scale of Sarason, which she translated into Japanese, the State-Trait Anxiety Scale (Spielberger et al., 1970), and a semantic differential attitude inventory of her own creation designed to measure student attitudes toward both end-of-term and entrance examinations. She administered these instruments to 418 Japanese students in Tokyo and Chibu (a nearby district) and 334 American students in the East Bay of the San Francisco area.

FIGURE 11.1
Three-way Interaction:
Ethnicity by Sex by Grade on Test Anxiety

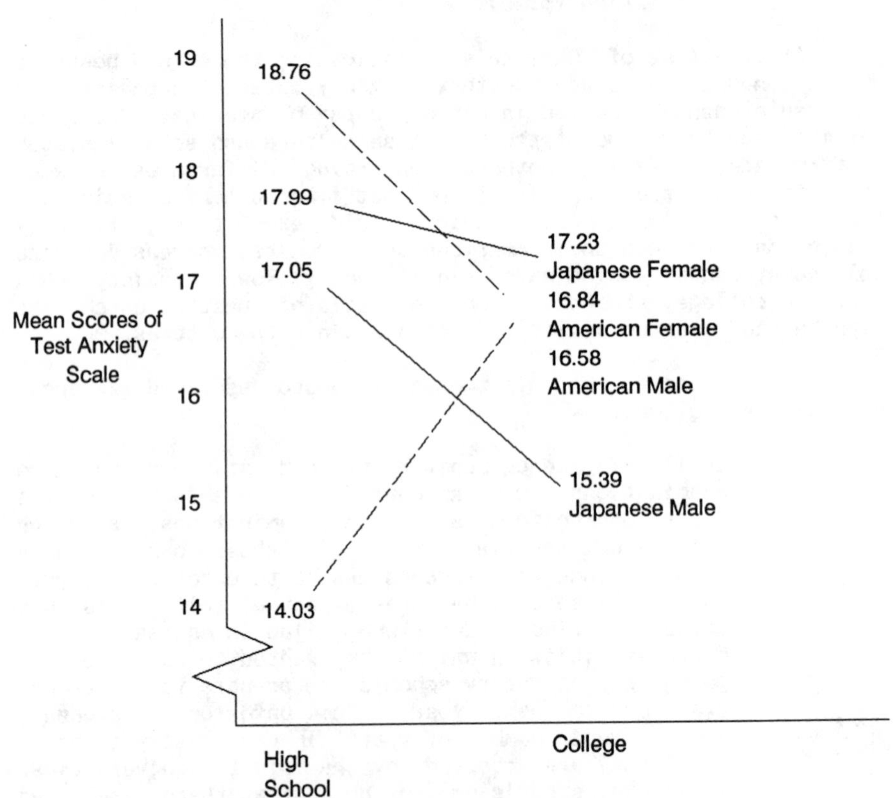

Three-way Interaction: Ethnicity x Sex x Grade
for the Test Anxiety Scale

Okamoto analyzed her data using both factorial analysis of variance and multiple regression. The independent variables in her ANOVA were national group membership, gender, and grade level. She included 35 predictor variables in her regression of test anxiety, including state and trait anxiety and attitudes toward college entrance and term examinations.

The results of Okamoto's data analysis generally supported her main hypothesis. However, there was an interesting departure from her predictions. Although Japanese students exhibited the expected drop in test anxiety between high school and college, the reverse was not true for American students (see Figure 11.1). American high school females exhibited the highest test anxiety of the eight subgroups, much higher than American high school males, who had the lowest levels of all subgroups. American college females showed considerably less test anxiety than their high school comparison group, although still slightly higher than their male college classmates. Thus, it appeared that American females experienced a pattern of test anxiety similar to that of both Japanese males and females, relatively high levels in high school and lower, more moderate levels in college. Okamoto speculated that perhaps the women's movement in America has created higher expectations for females in terms of both college and career achievement. This phenonenon might have affected their levels of anxiety.

The multiple regression analysis produced an R of .62 and accounted for 39% of the variance in test anxiety. Variables most predictive of test anxiety were general anxiety and attitudes concerning both college entrance and term examinations. A general conclusion is that both school testing practices and cultural expectations appear to influence patterns of test anxiety in both countries. American female high school students appear to be under greater stress than even Japanese high school students.

Statistics for Causal-Comparative Research

A very common statistic for testing differences between two groups is the *t-test*, sometimes called Student's t-test. The name Student does not signify use by students. Rather, "Student" is a pseudonym used by William Gossett, who worked for the Guinness Brewing Company and wrote under the pseudonym of Student because the brewery would not allow him to publish under his own name (Howell, 1987). This statistic, like its ubiquitous cousin, the *F-ratio* from analysis of variance, is based on a statistical theory involving true variance and error variance. The theory is quite simple yet profound:

Total Variance = True Variance + Error Variance

What this statement says is that all variance can be partitioned into two components, that which is true, or *systematic variance* and that which is due to unknown causes including *measurement error* and *individual differences* among subjects within a group. For example, in Okamota's study, we would say that the total variance of test anxiety (the fluctuation in scores among all the subjects) is composed of true differences between Japanese and American students plus differences due to measurement error and individual differences among members of the separate races. Another way of formulating variance theory is as follows:

Vt = Vb + Vw

This is simply a shorthand way of saying that total variance (Vt) is made up of variance between groups (Vb) plus variance within the groups (Vw). This latter component (Vw) often includes measurement error in actual research. When we conduct statistical tests between groups, such as in the example involving test anxiety, we typically formulate a ratio between Vb and Vw. That is, we seek to determine the extent to which variance between the groups (true variance) outweighs variance within the groups (error variance). Perhaps an analogy will help with this concept: You may be familiar with a method in the recording industry to describe the fidelity of recorded sound on tape and vinyl records. It is known as the *signal-to-noise ratio*. This ratio is based on a theory similar to the one above: total sound is composed of a true signal plus extraneous noise. With the development of compact disks, the signal-to-noise ratio has been greatly improved over previous technology. There is much less noise and therefore purer sound from CD music. In behavioral research, we seek to maximize true variance (the signal) and minimize error variance (the noise). To the extent we can do this, we can provide support for hypotheses and strengthen the theories by which we conduct and analyze human behavior.

The t-test

Before going directly to a computation of the t-ratio, it is worthwhile to consider further the concept of error variance. It was stated above that error variance is composed of both measurement error and individual differences. These separate aspects of error variance are equivalent to the *standard error of measurement* and the *standard error of the mean*. Let us exlore these two descriptive statistics in some detail:

The standard error of measurement, or more aptly the standard error of a single individual's score, is based on the reliability of the measuring instrument used. The formula for the standard error of measurement is:

SE(meas) = SD * Sqrt(1 - Rel)

This formula states that measurement error is equal to the standard deviation times the square root of 1 minus the reliability of the instrument. Consider a typical IQ test in which the standard deviation is 15 points and the reliability is .90. The Wechsler test is such an instrument. We can calculate the standard error of measurement for such a test as follows:

```
SE(meas) = SD * Sqrt(1 - Rel)
         = 15 * Sqrt(1 - .90)
         = 15 * Sqrt( .10 )
         = 15 * .33
SE(meas) =  5
```

The standard error of measurement is 5. What does this mean? It means that approximately two-thirds of the time, an individual's true IQ score is within plus or minus 5 points of the measured score. The standard error provides us with a measure of confidence in the test score. Remember that in research we often use the 95% confidence interval. This interval is roughly equivalent to two standard errors. Thus, we can be confident that 95% of the time an individual's true IQ lies within a 20-point band around his measured score (plus or minus 10 points).

How does the standard error of measurement compare with the standard error of a mean? The formula for the standard error of a mean is given below:

```
SE(mean) = SD / Sqrt(N)
```

This formula states that the standard error of a mean is equal to the standard deviation divided by the square root of N, the number of individuals in the sample. Let us perform a calculation for the same IQ test administered to 100 individuals:

```
SE(mean) = SD / Sqrt(N)
         = 15 / Sqrt(100)
         = 15 / 10
SE(mean) = 1.5
```

Now, how do we interpret this standard error statistic? Again, we have a number which provides us with a measure of confidence. But this time we are talking about confidence in a group's mean IQ score, rather than confidence in the score of a single individual. The standard error of 1.5 tells us that approximately two-thirds of the time the true mean IQ of our group lies within a 3-point band around the measured mean (plus or minus 1.5 points). Likewise, the 95% confidence interval is about twice this amount, plus or minus 3 IQ points. Notice that the amount of fluctuation in the group mean is considerably less than for the single IQ score. This is due to the law of large numbers, a major theorum of statistical theory.

Now, what has all this to do with the t-test? The answer is in the formula for the t-test, given below:

t = M1 - M2 / Sqrt(SE(mean1)**2 + SE(mean2)**2)

where M1 and M2 are the means of two separate groups, and SE(mean1) and SE(mean2) are the respective standard errors for the two group means. The formula tells us to first calculate the mean difference between two groups and then to divide that difference by a term analogous to the sum of the standard errors for each group. In other words we are creating a ratio between systematic variance and error variance, between a pure tone and noise. If the true difference between the groups outweighs the noisy differences within the groups themselves, then we can have great confidence when we make a claim for group differences.

Let's convert this statistical theory into a concrete problem. Assume we have two groups of school children, perhaps from different schools. We are interested in knowing whether the average IQ's of the two schools differ significantly. Suppose we have randomly sampled 100 children from each school. After testing the IQ's of the 200 children, we determine that the mean IQ for School A is 103 points; the mean for School B is 98 points. The t-test formula for use in this calculation is shown below:

t = M1 - M2 / Sqrt(SD**2/N1 + SD**2/N2)

Notice that this formula differs somewhat from the one given earlier. Compare the denominator of this formula with the one given for SE(mean) and you will see that it is really just a variant of the same t-test formula. With this formula we can calculate a t-ratio by knowing just the means, standard deviations and N's for each sample group:

	School A	School B
M	103	98
SD	15	15
N	100	100

```
t = M1 - M2 / Sqrt(SD**2/N1 + SD**2/N2)
  = 103- 98 / Sqrt(15**2/100+15**2/100)
  =     5   / Sqrt(  225/100+  225/100)
  =     5   / Sqrt(     2.25 +     2.25 )
  =     5   / Sqrt( 4.5 )
  =     5   /      2.12
t = 2.35 (df = N1 + N2 - 2 = 198)
```

The t-ratio is 2.35 with 198 degrees of freedom. To interpret this t-ratio we must enter a table of critical values for t. Turn to Appendix E for this table. Notice that Appendix E has significance levels (alpha levels) for both one-tailed and two-tailed tests. Since we did not hypothesize a specific direction for the difference between the schools, ours is a two-tailed test. Look below the .05 level for two-tailed tests and note how the critical values decrease from 12.706 for 1 degree of freedom to 1.960 for infinite degrees of freedom. Our df of 198 may be considered infinite; thus, we need a t-value of 1.96 or larger to reject the null hypothesis of no difference between the schools. Since our t-value is 2.35, we have exceeded the critical ratio of 1.96. We may, therefore, reject the null hypothesis with confidence and state that indeed the children from School A represent a different population of children from those of School B.

It may come as a surprise to you that a difference as small as five IQ points creates a significant difference between schools. This situation is due to the nature of statistical theory, which is based on the law of large numbers. Group sizes of 100 are considered quite large in statistical theory, and therefore relatively small differences between them are statistically significant. Although you will not usually have to carry out the numerical calculations for a t-test, you will better understand this statistical test if you do one or two by hand. Try the example above with a mean difference of 4 points. Is the result significant at the .05 level? What if you had hypothesized in advance that School A has a higher mean score? Would that make a difference?

The F-test and Analysis of Variance

We are indebted to yet another Britisher for an enormous contribution to the field of statistics. R.A. Fisher, for whom the F-test is named, developed the system of equations necessary for the analysis of variance (ANOVA). ANOVA is a general group-comparison method not limited to two groups. During the early part of this century Fisher was engaged in agricultural research in which it was necessary for him to make multiple comparisons between different plots of land to evaluate the effectiveness of different fertilizers, watering methods, etc. He developed ANOVA to fulfill his need for a single, overall test that would include multiple groups as well as multiple treatment effects and the interactions among them. ANOVA is a very powerful data analysis procedure on a par with regression analysis in its importance to behavioral science.

Though ANOVA has many forms and "designs," it is really just a conceptual extension of the t-test. In fact, in a two-group situation, F is mathematically equal to t squared. Another characteristic of ANOVA, not generally known, is its mathematical similarity to multiple regression. Let us begin with a three-group example and explore some of the characteristics of ANOVA.

In this fictitious example assume we are concerned with studying anxiety in three groups of education students--counselors, teachers, and school psychololgists. We believe that anxiety varies somewhat due to the nature of the students' programs. One important difference between programs is the thesis requirement. Counseling students have a choice between a counseling project and a traditional thesis. Student teachers have a similar choice between developing a course of study or evaluating an innovative curriculum. Student psychologists must write a traditional research thesis. We hypothesize a difference between these groups in their levels of anxiety concerning the successful completion of their thesis requirements. In order to test the hypothesis we devise a set of a dozen yes-no questions on thesis anxiety and administer them to five students in each program. A score of 12 indicates maximum anxiety.

Before we begin any calculations, recall that variance is defined as follows:

V = Sum(X - M)**2 / N-1

where X is a score, M is a group mean, and N is the number in a group. The formula tells us to sum the squared deviations from the mean and then divide that total by N-1. This produces a quantity which represents the extent to which individuals vary about the group mean. If individuals do not vary, then V=0.

In the analysis of variance it is customary to work with the *sum of the squares*, that is, the sum of the squared deviations from the mean. This value is the numerator in the above formula and it is abbreviated *SS*. Recall from the previous section that total variance is equal to variance between the groups plus variance within the groups (Vt=Vb+Vw). In ANOVA we use the pragmatic equivalent of this theoretical formula as follows:

SSt = SSb + SSw

Let us see how this formula applies to the data on the next page. The first thing to note about these data is that there is variance. Not all students have the same amount of anxiety. Our first task is to calculate the variance in terms of sums of squares for all students regardless of group membership. We do this by first summing the scores (column 1) and then computing the overall mean, sometimes referred to as the *grand mean*. The sum of the scores is 105. This value divided by the number of students equals seven, the mean.

The next step is to calculate deviation scores for each student (column 2). We simply compare a student's score to the grand mean and note the difference, positive or negative. Step three is to square the deviation scores and add them up (column 3)

Fictitious Thesis Data

Student	Anxiety Score X	Deviation Score (X-M)	Deviation Squared (X-M)**2
1.	1	-6	36
2.	5	-2	4
3.	4	-3	9
4.	3	-4	16
5.	2	-5	25
6.	4	-3	9
7.	8	+1	1
8.	10	+3	9
9.	11	+4	16
10.	7	0	0
11.	8	+1	1
12.	11	+4	16
13.	12	+5	25
14.	9	+2	4
15.	10	+3	9
	---		---
Sum =	105		180 = SSt
M =	7		

- -

to produce SSt, the sum of the squared deviations from the grand mean. We now have the first component of our variance equation, SSt.

The next component of the equation is SSb, the equivalent of variance between the groups. Notice that if we calculate either SSb or SSw, we can determine the other through subtraction, since they add up to SSt. We will proceed to calculate SSw, the sums of squares within the groups. SSw is equivalent to the sum of the separate group variances expressed as sums of squares:

SSw = SS1 + SS2 + SS3

where SS1=Sum(X-M)**2 for Group 1, the counseling students, and SS2 represents the same quantity for Group 2, the student teachers, and SS3 is the same for school psychology students. The calculations for Group 1 are shown below:

Group 1: Counseling Students	Anxiety Score X	Deviation Score (X-M)	Deviation Squared (X-M)**2
1.	1	-2	4
2.	5	2	4
3.	4	1	1
4.	3	0	0
5.	2	-1	1
	--		--
Sum =	15		10 = SS1
M =	3		

Note that these calculations are made in exactly the same way as SSt, except that scores for only one group of students are used each time. Because SSw represents variance within the groups, we use individual group means to determine deviation scores for each respective group, rather than the grand mean as we did for SSt. We can now formulate SSw as follows:

SSw = SS1 + SS2 + SS3
SSw = 10 + 30 + 10
SSw = 50

Notice that one of the groups has a considerably larger sum of squares than the others. This indicates that Group 2 has more fluctuation in anxiety scores than groups 1 and 3. Look back at the list of raw scores and you will see this to be true. The range of scores for Group 2 is seven points and only four points for groups 1 and 3. In calculating SS1 we discovered Group 1's mean to be 3. The calculations for groups 2 and 3 are similar. Their means are 8 and 10, respectively.

Now that we have computed SSw, we can calculate SSb by subtraction as follows:

SSt = SSb + SSw
SSb = SSt - SSw
SSb = 180 - 50
SSb = 130

We now have all the pieces of the puzzle necessary to perform the analysis of variance. That is, we can now formulate an F-ratio to determine whether a significant difference exists between any pair of group means. The question we are asking is: Given the amount of group variation present, is there a significant difference among the anxiety means of 3, 8, and 10? We answer this question by constructing an ANOVA summary table as follows:

ANOVA Summary

Sources		df	SS	MS	F
Between	(K-1)	2	130	65	15.6
Within	(N-K)	12	50	4.17	
Total	(N-1)	14	180		

You will notice that this table contains one additional term not discussed above. This is the *mean square*, *MS*. The mean square for a particular source of variance is derived by dividing SS by its corresponding degrees of freedom. That is, MS=SS/df. For example, MSb=SSb/K-1, where K equals the number of groups. Thus, MSb=130/2, or 65. Likewise, MSw=SSw/N-K, or 50/12=4.17. Once the mean squares are calculated, the F-ratio is determined by MSb/MSw. That is, the "average" variance between groups is divided by the average variance within groups. The greater the between-groups variance compared with the within-groups variance, the more likely a significant difference exists between the groups. In other words, the higher the F-ratio, the more likely a significant difference.

In order to evaluate a given F-ratio, one must consult a table of critical values of F. Turn to Appendix F for such a table. Enter the table with 2 degrees of freedom for the numerator (along the top of the page) and 12 df for the denominator (down the left side). You will find four critical values representing the .25, .10, .05, and .01 levels of significance. Since our F ratio of 15.6 exceeds the highest of these values, 6.93, we may reject the null hypothesis with considerable certainty. Our F-ratio of 15.6 is significant beyond the .01 level. There is indeed a significant difference in anxiety levels among the three student groups.

While we now know that the three educational programs are not equivalent with respect to mean anxiety levels of the students, unfortunately, the overall F-test does not give us information about all possible differences between groups. What we now know for sure is that Group 1, with a mean of 3, differs significantly from Group 3 with a mean of 10 on the anxiety scale. But what about Group 2? How does a mean of 8 compare with a mean of 2 or a mean of 10? With 3 groups there are three comparisons possible. As the number of groups increases, the number of possible comparisons rises rapidly. In a 5-group ANOVA, not an unusual situation, the number of possible comparisons is 10.

The discerning reader might wonder why we bother doing an F-test in the first place if it gives us information only about the two extreme groups. Why not simply crank out a series of t-tests between all possible groups? The reason is that we run the risk of inflating our alpha level by performing multiple t-tests. In a 5-group situation, if we establish the significance level at .10, it is likely that one of the ten t-tests will be significant by chance alone. With ANOVA the significance level is preserved, and the danger of falsely rejecting a null hypothesis is greatly reduced.

But how then do we draw conclusions about all the groups in an analysis? Are student teachers different from student counselors in thesis anxiety? Are they different from student psychologists? The answer to our dilemma is an *a posteriori contrast*, more commonly called a *post hoc test*. Many statisticians have worked on the problem of how to correctly compare all the groups in an ANOVA. Several of them have devised specific tests for this purpose. The researcher has a choice of seven different post hoc tests in SPSS. The most commonly used post hoc test is the *Scheffe Test*, named after its inventor. Another common post hoc test is the *Duncan Multiple Range Test*, also named for its originator. The Scheffe test is used more often because it is the more conservative test. That is, it is less likely to lead to the false rejection of a null hypothesis.

While it is instructive to carry out hand calculations to understand the theory underlying a statistical procedure, the student's time is best spent in learning to interpret computer output. Figures 11.2 and 11.3 show output from an SPSS run of the ONEWAY program below:

```
10.     DATA LIST
10.005 FIXED(1)/1 ANX 1-2, GRP 3-4
15.     ONEWAY
15.005 ANX BY GRP(1,3)/
15.010 RANGES=SCHEFFE
20.     STATISTICS
20.005 1
```

This program is designed to perform a one-way ANOVA followed by a Scheffe post hoc test. In one-way ANOVA there is only one independent variable, in this case, group membership in one of three educational programs. The dependent variable is thesis anxiety. The DATA LIST specification indicates an anxiety score in columns 1-2 and a group number in column 4. Line 15.005 informs SPSS that there are three "levels" for the group variable. The next line invokes the Scheffe test following RANGES=. STATISTICS 1 provides means and standard deviations for the groups.

Figure 11.2 shows the SPSS output for the first part of the program. The only real difference between the SPSS ANOVA summary table and the one presented above is the F PROB statistic provided by SPSS. This statistic gives us the exact probability of the F-ratio and eliminates the need to use a table of critical values.

FIGURE 11.2
ANOVA Summary for One-Way Example

CPU TIME REQUIRED .097 SECONDS

ONEWAY

00053000B CM NEEDED FOR ONEWAY

END OF FILE ON FILE ANXDAT

AFTER READING 15 CASES FROM SUBFILE NONAME

VARIABLE ANXIETY THESIS ANXIETY
BY GROUP PROGRAM

ANALYSIS OF VARIANCE

SOURCE	D. F.	SUM OF SQ	MEAN SQ	F RATIO	F PROB
BETWEEN GROUPS	2	130.000	65.000	15.600	.0005
WITHIN GROUPS	12	50.000	4.167		
TOTAL	14	180.000			

GROUP	COUNT	MEAN	STAND. DEV.	STAND. ERROR	MIN.	MAX.	95 PERCENT CONF INT FOR MEAN		
GRP001	5	3.00	1.58	.71	1.00	5.00	1.04	TO	4.96
GRP002	5	8.00	2.74	1.22	4.00	11.00	4.60	TO	11.40
GRP003	5	10.00	1.58	.71	8.00	12.00	8.04	TO	11.96
TOTAL	15	7.00			1.00	12.00			
UNGROUPED			3.59	.93			5.01	TO	8.99

FIGURE 11.3
Scheffe Post Hoc Test for One-Way ANOVA

```
VARIABLE ANXIETY              THESIS ANXIETY
BY GROUP                      PROGRAM

MULTIPLE RANGE TEST

SCHEFFE PROCEDURE
RANGES FOR THE                .050 LEVEL -
           3.94               3.94

THE RANGES ABOVE ARE TABULAR VALUES.
THE VALUE ACTUALLY COMPARED WITH MEAN (J) - MEAN (I) IS
           1.4434 * RANGE * SQRT (1/N(I) + 1/N(J))

 (*) DENOTES PAIRS OF GROUPS SIGNIFICANTLY DIFFERENT AT THE .050000 LEVEL

                                  G  G  G
                                  R  R  R
                                  P  P  P
                                  0  0  0
                                  0  0  0
                                  1  2  3
       MEAN         GROUP

        3.0000      GRP001
        8.0000      GRP002        *
       10.0000      GRP003        *


HOMOGENEOUS SUBSETS (SUBSETS OF GROUPS, WHOSE HIGHEST AND LOWEST
MEANS DO NOT DIFFER BY MORE THAN THE SHORTEST SIGNIFICANT RANGE FOR
A SUBSET OF THAT SIZE)


    SUBSET 1

    GROUP        GRP001
    MEAN         3.0000
  ----------   ----------

    SUBSET 2

    GROUP        GRP002       GRP003
    MEAN         8.0000       10.0000
  ----------   ----------   ----------
```

The F PROB of .0005 indicates that we would be taking only 5 chances in 10,000 of being wrong if we reject the hypothesis of no differences. Below the summary table are descriptive statistics for each group including means, SD's, and standard errors.

Figure 11.3 shows the output for the Scheffe test. From two different sets of information we can tell that groups 2 and 3 differ from Group 1, but not from each other. The first indication is in a square matrix in which differences are shown by an asterisk. Note the asterisks next to groups 2 and 3 and below Group 1. At the bottom of the printout this same information is repeated in the form of subsets. Subset 1 is composed of Group 1 only. Subset 2 is composed of both groups 2 and 3. Thus, we conclude that counseling students have significantly less thesis anxiety than either student teachers or psychologists. And, although psychologists have more anxiety than teachers, the two point difference between them is not meaningful statistically.

ANOVA vs. Multiple Regression and Correlation (MRC)

An important difference between ANOVA and MRC is that the latter is ideally used with interval variables while ANOVA commonly employs nominal independent variables. That is, MRC is often used with continuous, metric variables such as test scores and personality scales while ANOVA uses classifactory variables such as race, political party, and other group membership variables. However, it is not essential to constrain MRC to continuous variables as predictors. It is possible to use nominally scaled "dummy" variables as predictors in a regression equation.

Consider the example of thesis anxiety above. It is possible to analyze the anxiety data using MRC as follows: First, one must recast the single group membership variable into two dummy predictor variables as shown on the next page. MRC dummy variables are created by assigning a 1 for group membership and a 0 for non-membership. The first predictor contains the information for Group 1 and the 2nd predictor for Group 2. Both predictors contain information on Group 3 (the double zero configuration). There is always one less predictor than the number of groups in ANOVA.

The MRC data were analyzed using this SPSS program:

```
10.     DATA LIST
10.005 FIXED(1)/1 ANX 1-2, PRED1 4, PRED2 6
15.     NEW REGRESSION
15.005 VARIABLES=ANX, PRED1, PRED2/
15.010 STATISTICS=DEFAULTS/
15.015 DEPENDENT=ANX/ENTER/
```

	ANOVA Data		MRC Data		
	D.V.	I.V.	D.V.	I.V.1	I.V.2
Subject	ANX	GRP	ANX	PRED1	PRED2
1.	1	1	1	1	0
2.	5	1	5	1	0
3.	4	1	4	1	0
4.	3	1	3	1	0
5.	2	1	2	1	0
6.	4	2	4	0	1
7.	8	2	8	0	1
8.	10	2	10	0	1
9.	11	2	11	0	1
10.	7	2	7	0	1
11.	8	3	8	0	0
12.	11	3	11	0	0
13.	12	3	12	0	0
14.	9	3	9	0	0
15.	10	3	10	0	0

Codes: D.V. = dependent variable
I.V. = independent variable
ANX = ANOVA and MRC variable names for D.V.
GRP = ANOVA variable name for single I.V.
PRED1 = MRC variable name for 1st predictor
PRED2 = MRC variable name for 2nd predictor

- -

This program is similar to those shown in the previous chapter with one exception. The last statement, 15.015, calls for a "forced" regression rather than a stepwise regression. The ENTER command assures that all variables will enter the equation regardless of their relative contributions. The results of this regression analysis are shown in Figure 11.4. Note the high R value of .849. The R SQUARE of .722 means that our knowledge of students' group membership, i.e. educational program, accounts for 72% of the variance in thesis anxiety. The standard error of 2.04 indicates that about two-thirds of the time our regression equation would estimate a subject's anxiety score within two points of his true score given knowledge of group membership.

The analysis of variance summary table is identical to that of the ANOVA printout except for the names given to the sources of variance. Between-groups variance is termed "regression," and within-groups variance is called "residual." The group means can be obtained by using the b-weights in the equation. The constant value of 10 is the mean for Group 3. The values for groups 1 and 2 are given by PRED1 and PRED2 in relation to Group 3. That is, 10-7=3 is the mean for Group 1, and 10-2=8 is the mean for Group 2.

FIGURE 11.4
Regression Analysis of One-Way ANOVA

MULTIPLE REGRESSION

VARIABLE LIST NUMBER 1. LISTWISE DELETION OF MISSING DATA.

EQUATION NUMBER 1.

DEPENDENT VARIABLE ANXIETY THESIS ANXIETY

BEGINNING BLOCK NUMBER 1. METHOD: ENTER

VARIABLE(S) ENTERED ON STEP NUMBER

1	PRED2	VECTOR 2
2	PRED1	VECTOR 1

MULTIPLE R	.84984
R SQUARE	.72222
ADJUSTED R SQUARE	.67593
STANDARD ERROR	2.04124

ANALYSIS OF VARIANCE

	DF	SUM OF SQUARES	MEAN SQUARE
REGRESSION	2	130.00000	65.00000
RESIDUAL	12	50.00000	4.16667

F = 15.6000 SIGNIF F = .0005

VARIABLES IN THE EQUATION

VARIABLE	B	SE B	BETA	T	SIG T
PRED2	-2.00000	1.29099	-.27217	-1.549	.1473
PRED1	-7.00000	1.29099	-.95258	-5.422	.0002
(CONSTANT)	10.00000	.91287		10.954	.0000

FOR BLOCK NUMBER 1 ALL REQUESTED VARIABLES ENTERED.

CPU TIME REQUIRED .221 SECONDS

Thus we see that multiple regression and analysis of variance accomplish the same purpose. The purpose of this demonstration was not to persuade you to use MRC rather than ANOVA, but rather to show that these two systems of data analysis are simply different ways of conceptualizing similar research problems. It is often quite helpful in research thinking to consider a problem from both points of view. Sometimes it is even helpful to analyze a problem using both methods as we have here. Most often, however, researchers choose one method or the other because of their special advantages. MRC is well-suited for exploratory analyses using many variables. ANOVA is better suited to more limited analyses in which the interaction between variables is of special interest. We will discuss the topic of statistical interaction in a later section.

ANOVA Measures of Association

An ANOVA statistic analogous to R in multiple regression is *E*, the *correlation ratio*. This is a useful measure of association between an independent and dependent variable. The formula for E is:

$$E = Sqrt(SSb / SSt)$$

where SSb equals the sum of squares for the between-groups source of variance, and SSt is the total sum of squares. In our thesis anxiety example, the correlation ratio would be computed as follows:

$$E = Sqrt(130 / 180)$$
$$E = Sqrt(.72)$$
$$E = .85$$

Thus, the correlation ratio between thesis anxiety and type of student program is .85. This statistic is similar to the Pearson r except that it is not dependent on a linear relationship. When E is squared we get a statistic equivalent to R squared. E squared is a measure of variance accounted for. Since E squared is .72, we would conclude that 72% of the variance in thesis anxiety is accounted for by knowledge of students' participation in one of the three programs.

The fact that ANOVA reveals associations not dependent on a linear relationship between variables is an important distinction between ANOVA and regression analysis. Recall from the previous chapter the analysis of sexual behavior of respondents to the happiness questionnaire. After analyzing the Pearson coefficient of correlation between V42, number of sex partners and V49, age, it was concluded that a significant relationship did not exist between these variables. This conclusion was correct in terms of a linear relationship. That is, there was no evidence of increasing numbers of partners with corresponding increases in age, as one might expect. However, when number of partners is analyzed in terms of age groups with ANOVA, a somewhat different picture emerges. This becomes evident through the calculation of E, the correlation ratio:

$$
\begin{aligned}
E &= \mathrm{Sqrt}(\ SSb\ /\ SSt\ ) \\
&= \mathrm{Sqrt}(\ 74.845\ /\ 821.728\ ) \\
&= \mathrm{Sqrt}(\ .091\ ) \\
E &= .301
\end{aligned}
$$

where SSb equals the sum of squares between age groups, and SSt is the total sum of squares in the dependent variable, number of sex partners. The correlation ratio of .30 is significant beyond .001. Thus, there is a definite relationship between age and number of sex partners. How can contradictory conclusions be derived from different statistical methods? The reason for the apparent contradiction becomes clear when we look at a graph of the mean number of sex partners by age group below:

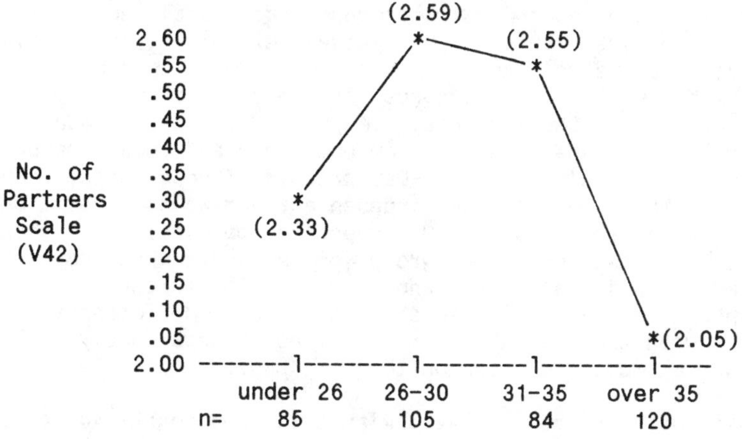

Age Groups (N=394)

This graph shows a significant difference among the four age groups with respect to mean number of sex partners. It is not difficult to see why a Pearson r for such data would be insignificant. A regression line cannot be fit well through the four points in the graph. When such a line is fit, the resultant r is near zero. What we have here is a curvilinear relationship in which number of partners is highest in the two middle age groups and lowest in the youngest and oldest subjects. It seems apparent that the sexual revolution did not affect the behavior of subjects over 35 to the extent it has affected younger subjects.

Another statistic used in conjunction with ANOVA is *omega squared.* This statistic is used in the same way as E squared, but is more conservative. Some statisticians consider it to be a better estimate than E squared. The formula for omega squared is as follows:

Omega Squared = SSb - (k-1)*MSw / SSt + MSb

where k equals the number of groups, and the other terms represent sums of squares and mean squares for the different sources of variance in an ANOVA summary table. The application of this formula produces a value of .70, vs. .72, for the proportion of variance accounted for in the thesis anxiety example above.

Two-Way ANOVA

While one-way ANOVA is indeed a useful method of data analysis, the real power of ANOVA becomes apparent in two-way and n-way designs in which independent variables are allowed to interact with one another to produce additional sources of variance. Consider this hypothetical example from social psychology: Assume we have attitude measures concerning equal opportunity for women. Our measures are on a 50-point scale, in which 50 represents the most positive attitude toward equality. We have collected these measures from both male and female members of three political parties--Democrats, Independents, and Republicans. Thus, we have two independent variables, political party affiliation and gender. Our question becomes: Are there differences in attitudes among groups of subjects when they are categorized by political party and gender? And furthermore, do the two independent variables interact to produce differences not discernible when the variables are analyzed independently? The data for our example are shown on the next page.

These data may be analyzed with SPSS subprogram ANOVA as follows:

```
10.     DATA LIST
10.005 FIXED(1)/1 ATT 1-2, POLPAR 4, GENDER 6
15.     ANOVA
15.005 ATT BY POLPAR (1,3), GENDER (1,2)
```

The output from this program produces the summary table below:

Subject	Attitude Toward Women's Equality	Political Party Affiliation	Gender
1.	50	1	1
2.	49	1	1
3.	48	1	2
4.	47	1	2
5.	46	2	1
6.	45	2	1
7.	44	2	2
8.	43	2	2
9.	42	3	2
10.	41	3	2
11.	40	3	1
12.	39	3	1

Code: Political Party
1=Democrat
2=Independent
3=Republican

Gender
1=Female
2=Male

- -

ANOVA Summary

Source of Variation	Sum of Squares	df	Mean Square	F	Sig of F
Main Effects					
POLPAR	128.000	2	64.000	128.000	.001
GENDER	1.333	1	1.333	2.667	.154
2-Way Interaction					
POLIPAR by GENDER	10.667	2	5.333	10.667	.011
Explained	140.000	5	28.000	56.000	.001
Residual	3.000	6	.500		
Total	143.000	11	13.000		

The elements of this table are quite similar to those from the ONEWAY printout. The ANOVA program lists independent variables under the heading "Main Effects." All sources of variance are combined under the heading "Explained" variance. Explained variance is equivalent to between-groups variance in a one-way design. Residual variance, the difference between explained and total variance, is equivalent to within-groups variance in the one-way model. Notice that the various sources of variance add up numerically in the form of sums of squares. So too do the degrees of freedom. The F-ratios are computed by dividing each mean square by the residual mean square.

Notice in the two-way model that there are three sources of variance, and therefore three F-ratios. This is because the interaction term functions as a separate source. Let's interpret this table: First, we notice that the political party variable is significant at .001. The gender variable is not significant, but the interaction of political party and gender is significant at .011. What does this mean? This outcome tells us that while political party affiliation is important to one's attitude toward women's equality, we cannot make a general statement about party membership. We cannot say, for example, that all Independents have a more supportive attitude than Republicans. It depends to some degree on a person's gender. To properly understand these results, we must investigate the "cell means." These are the subgroup means shown in the table below:

		Political Party			
		Dem	Ind	Rep	
Gender	female	49.5	45.5	39.5	44.83
	male	47.5	43.5	41.5	44.17
		48.5	44.5	40.5	

From this table of cell and marginal means (rows and columns), we can see that there is a constant difference between the political parties with Democrats being the most positive and Republicans the least positive in their attitudes. Independents are exactly in between. Overall, there is little difference beween the sexes. Males and females differ by only a fraction of a point. Notice, however, that within the Democratic and Independent parties there is a 2-point difference between men and women, with women having the more positive attitude. In the Republican Party, on the other hand, the attitude of men is more positive than that of women by two points. This reversal of the trend between women and men is what accounts for the significant interaction in our ANOVA summary table. The relationship between gender and attitude is not uniform across the political parties. Thus, although there is a significant difference between the parties in their view of women's rights, there is something else going on as well. While women are typically more favorable than men, that is not the case among Republicans. If it were, gender would also be a significant main effect, and no interaction would exist between the independent variables.

The concept of interaction is not an easy one to understand. It becomes even more difficult as additional variables are added to ANOVA models. In a 3-way design there are three 2-way interactions and an additional 3-way interaction for a total of seven sources of variance. While 4-way and 5-way designs are sometimes used, they are relatively infrequent. Quite often, too, higher order interactions are not significant. Therefore, they don't present problems in interpretation. It is important to understand, however, that research designs with multiple independent variables are inherently better than 1-way designs. This is because the error variance is reduced each time a new variable is added to the model. By reducing error variance, we reduce the "noise" in the system and thereby create more sensitive tests of all hypotheses. These concepts of n-way ANOVA should become clearer in the next section, which provides some actual results from the happiness data. A further discussion of ANOVA and its cousin, the analysis of covariance (ANCOVA), will also be presented in the next chapter on experimental methods.

Research Results from the Happiness Questionnaire

At the beginning of this chapter it was stated that causal-comparative research should be built on theory and prior research findings. Because of the complex connection between cause and effect in this type of research, it should not be undertaken in a haphazard or frivolous manner. One should not merely look for all possible differences between groups and report them. Such differences, in order to have important meaning, must be hypothesized in advance and based on existing theory and empirical knowledge. Let us explore the genesis of a theory-based investigation of the happiness data.

Geographic Mobility

Prior research by Fried (1972) and Whalen and Fried (1973) explored the nature of geographic mobility and its effect on educational achievement among high school students. A review of the literature on mobility (changing one's place of residence) showed conflicting results. Some researchers concluded that high mobility had adverse effects on achievement. Others found that achievement was positively affected by mobility. Still others found no relation between mobility and academic achievement.

In an effort to clarify these equivocal results, Whalen and Fried designed a multivariate study of mobility patterned after Gilliland's (1967) investigation of elementary school children. In addition to the mobility variable, the researchers included intelligence and socio-economic status as main effects in a 3-way ANOVA design. Results of this study showed that while mobility itself was not significantly related to measured achievement, it interacted with IQ in a significant way. Even after the normal relationship between IQ and academic achievement was taken into account, a considerable difference existed between two groups of highly mobile students. Among students who had attended schools in four or more cities, those with high IQ appeared to benefit significantly from their mobility, while those of low IQ showed a decrement in academic performance. Among the students who had not changed residences at all during their school years, there were no differences between predicted and actual achievement for either group.

Thus, it appears that mobility--moving around during childhood--has different effects on different people. It is possible that the interests and attitudes of more intelligent children are stimulated by frequent geographic relocations. Perhaps the more capable students have more confidence to meet the challenge of a new environment. Less capable students may find frequent moves too bewildering to cope with. Their academic performance may suffer accordingly.

There are undoubtedly other variables that play a part in the effect that mobility has on individuals. Perhaps it isn't mobility per se that affects children so much as it is the reason or reasons why mobility occurred. If a child's family is forced to relocate for financial reasons or because of a marital break-up, might this produce a more negative outcome than a well-planned move in which the family members look forward to a new home in a different environment? Family size is another variable that could be important in moderating the effects of mobilty. A child who has moved into a new community with siblings may have fewer adjustments to make than an only child who lacks a sibling support group.

The happiness questionnaire contains many items which bear on possible causes and effects of mobility. Let us proceed to investigate some of these. First, let's look at Item 28, which asks: How many times before the age of 18 did you move from one community to another? The scale for this item ranges from (1) Never to (6) Five or more times, and there is considerable variance in student responses. In order to maximize the variance, and thus the effect of mobility, we will select from the total distribution only those individuals who responded with a 1 or a 6. Group 1, which I will call the non-mobile group, consisted of 90 individuals who did not move at all during childhood. Group 2, the high-mobile group, consisted of 82 students who moved five or more times.

Univariate Hypotheses

Having constructed these extreme groups, how should we expect them to differ? Based on our theoretical and empirical knowledge of mobility along with some educated guesses and intuitive hunches, what hypotheses can we make concerning other variables on the questionnaire? We might expect high-mobiles to have experienced divorce to a greater extent (items 23 and 25). We might expect non-mobiles to recall their parents' relationship in more positive terms (Item 24). Since divorce often occurs relatively early in a marriage, there might be more first-born children in the high-mobile group (Item 26). We might expect high mobiles to report a less supportive relationship with their father (Item 31) and, perhaps, their mother as well (Item 30). Perhaps high-mobiles come from a lower socio-economic background (Item 27). Gilliland (1967) found this to be true. And, finally, we might well expect high-mobile students to recall a significantly less happy childhood (Item 34).

Interaction Hypotheses

In addition to the above univariate hypotheses, we want to stipulate some hypotheses based on the interaction effects of mobility. Specifically, we shall hypothesize that when mobility is combined with both divorce and socio-economic status (SES) in a 3-way ANOVA with childhood happiness as the dependent variable, the following outcomes are likely to obtain: (1) students who experienced both mobility and divorce will recall significantly less happy childhoods than students who have experienced only one or neither of these conditions, and (2) students who grew up in a lower SES environment and also experienced high mobility will recall significantly less happy childhoods than those in other 2-way categories of SES and mobility.

These additional hypotheses represent two of the three possible 2-way interactions in a 3-way ANOVA. The third 2-way interaction involves that between SES and divorce, not including mobility. Because our study focuses on mobility, and also because we don't have a strong theoretical basis for making a prediction about this effect, we elect not to make a hypothesis concerning this interaction. In a similar fashion, we choose not to stipulate a prediction for the 3-way interaction of mobility, SES, and divorce. These effects will still be present in our ANOVA model, and they will benefit our analysis; but we must be circumspect about any significant outcomes obtained from them.

The SPSS T-TEST Program

These are our hypotheses. How can we test them? We will proceed with the univariate hypotheses by doing a series of t-tests between the two mobility groups on each of the above items. Because we have the power of a computer at our disposal, it is just as easy to test all the questionnaire items rather than the selected few. This will provide us with even more information, but we must remember to be wary of serendipitous results. The SPSS t-test program is shown below:

```
 5.     DATA LIST
 5.005 FIXED(1)/1 V1 TO V80 1-80
10.     MISSING VALUES
10.005 V1 TO V46 (0, 7 THRU 9)/ V47 (0, 5 THRU 9)/
10.006 V48 (0, 3 THRU 9)/ V49 TO V80 (0, 7 THRU 9)
```

```
12.     RECODE
12.005 V28 (1=1)(2 THRU 5=0)(6=2)
15.     T-TEST
15.005 GROUPS=V28/VARIABLES=V1 TO V80
```

You are already familiar with the first part of this program, blocks 5 and 10. Block 12, the RECODE statement, shows how to create the extreme groups on mobility. Since students with responses of 2 through 5 are assigned a new value of 0, they will be excluded from the analysis. As far as SPSS is concerned they are "missing values." In the T-TEST specification it is necessary to first inform SPSS of the grouping variable, V28, and then to indicate on what variables the groups shall be compared, V1 TO V80. This last specification actually includes the meaningless comparison on V28, itself; but we will ignore that on the printout. SPSS doesn't mind making meaningless comparisons.

Figure 11.5 shows SPSS output for two of the hypothesized items, 24 and 25. The top part of the t-test printout gives descriptive statistics for the two mobility groups. For Item 24, parents' relationship, note that Group 1, the non-mobile group, has a lower mean than Group II indicating a more loving relationship. The question is whether the mean difference of approximately .4 units is significant. The answer to this question is contained in the lower portion of the printout, which provides two different estimates of the t-ratio, the pooled variance and separate variance estimates.

When the variances of two groups are statistically similar, it is proper to "pool" the within-group variances to estimate the standard error of the mean differences. If the variances are not similar, the proper t-test is made with a separate-variance estimate. The researcher must first determine if the group variances are similar before choosing which estimate to use. This information is given to the left of the pooled variance estimate on the printout. An F-value and associated probability indicate whether the variances should be considered equivalent. If the 2-tailed probability is .05 or less, then we must reject the hypotheses of equivalent variances and use the separate-variance t-test. If the probability of F is greater than .05, we may assume the variances to be equivalent and use the pooled-variance estimate for the t-test.

The F probability for Item 24 of .780 is well above the critical value of .05. Therefore, it is proper to use the pooled variance t-test. Figure 11.5 shows a t-value of 1.69 (ignore the sign) with an associated probability of .092. If we had not formulated a directional hypothesis, the probability of .092 would not allow us to reject the null hypothesis, since it is above .05. However, since we did formulate a directional hypothesis, we are entitled to conduct a 1-tailed test of significance. This is

FIGURE 11.5
SPSS t-Test Output for Two Mobility Hypotheses

VARIABLE V24	NUMBER OF CASES	MEAN	STANDARD DEVIATION	STANDARD ERROR
GROUP 1	90	2.6333	1.487	.157
GROUP 2	81	3.0247	1.533	.170

		POOLED VARIANCE ESTIMATE			SEPARATE VARIANCE ESTIMATE		
F Value	2-Tail Prob.	T Value	Degrees Freedom	2-Tail Prob.	T Value	Degrees Freedom	2-Tail Prob.
1.06	.780	-1.69	169	.092	-1.69	165.93	.093

VARIABLE V25	NUMBER OF CASES	MEAN	STANDARD DEVIATION	STANDARD ERROR
GROUP 1	81	5.7284	1.000	.111
GROUP 2	74	4.5405	1.852	.215

		POOLED VARIANCE ESTIMATE			SEPARATE VARIANCE ESTIMATE		
F Value	2-Tail Prob.	T Value	Degrees Freedom	2-Tail Prob.	T Value	Degrees Freedom	2-Tail Prob.
3.43	.000	5.03	153	.000	4.90	109.96	.000

accomplished simply by dividing the t-test probablity by 2; .093/2=.046. Therefore, since our 1-tailed t-test probability is equal to or less than .05, we may reject the null hypothesis. The group means do in fact differ. High mobile subjects perceive their parents' relationships as less loving.

A much greater difference exists between the group means for Item 25 on divorce. The mean of 5.78 for Group I indicates that most individuals in the non-mobile group did not experience divorce. The mean of 4.54 for Group 2 indicates the average high-mobile respondent experienced divorce during the early teen-age years. A check of the F value for Item 25 shows the variances of the two groups to be quite different, F=.000. It is necessary, therefore, to use the separate-variance estimate for the t-test. The t-value of 4.90 with a probability of .000 is highly significant. We must reject the null hypothesis and conclude that these two groups of subjects represent very different populations with respect to the occurrence of divorce in their childhoods.

Table 11.1 summarizes the results of the eight univariate hypothesis tests. Six of the eight research hypotheses were supported (Items 23 and 25 actually dealt with the same variable--divorce). From these tests we may conclude that high mobiles tend to be children of divorce, they sense a less loving relationship between their parents, they tend to be first- or second- rather than later-born children, they have less supportive

TABLE 11.1
Results of Univariate Hypotheses Tests

Item No.	Group 1 M	Group 1 SD	Group 2 M	Group 2 SD	t-ratio
23	1.18	0.63	1.72	1.23	3.58
24	2.63	1.49	3.02	1.53	1.69
25	5.73	1.00	4.54	1.85	4.90
26	2.59	1.69	2.01	1.27	2.54
27	3.64	1.04	3.59	1.18	0.35 (ns)
30	2.11	1.44	2.26	1.31	0.69 (ns)
31	2.33	1.53	3.28	1.65	3.92
34	2.48	1.49	3.04	1.49	2.46

relationships with their fathers, and, perhaps most importantly, they recall significantly less happy childhoods. They do not, as hypothesized, necessarily come from lower class environments. Nor do they have any less supportive relationships with their mothers.

In addition to these results, there were some other questionnaire items which showed significant differences between the mobility groups. These were items 9, 39, and 47. High mobiles rated their financial situations as more important to their happiness than non-mobiles, they reported getting drunk or loaded more often, and they were less sure about the existence of life after death. While these characteristics seem to fit plausibly into our profile of the highly mobile child-turned-adult, we must be very careful about attaching a causal link between mobility and these behaviors. It is quite possible, perhaps even probable, that such characteristics are part of a personality "package" which happens to correlate with the mobility phenomenon.

The SPSS ANOVA Program

In order to test our interaction hypotheses, we must construct a 3-way ANOVA design. We previously decided to use extreme groups on the mobility factor, thus reducing our sample of 400 down to about 170 subjects. Although the use of extreme groups is quite effective, it is wasteful of data and cannot be used for all the independent variables. A prudent way to retain subjects and assure a reasonable number in all subgroups (cells) is to collapse the SES and divorce variables into two categories each. The recoding of these variables is shown in the SPSS program below:

```
12.     RECODE
12.005 V28 (1=1)(2 THRU 5=0)(6=2)
12.010 V25 (1 THRU 5=1)(6=2)
12.015 V27 (1,2,3=1)(4,5,6=2)
15.     ANOVA
15.005 V34 BY V28(1,2), V25(1,2), V27(1,2)
20.     STATISTICS
20.005 1
```

Note that Item 25 was used for the divorce factor. Original categories 1 through 5 are indicative of a divorce or separation at different age periods during childhood. Category 6 represents no divorce or separation. By recoding this variable we have divided subjects into two groups-- divorce and no-divorce. Item 27, the SES factor, was recoded so that a new Group 1 includes individuals from lower class poverty to lower middle class and new Group 2 contains subjects from middle class through upper class. We have created what is often referred to as a 2-by-2-by-2 ANOVA design. Each of the 3 factors has two levels, or categories. This is in contrast to the 3-by-2 design we used for the fictitious women's lib data in which the main effects were political party (three levels) and gender (two levels).

When the above program is run, it first produces the cell means and counts shown in Figure 11.6. The grand mean for childhood happiness, 2.76, is shown under TOTAL POPULATION. This indicates that average childhood happiness was close to "slightly happy." The number in parentheses below the grand mean (155) is the number of subjects included in the analysis. Next is shown a breakdown of the mobility variable, V28. Group 1, the non-mobile subjects, have a mean of 2.52 compared with 3.03 for Group 2, the high-mobiles. Similar breakdowns and counts are given for the other main effects. Notice that V25, divorce, has a rather uneven numerical split between groups 1 and 2, 42 vs. 113 subjects. Only 42 of the 155 subjects experienced divorce in childhood. This uneven split, when combined with other variables, produces a situation in which only eight individuals are classified as both non-mobile and divorced (see the 2-way breakdown for V28 and V25). This situation of disproportionate cell sizes poses a threat to the proper use and interpretation of analysis of variance.

ANOVA with Unequal Cell Sizes

Because the analysis of variance was developed for use in experiments where there is an equal distribution of subjects in cells, it is not always appropriate for causal-comparative research. Due to the way variance is partitioned in the classical, experimental version of ANOVA, it is important that independent variables be *orthogonal* to one another. That is, independent variables should be uncorrelated with one another. In a typical *factorial* experiment with multiple independent variables, the researcher assigns equal numbers of subjects to different experimental conditions. For example, in a 2-by-2 design to study the effects of motivation on achievement, an equal number of subjects might be exposed to the presence or absence of verbal and non-verbal rewards. Such assignment of subjects to treatments guarantees the condition of orthogonality.

In *ex-post-facto* research, however, in which attribute variables are used, it is not often possible to guarantee an equal distribution of subjects in cells. Attribute variables, in contrast to active or manipulated variables, are those which subjects bring with them to the research situation. Kerlinger (1973) defines attribute variables and discusses their use in research:

> *Attribute variables* are measured variables. Intelligence, aptitude, social class, and many other similar variables cannot be manipulated; subjects come to research studies, so to speak, with the variables. They can be assigned to groups on the basis of their possession of more or less intelligence or on the basis of being members of middle-class or working-class families. When there are two or more

FIGURE 11.6
Cell Means and Counts for 3-Way ANOVA
Mobility by SES by Divorce on Childhood Happiness

CELL MEANS
V34
BY V28
V25
V27

TOTAL POPULATION

2.76
(155)

V28

1	2
2.52 (81)	3.03 (74)

V25

1	2
3.33 (42)	2.55 (113)

V27

1	2
3.11 (62)	2.53 (93)

V28 \ V25	1	2
1	2.25 (8)	2.55 (73)
2	3.59 (34)	2.55 (40)

V28 \ V27	1	2
1	3.12 (34)	2.09 (47)
2	3.11 (28)	2.98 (46)

V25 \ V27	1	2
1	3.24 (17)	3.40 (25)
2	3.07 (45)	2.21 (68)

V27 = 1

V28 \ V25	1	2
1	2.80 (5)	3.17 (29)
2	3.42 (12)	2.88 (16)

V27 = 2

V28 \ V25	1	2
1	1.33 (3)	2.14 (44)
2	3.68 (22)	2.33 (24)

such variables in a study and, for analysis of variance purposes, the subjects are assigned to subgroups on the basis of their status on the variables, it is next to impossible, without using artificial means, to have equal numbers of subjects in the cells of the design. This is because the variables are correlated, are not independent. The variables intelligence and social class, for instance, are correlated. To see what is meant and the basic difficulty involved, suppose we wish to study the relations between intelligence and social class, on the one hand, and school achievement, on the other hand. The higher intelligence scores will tend to be those of middle-class children, and the lower intelligence scores those of working-class children. (There are of course many exceptions, but they do not alter the argument.) The number of subjects, therefore, will be unequal in the cells of the design simply because of the correlation between intelligence and social class (Kerlinger, 1973, p. 7).

The situation described by Kerlinger is the very one we are faced with in the present analysis. By combining three attribute variables, in this case, we have exacerbated the problem of correlation among the independent variables. Divorce, low SES, and high mobility are common conditions to some degree; the variables are correlated with one another. By "assigning" subjects to various categories on these variables, we have reproduced a natural condition of imbalance among the categories. Because this condition of imbalance is not compatible with the mathematics of experimental ANOVA, we must resort to an alternative form of ANOVA, in this case the regression approach. Kerlinger (1973) has this to say about regression analysis:

> Researchers commonly partition a continuous variable into high and low, or high medium and low groups--high intelligence-low intelligence, high authoritarianism-low authoritarianism, and so on--in order to use analysis of variance. Although it is valuable to conceptualized design problems in this manner, it is unwise and inappropriate to analyze them so (because of the problem of unequal cell sizes).
>
> Such problems virtually disappear with multiple regression analysis. In the case of the dichotomous variables, one simply enters them as independent variables....Experimental treatments, too, are handled as variables. Although the problem of unequal n's, when analyzing experimental data with multiple regression analysis, does not disappear, it is so much less a problem as to be almost negligible (Kerlinger, 1973, pp. 8-9).

Different Forms of the Analysis of Variance

Because the originators of SPSS were cognizant of the problems associated with analysis of variance in social research, they provided for different forms of the analysis in their package. There are actually three different types of ANOVA in SPSS. These are the *experimental approach*, the *hierarchical approach*, and the *regression approach*.

Without becoming too technical, these approaches differ in the way they assign sums of squares to the sources of variance in a design. If a design is perfectly orthogonal (equal cell sizes), there is no difference between the three methods. They will all produce the same results. However, when there is intercorrelation of the independent variables (unequal cell sizes), the researcher must choose between the hierarchical and regression forms of analysis. The hierarchical approach is approporite when one is testing a theory based on a definite causal chain. If there is little doubt that variable A precedes variable B in time, and, similarly, that variable B precedes variable C historically, then the hierarchical approach is correct. If, however, one cannot determine a logical order of precedence for the variables, then the regression approach is more appropriate.
The interested reader is referred to Overall and Spiegel (1969) and Applebaum and Cramer (1974) for more detailed discussions of these approaches.

Because our present research problem can be characterized as having intercorrelations among the independent variables but no clear causal order among the variables, we shall use the regression approach to the analysis of variance. In SPSS, this can be accomplished very easily by selecting Option 9 for the ANOVA program. The program statements for this option are shown below:

```
15.     ANOVA
15.005 V34 BY V28(1,2), V25(1,2), V27(1,2)
18.     OPTIONS
18.005 9
```

The SPSS-X version is quite similar:

```
ANOVA  V34 BY V28(1,2), V25(1,2), V27(1,2)
OPTIONS 9
```

Figure 11.7 shows the output from this program. Note that no cell means are present. The regression version of ANOVA produces only an ANOVA summary table. But we can use the cell means from Figure 11.6 to help interpret the summary table. This table is quite similar to the one shown previously for a 2-way ANOVA. One difference, apart from the greater number of sources of variance,

FIGURE 11.7
SPSS Output for 3-Way ANOVA
Using the Regression Approach

ANOVA

00051700 CM NEEDED FOR ANOVA

END OF FILE ON FILE HAPPY
AFTER READING 402 CASES FROM SUBFILE NONAME

ANOVA TABLE

V34
BY V28
V25
V27

SOURCE OF VARIATION	SUM OF SQUARES	DF	MEAN SQUARE	F	SIGNIF OF F
MAIN EFFECTS	25.606	3	8.535	4.274	.006
V28	9.965	1	9.965	4.990	.027
V25	.620	1	.620	.311	.578
V27	9.380	1	9.380	4.697	.032
2-WAY INTERACTIONS	22.136	3	7.379	3.695	.013
V28 V25	11.412	1	11.412	5.715	.018
V28 V27	6.018	1	6.018	3.014	.085
V25 V27	.172	1	.172	.086	.770
3 -WAY INTERACTIONS	1.859	1	1.859	.931	.336
V28 V25 V27	1.859	1	1.859	.931	.336
EXPLAINED	56.609	7	8.087	4.050	.001
RESIDUAL	293.559	147	1.997		
TOTAL	350.168	154	2.274		

402 CASES WERE PROCESSED.
247 CASES (61.4 PCT) WERE MISSING.

CPU TIME REQUIRED 4.718 SECONDS

is that F-values are given for the collective main effects and interactions. These values and their associated significance levels are not always shown in summary tables because they are of limited use. SPSS provides them in case the researcher wants to test a hypothesis about the collective action of all main effects or interaction terms.

Figure 11.7 shows that two of the main effects are significant at .05 or beyond. These are V28, mobility, and V27, SES. However, there is a significant interaction between V28 and V25, mobility and divorce. And, there is a nearly significant interaction between V28 and V27, mobility and SES. Thus, we cannot say simply that mobility and SES are important to childhood happiness. They are, but the situation is not that simple. We must take into account how they interact together on happiness and also how they each interact with divorce to produce different degrees of childhood happiness. Let us look first at the significant interaction between mobility and divorce on childhood happiness. An indispensable tool for studying interactions is the graph. The graph in Figure 11.8 was constructed by using the cell means from Figure 11.6.

From Figure 11.8 it is pretty clear that when divorce is combined with high mobility there is an adverse impact on childhood happiness. It is only the group of subjects who experienced both divorce and high mobility that reported low levels of childhood happiness. Among subjects from intact families there is no difference in childhood happiness between those who experienced mobility and those who did not. The non-mobile divorced subjects actually reported slightly higher levels of happiness than their non-divorced counterparts. This difference is slight, however, and may be due to sampling error since only eight individuals were included in the non-mobile, divorced group.

Although the interaction between SES and mobility was not quite significant, it is worth investigating its characteristics,especially since it involves our second interaction hypothesis. It is shown graphically in Figure 11.9. Here we see that the significant difference between high- and low-SES subjects on childhood happiness is due largely to the elevated happiness scores for the non-mobile, high-SES subjects. That is, high-SES subjects who experienced high mobility were not significantly happier as children than low-SES subjects, regardless of the latter group's mobility.

How do these results bear on our interaction hypotheses? Here are the hypotheses: (1) students who experienced both mobility and divorce will recall significantly less happy childhoods than students who have experienced only one or neither of these conditions, and (2) students who grew up in a lower SES

FIGURE 11.8
Two-way Interaction of Divorce and Mobility

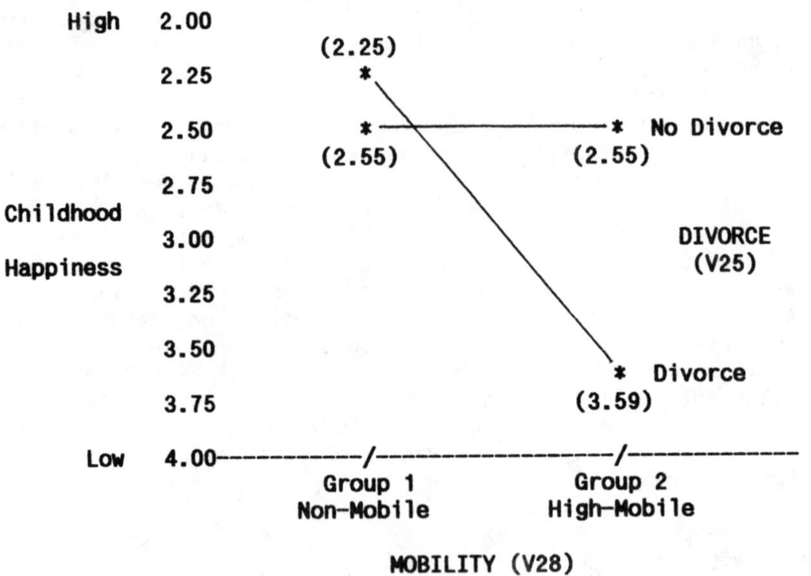

FIGURE 11.9
Two-Way Interaction of SES and Mobility

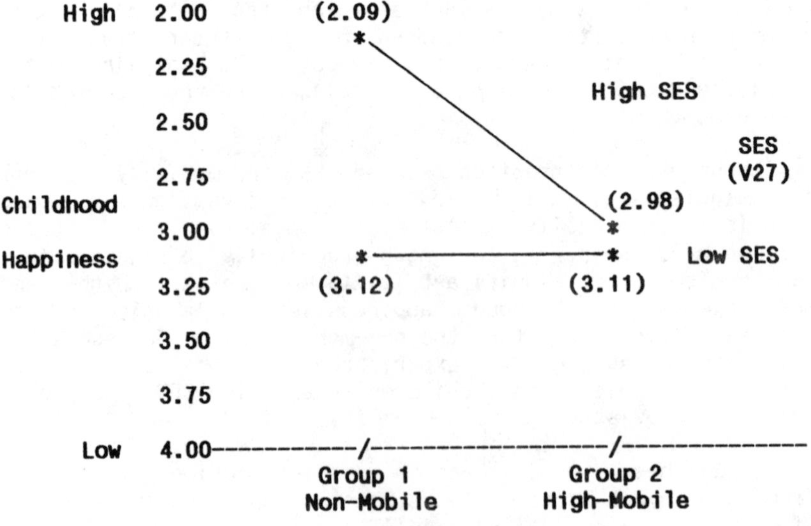

environment and also experienced high mobility will recall significantly less happy childhoods than those in other 2-way categories of SES and mobility. The first interaction, between mobility and divorce was significant, and the nature of the interaction was exactly as we had predicted. The second interaction was not significant, and therefore our research hypothesis was not supported. However, it appears that further research on the interaction between SES and mobility is warranted. There was a strong interactive trend in these variables, although the nature of the interaction was not exactly as predicted.

A final word before closing this chapter: The discerning reader may recall that divorce was a highly significant univariate outcome and may wonder why it was not a significant main effect in the 3-way ANOVA. The reason has to do with the way multiple regression works. In the regression approach to ANOVA each effect is adjusted for all other sources of variance. If a particular source of variance, in this case divorce, is highly correlated with other sources, then its unique effect is reduced accordingly. Because divorce is correlated with both mobility and SES in the 3-way design, its individual contribution was not sufficient to be significant as a main effect. However, it remains an important factor in terms of its significant interaction with mobility. Another difference between the univariate and 3-way analyses is that SES is now significant, whereas before it was not. This is due to the fact that six additional sources of variance were added to the model. The presence of these additional terms reduced the error variance substantially such that the F-ratio for SES, in contrast to the earlier t-ratio, is now significant.

This chapter has explored data analysis procedures for causal-comparative research. It was shown that the analysis of variance is a logical extension of the t-test and that it shares some features in common with multiple regression. In fact, ANOVA is a special case of multiple regression and correlation (MRC). The use of post hoc tests and measures of association were demonstrated. Considerable emphasis was given to the use of ANOVA to test interaction hypotheses in 2-way and 3-way designs. Finally, it was pointed out that in much causal-comparative research, classical ANOVA procedures are often inappropriate. The regression approach to ANOVA is necessary when independent variables are correlated with one another.

CHAPTER TWELVE

EXPERIMENTAL METHODS

This chapter begins with a prototypic quasi-experimental study. The example investigation is followed by sections on experimental design theory and program evaluation. The chapter concludes with statistical examples from the happiness questionnaire and a final section on recent developments in data analysis.

Although some considerable space in this chapter is devoted to methods of conducting a true experiment, this type of research, with the exception of laboratory research in psychology, is relatively infrequent in behavioral science. However, it is important for the student to understand the principles of experimental research in order to design better quasi-experimental and correlational studies. The research examples provided will be of the latter two types.

Research Example: The Effects of Transcendental Meditation on Three Factors of Personal Discontent

In the early 1970's it was fashionable to use many different forms of psychotherapy for the alleviation of personal problems. Some of these "therapies" originated outside mainstream psychology and achieved considerable popularity and status. One of them, transcendental meditation (TM), enjoyed much notoriety and was actually used in some public schools to improve students' mental health and educational achievement.

This author, ever skeptical of huge claims of success for a single therapeutic intervention, decided to investigate the efficacy of TM. He teamed up with a graduate student who was engaged in the practice of TM and had access to local TM sites. The researchers designed a quasi-experimental investigation to study the effects of TM on three psychological variables: hostility, anxiety, and depression. The investigation led to a paper presentation at the California Educational Research Association (Hahn & Whalen, 1974) and the senior author's master's thesis (Hahn, 1975). The summary which follows was extracted from these sources.

Transcendental meditation is a relatively simple form of meditation which involves the silent repetition of a "mantra" to quiet the mind and rid it of negative thoughts. Individuals who want to practice TM usually attend a short course in which they are assigned a mantra and receive instruction in the practice and theory of TM. Regular use of TM involves a total of 30 to 40 minutes of daily meditation usually divided between morning and evening sessions.

At the time of the investigation, several independent evaluations of TM's effects had already been completed. Initial studies focused on physiological effects. Some of the conclusions drawn were that: (1) meditators have a faster reaction time than non-meditators, suggesting better coordination between perceiving and responding, (2) the number of galvonic skin responses decreased with TM, showing a possible higher tolerance for environmental stress among meditators, an (3) meditators exhibited a lower rate of breathing and oxygen consumption, and also showed a reduction in the level of blood lactate, a condition which has been linked to stress, irritability, and tension.

A few psychological studies had been reported, but they were generally weak in controlling for confounding variables. A New York psychiatrist concluded that TM was highly beneficial for many of his clients. A comparison of meditators and non-meditators using Shostrom's Personal Orientation Inventory indicated that meditators were more self-actualized, having greater inner direction, self regard, acceptance of aggression, capacity for intimate contact, and acceptance of self.

Some other studies related TM to the use of drugs. Reductions in use and trafficking were observed among practitioners. It was partly on the basis of these findings that TM was introduced to the schools. Driscoll (1972) looked at TM in educational settings and found that grades improved, relationships with family, teachers, and peers were better, and drug abuse decreased.

The present study was designed as follows: Volunteer subjects were recruited from two TM sites in the San Francisco Bay Area. The control subjects were two classrooms of community college students in general psychology at a nearby location. They were judged to be similar in age and educational background to the experimental subjects. Although the experimental subjects were not selected randomly from a larger population of meditators, it was felt that they were representative of a typical group of young adults starting TM during the first six months of 1974 in the San Francisco area.

The instrument used for data collection was the Multiple Affect Adjective Check List (MAACL), an instrument the investigators felt was perhaps more reliable than some others used in previous research. The MAACL (Zuckerman & Lubin, 1965) is a list of 132 adjectives alphabetically arranged. It was designed to fill a need for a self-administered test which would provide valid measures of three of the clinically relevant negative effects: hostility, anxiety, and depression (HAD). Some examples of adjectives which subjects endorsed on a 2-point scale are "afraid," "angry," "blue," "cheerful," and "contented."

In an effort to control for the sensitization of experimental subjects which sometimes results from pretesting, the researchers utilized a variant of the so-called Solomon Four-Group Design. This is a procedure in which the experimental and control groups are divided into two subgroups each. One of the groups is pretested, i.e., administered the test prior to the treatment, and one is not. In this way, if subjects experience some sort of reaction to the test, this effect can be separated from that of the treatment. The first experimental group, composed of 54 subjects, was tested the day of their initiation into TM and then again in three months. The second experimental group, composed of 37 subjects, had already practiced meditation for three months and was posttested at that time. The first control group (N=52) was pre- and posttested at the same time as the first experimental group. The second control group (N=37) was tested only once, at the same time as the second experimental group. In addition to these four groups, a fifth group of long-term meditators (N=43) was tested after one or more years of meditation.

Analysis of variance was used to determine if significant differences in HAD existed between meditators and non-meditators. Duncan's Multiple Range Test was utilized to determine exactly where the differences occurred. A further analysis was made to determine which specific adjectives changed significantly in endorsement frequencies from pre- to posttest. Finally, three additional independent variables were analyzed for differences. These were age, sex, and regularity of meditation. Subjects rated themselves on this last variable and were dichotomized accordingly.

Figures 12.1 and 12.2 provide a visual summary of the major results. Figure 12.1 shows that after three months of meditation, a significant difference was noted in HAD between regular and irregular meditators. Figure 12.2 shows reductions in HAD for both groups, but shows that the the pre-to-post reductions were not as strong among irregular meditators. In fact, their reductions were not significantly different from those of the pretested control group. Some additional findings of note were: (1) pretest scores for experimental and control groups did not differ significantly, indicating that subjects who chose to meditate were not different in HAD from control subjects who had not thought of meditating, (2) long-term meditators had significantly lower HAD than the three-month meditators, and (3) age and sex did not influence the effects of TM on one's level of HAD.

FIGURE 12.1
Comparison of the Mean Scores of
Regular and Irregular Meditators (E_1-post + E_2)*

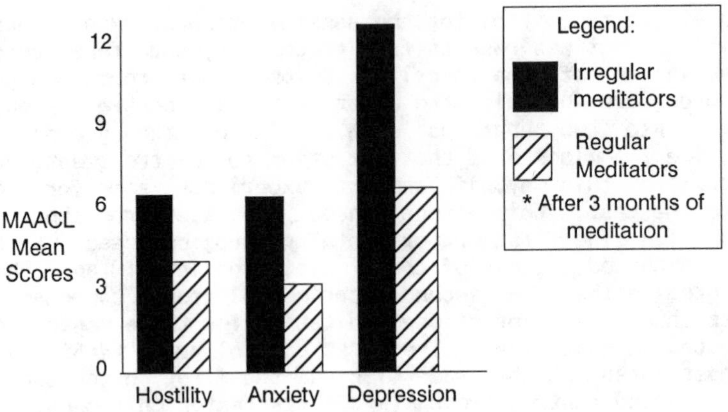

FIGURE 12.2
Pre-test (E_1) and Post-test (E_1-post + E_2) Mean Scores
for Regular and Irregular Meditators

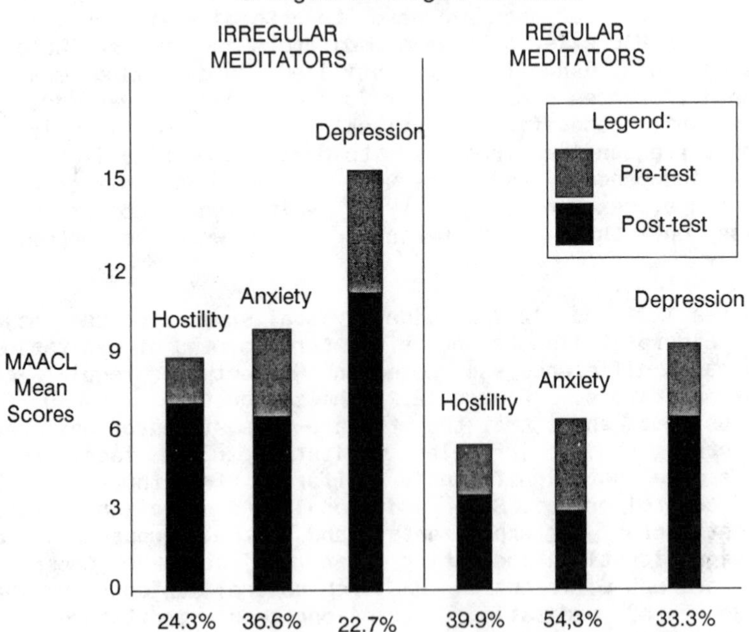

In conclusion, it was the researchers' judgment that transcendental meditation does appear to embody certain beneficial therapeutic effects which can substantially reduce the psychological states of hostility, anxiety, and depression. Further, the benefits from TM appear to be proportionate to the time spent in meditation; they were more evident in regular meditators than in those who practiced intermittent meditation.

Research Design Theory

The field of behavioral research is indebted to Campbell and Stanley (1963) for their work in systematizing the sources of extraneous variance which may jeopardize the validity of experiments. In their chapter on *Experimental and Quasi-Experimental Designs for Research*, which first appeared in the *Handbook of Research on Teaching* (1963), they presented 16 experimental designs coupled with their common threats to validity. This body of experimental theory provided a foundation for technical and theoretical advances in empirical methods during the past 25 years. This section will summarize this theory by presenting some of the more common factors jeopardizing experimental validity. This will be followed by a presentation of commonly-used research designs together with their advantages and pitfalls.

Internal and External Validity

A useful distinction is that between internal and external validity. Internal validity is defined by Campbell and Stanley (1963) as "the basic minimum without which any experiment is uninterpretable." Internal validity involves the question of whether the experimental treatment actually made a difference in a specific study. External validity, on the other hand, poses a question about generalizability: "To what populations, settings, treatment variables, and measurement variables can this effect be generalized?" (Campbell and Stanley, 1963, p. 5). These concepts are somewhat analogous to reliability and validity in measurement theory. In order for a test to be valid, it must first be reliable. Likewise, in order for an experiment to have generalizability, it must be internally valid. Let us first explore some threats to internal validity.

Some Threats to Internal Validity

1. *History*: events occurring between the first and second measurements in addition to the treatment variable.
2. *Maturation*: organismic processes within the research subjects operating as a function of the passage of time including growing older, growing hungrier, becoming more drowsy, etc.

3. *Testing*: the effects of taking a test upon the scores of a second testing.

4. *Instrumentation*: changes in the process of measurement which may occur during an initial observation period or between successive observations. Consider, for example, the grading of essays and how a reader might change his criteria as he proceeds through a set of papers.

5. *Statistical regression*: natural movement of a group mean from an initial extreme postion toward its population mean without an intervening treatment.

6. *Selection bias*: initial differences between experimental and control groups.

7. *Experimental mortality*: differential loss of subjects from comparison groups over the course of a longer-term investigation.

Some Threats to External Validity

1. The *reactive effect of testing*: an interaction between pretesting and a subsquent treatment on the final experimental outcome. Although both experimental and control groups may experience a similar reaction to pretesting, a condition which would not jeopardize internal validity, it may not be possible to generalize experimental results to the unpretested population from which the experimental subjects were sampled.

2. The *reactive effect of selection*: an interaction between subject selection and a subsequent treatment. For example, in Hahn and Whalen's (1974) study of transcendental meditation, in which the subjects selected themselves into treatment groups, it is not possible to generalize the findings to the universe of subjects who do not choose TM.

3. The *reactive effect of experimental arrangements*: an interaction between the research setting and a treatment which would preclude generalization about the effect to subjects in a different setting. Subjects who know they are involved in an experiment may react in accordance with their perceptions of the experimentor's "demands." The famous *Hawthorne Effect* was due to this characteristic of experiments. Workers at the Hawthorne plant of the Western Electric Company improved their work output regardless of which treatment was used because they knew they were getting special treatment.

Experimental Research Designs

The rather brief explication of threats to validity will be amplified in this section on research designs. Eight designs will be presented. The first two are termed weak designs and correspond to Campbell and Stanley's pre-experimental designs. They are included for two reasons: they nicely illustrate many of the threats to validity, and they continue to be used by researchers. The next three designs are termed strong designs and correspond to Campbell and Stanley's true experimental designs. The last three designs are called compromise designs. They correspond to Campbell and Stanley's quasi-experimental designs.

A few words need to be said about notation conventions for experimental designs. Although there is not total uniformity among writers in the use of symbols to represent designs, it is common for an "X" to represent a treatment variable and "Y" to represent an observed or measured dependent variable. There may be more than one X or Y in a given design so that Y1 and Y2 may refer to a pre- and posttest for one group and Y3 and Y4 would be similar measurements of a control group. The letter "R" stands for random assignment of subjects to groups. The passage of time is portrayed by a left to right sequencing of these symbols. Each experimental group resides on a single horizontal line.

Weak Designs

The One-Group Pretest-Posttest Design. Because this design does not utilize a control group, it is very weak in internal validity. The design is used rather extensively in education because of the difficulty in finding cooperative control groups. It is diagrammed as follows:

Y1 X Y2

The symbols indicate that a single group receives a pretest, Y1, followed by a treatment and then a posttest, Y2. Consider the following examples: An attempt to improve the physical fitness of junior high school students by introducing a new series of aerobic exercises; determining shifts in political attitudes after a certain candidate's big speech; measuring change in racial attitudes after a documentary film on race relations. In all these examples the same measuring instrument would be used before and after the treatment.

It is not difficult to imagine a number of rival hypotheses which could account for a significant change from pretest to posttest in the absense of any treatment. History is an uncontrolled factor which might affect the validity of a change in political attitudes, quite apart from a candidate's speech. The longer the lapse of time between pre- and posttest, the more likely history becomes a rival hypothesis. Maturation could be a factor in the physical prowess of students, especially if the treatment is extended over an entire school year. Testing is a third counfounding variable which might account for significant change. It is well known that students learn something by taking a test for the first time. In the case of an attitude "test," subjects might be sensitized to the experiment and act accordingly.

Instrumentation is not likely to play a part in these examples if sound measurement procedures are used. But statistical regression could be a problem if subjects were chosen for a program because they "needed" the treatment. For example, if only the lowest-performing children on the physical pretest were selected for participation, there would almost certainly be an improvement in their posttest scores regardless of an experimental intervention. Because so many educational and counseling programs are designed to meet the needs of individuals who are in special need, statistical regression is a real bugaboo to researchers who cannot muster a control group. Subjects who are extremely high or low on a pretest measure will almost certainly receive a more moderate score on the posttest. If there is a way to predict the extent of regression to the mean, and therefore remove it from any treatment effect, then this design might be considered. Otherwise it should be avoided.

The Static Group Comparison. Another weak design is one in which a comparison group is used, but assignment to groups is not under the control of the researcher.

X Y1

Y2

Some examples of this design are a comparison of students from an accredited college vs. students from a non-accredited institution, a comparison of couples who have experienced "marriage encounter" vs. those who haven't, freshman vs. senior college women in terms of physical attractiveness.

The most likely source of invalidity for this design is selection, the differential recruitment of individuals into the comparison groups. It seems obvious that a comparison of any two colleges in terms of, say, SAT averages is plagued by many potentially confounding variables beyond a difference in accreditation status. It may not be so obvious why freshmen women are more glamorous than their senior classmates. We hate to think it was our educational programs that debeautified them rather than an early trip to the alter. Differential mortality, then, becomes the most plausible rival hypothesis to explain this difference.

Although the static group comparison design has a "control" group, unless that group can be considered equivalent in most ways to the experimental group, this design should be avoided. An attempt to "match" subjects on background characteristics is usually not effective and can be misleading. Without good knowledge concerning pretreatment equivalence of groups, this design produces meaningless results.

Strong Designs

The following three designs correspond to Campbell and Stanley's true experimental designs. Because they are more complex than the weak designs, some attention will be given to the proper analysis of data for these designs. Actual examples of analyses using SPSS will be presented later in the chapter.

The Pretest-Posttest Control Group Design. This is probably the most-used experimental design. During the early part of this century, behavioral researchers apparently realized the weakness of the one-group pretest-posttest design, and they added a control group to it. This popular experimental design takes this form:

R Y1 X Y2

R Y3 Y4

The R's at the beginning of each line signify that subjects are assigned from a common pool to the two groups at random. It should be noted that random assignment is not the same as random sampling. Much psychological research utilizes a subject pool of undergraduate students who are assigned randomly to experimental and control groups. While this procedure is vital to internal validity, it does not assure external validity. Strictly speaking, one cannot generalize the results of such research to all college students, let alone the general population. However, campus researchers are often more desirous of assuring good internal validity, with the hope that replications of their experiments on different populations will eventually provide external validity.

Another requirement of this design, in order for it to be truly experimental, is that subjects must not all receive the treatment together in a single session. This restriction rules out most educational and other research in which the treatment is provided through group instruction. (There is a quasi-experimental version of this design to be discussed in the next section.) The reason for this requirement is that intrasession history could become a rival hypothesis to the treatment effect. Page (1968) has referred to this phenomenon as the "lawn mower" effect. Consider how students in an experimental classroom might be adversely affected by a power lawn mower outside their window on the day the special lesson (treatment) is given.

For the above design to be truly experimental, the treatment should be administered to each subject individually by the same experimenter(s) using standard procedures. In addition, if a placebo treatment is used with a control group, it should be applied simultaneously and in like manner to that of the experimental group. Naturally, the pre- and posttests, or other observation procedures, should also be conducted simultaneously as well by the same experimenter(s). This last requirement is almost impossible to fulfill and is rarely achieved. With such stringent requirements it is not difficult to understand why quasi-experiments outnumber true experiments in behavioral research.

The two-group pre-post design controls very well for all sources of internal validity. Its major limitation concerns external validity. Because both experimental and control subjects are pre-tested, the researcher can never be completely sure that his results will generalize to an unpretested population. This may not be a problem in many settings. If the pretest is used routinely as part of a treatment program, as in the form of a counseling intake questionnaire, then it is not likely to affect experimental results. Nor will its future use in conjunction with a new treatment population pose a problem. It is best to think of a pretest as part of a treatment package. Recommendations based on research results should include the use of the pretest as part of the treatment.

The proper analysis of data for the pretest-posttest control group design is a bit more complicated than one might expect. The crucial test of significance is between Y2 and Y4, the two posttests. A t-test for independent groups or an F-test from ANOVA may be used for this purpose. Both of these tests naturally assume an equivalence of Y1 and Y3. That is, if randomization has worked, then the two groups should be nearly equivalent on the pretest. Such equivalence is more likely with large groups--25 to 30 or more per group. If smaller groups are used, then a test of the Y1 vs. Y3 difference should be made to verify equivalence.

The difficulty in data analysis with this design comes when the groups are determined not be equivalent on the pretest. Some would also argue that even if there is an insignificant difference between Y1 and Y3, that difference should be taken into account when testing for the Y2 vs. Y4 difference. How can a pretest difference between the groups be handled? There are two possibilities: The first is to compute a "gain" score for each subject. This score, which represents the difference between a subject's pre- and posttest scores, usually a positive gain, becomes the new dependent variable for a Y2 vs. Y4 significance test. A second and preferable method is the analysis of covariance (ANCOVA). This technique involves the use of the pretest as a predictor of posttest performance. A residual score representing the difference between a subject's predicted and actual posttest score is then used for the Y2 vs. Y4 comparison. This method will be illustrated later in the chapter.

The Posttest-Only Control Group Design. For those situations in which fairly large numbers of subjects are assigned to experimental and control groups, the posttest only design has some advantages over the previous design.

R X Y1

R Y2

This design, diagrammed above, has several positive characteristics which should be considered. First, the statistical test is straightforward and uncomplicated. A t-test or F-test may be made for the Y1 vs. Y2 comparison. Because no pretest is administered, there is no possiblity of a testing-treatment interaction effect, and greater external validity is attained. With this design there is no problem in generalizing the results to the population from which the subjects were selected. Another advantage of this design is that subject anonymity can be preserved, a feature of considerable importance in the human subjects review process required for approval of one's research study. In a pretest-posttest design one must be able to link a subject's pre- and posttest scores. That requires subject identification in some fashion, whether by name or number. Although steps can be taken to maximize confidentiality, there is always a lurking doubt that someone will learn the identity and performance of some or all of the subjects.

In addition to the lack of pre-treatment knowledge of subjects' performance levels, there is one major disadvantage to the posttest-only design. The statistical test of significance, while quite elegant, lacks power. There is no reduction in error variance as is achieved with a pretest covariate in the pre-post design. This deficiency can be remedied through the use of a separate covariate or "blocking" factor. For example, in a study of the effect of a new algebra curriculum, a prior grade point average or math ability rating might be used to block students into high, medium, and low ability groups. This creates a factorial ANOVA design in which ability becomes a second main effect along with the treatment variable. Any variance in posttest scores due to subject differences in ability can be factored from the error variance, thus improving the power of the F test for the treatment effect. Another important by-product of such a factorial design is the ability to test for a possible interaction between treatment and ability level. It would be extremely important to know, for example, that a new instructional method works well only for medium and high ability students.

The posttest-only control group design is very strong in both internal and external validity. It avoids the sensitizing effect of a pretest. When used with one or more blocking factors such as ability, SES, or severity of clinical problem, this design can produce a powerful factorial model for the analysis of research data.

The Solomon Four-Group Design. This design is named for the sociologist who first presented it as a means for better controlling a potential testing effect. The diagram below shows this to be a combination of the two previous designs.

R	Y1	X	Y2
R	Y3		Y4
R		X	Y5
R			Y6

The first two lines above represent the pretest-posttest control group design; the last two lines, the posttest-only control group design. With the Soloman design it is possible to control for a pretesting effect in two ways. Since groups 3 and 4 are not pretested, the effect of pretesting is eliminated as a confound of the Y5 vs. Y6 comparison. But if the pretest does cause a reaction, its effect can be determined through a comparison of Y2 with Y5. In addition, one can control for maturation and history by comparing Y6 with Y1 and Y3.

The main drawbacks of this design are the larger number of subjects needed and the fact that no statistical model will work for all comparisons simultaneously. It is possible to analyze the posttest scores with a simple 2-by-2 ANOVA as follows:

	X	No X
Pretested	Y2	Y4
Unpretested	Y5	Y6

With this two-way ANOVA one can determine the treatment effect by comparing the column means for X and No X (the average of Y2 and Y5 vs. Y4 and Y6). A comparison of the row means will indicate the main effect of pretesting (the average of Y2 and Y4 vs. Y5 and Y6). Finally, the cell means will indicate the presence of a significant pretesting-by-treatment interaction. If the main and interactive effects of pretesting are not significant, the researcher may desire to perform an analysis of covariance on Y4 with Y2 as the covariate. This strategy will serve to increase the power of the test for a treatment effect, possibly improving the results obtained previously.

The Solomon Four-Group Design is an extremely powerful research design which combines the virtues of the pretest-posttest and posttest-only designs discussed above. It is most effectively employed in attitude research where subjects may be unduly sensitized by a pretest. When a true experiment is not possible, this design may be used in its quasi-experimental form as in the study on transcendental meditation described at the beginning of the chapter.

Compromise Designs

Three designs are presented in this section. They are judged by the author to be among the most common and useful of the twelve quasi-experimental designs presented by Campbell and Stanley. These designs are referred to as compromise designs because, while they lack the rigor of true experimental designs, they are decided improvements over the weak designs presented earlier.

The Single Group Time Series Design. According to Campbell and Stanley (1963) the time series experiment typified much of 19th century research in the physical sciences and biology. The design is diagrammed below:

Y1 Y2 Y3 Y4 X Y5 Y6 Y7 Y8

The Y's represent a series of observations or measurements over time. Although eight measurements are shown here, the number may be fewer or greater. With only two such measurements we have the equivalent of the one group pretest-posttest design, a weak design. Thus, the minimum number of Y's for this design should probably be three, two prior to treatment to form a trend line, and one after the treatment to show evidence of a departure from the trend. The strength in this design in comparison with the one-group pretest-posttest is its ability to vitiate history as a rival hypothesis for the treatment effect. That is, a rival hypothesis exists that some event simultaneous to X produced a change which is mistaken for X. Obviously, the more measurements available to establish a trend, the less likely history is as a rival hypothesis. The other sources of invalidity are logically discounted in a manner similar to that of history.

This design is probably best used in institutional research where data are collected in a periodic and routine fashion. For example, a researcher might use yearly traffic fatalities to determine the effect of a compulsory seatbelt law. Because the law affects all motorists in a given state, no control group is possible; and other states are not deemed equivalent for comparison. Other examples are the effect on school absenteeism of a tough new truancy law, or the effect on disciplinary referrals after a new vice principal is appointed. Though there are problems in drawing conclusions from such studies, the time series design sometimes offers the only method of investigation. As Campbell and Stanley stated:

> *Where nothing better controlled is possible*, we will use it. We will organize our institutional bookkeeping to provide as many time series as possible

> for such evaluations and will try to examine in more detail than we have previously the effects of administrative changes and other abrupt and arbitrary events as Xs. But these will not be regarded as definitive until frequently replicated in various settings (Campbell & Stanley, 1963, p.42).

Although the concept of a time series design is quite simple, the analysis of data produced by this design is fraught with difficulty. Statisticians are not in agreement about appropriate tests of significance for time series data. One of the reasons for this is the variety of outcomes which can be produced from such an experiment. Figure 12.3, taken from Campbell and Stanley (1963, p. 38), shows eight possible results for time series data. Not all of these outcomes represent significant treatment effects. Probably both A and B are significant, and possibly C, D, and E, as well. Outcomes F, G, and H show patterns apparently undisturbed by the treatment, X.

One method that has been used to analyze time series data is a type of analysis of variance known as repeated measure ANOVA (cf. Bruning and Kintz, 1977, pp. 44-83). Thus far in this book we have utilized one-way and factorial ANOVA, both of which assume that scores in different cells come from different groups of subjects. In repeated measures ANOVA the assumption is that data in different cells come from the same subjects. The cells represents a group of successive measurements for individuals over time. Thus, for the outcomes shown in Figure 12.3, we would have a repeated measures ANOVA with eight cells. An F test would indicate a significant difference among the means in those eight cells. An SPSS example of this method will be shown later.

The Two-Group Time Series Design. This is a logical extension of the previous design for one group. It is diagrammed thusly:

```
Y   Y   Y X Y   Y   Y
- - - - - - - - - - -
Y   Y   Y   Y   Y   Y
```

The two-group time series can be used in two somewhat different ways. First, in conjunction with the examples cited for the one-group time series design, if a comparable institution can be found, it should be used as a control group. In the seat-belt example, if another state can be found which has a similar history of traffic fatalites but which does not require seat belts, then its records may be used to strengthen the case against history as a rival hypothesis. Once again, the number of pre- and post-treatment measures may vary somewhat. It should be noted, however, that multiple measures taken after the treatment serve to demonstrate the permanence of a new behavior.

FIGURE 12.3 *

Possible Outcomes of Time Series Experiments

Donald T. Campbell and Julian C. Stanley

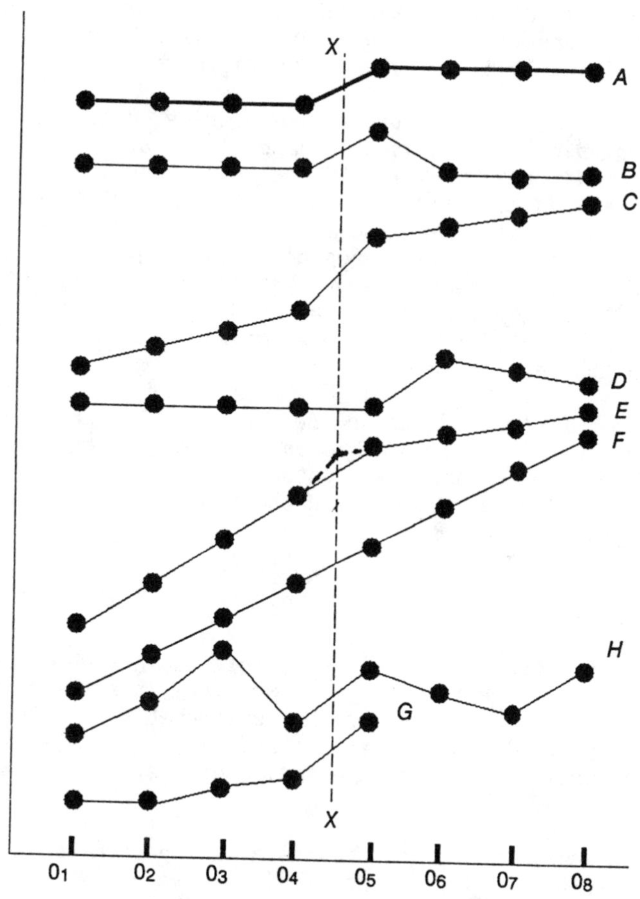

Some Possible Outcome Patterns from the Introduction of an Experimental Variable at Point *X* into a Time Series of Measurements, O_1 - O_8. Except for *D*, the O_4 - O_5 gain is the same for all time series, while the legitimacy of inferring an effect varies widely, being strongest in *A* and *B* and totally unjustified in *F*, *G*, and *H*.

* reprinted by permission of the American Educational Research Association

The two-group time series design can be used also to compare subjects within a group. For example, suppose an elementary teacher identifies six boys and an equal number of girls who are guilty of excessive out-of-seat behavior. Working with a school psychologist, he constructs a behavioral treatment involving positive reinforcement for on-task performance and the ignoring of out-of-seat behavior. After recording out-of-seat behavior for several days during a baseline period, he begins the treatment and continues to monitor out-of-seat behavior. A question of interest is whether the treatment works equally well for both sexes. The two-group design allows for such a comparison.

The analysis of multiple time series data is not too different from single group data. Campbell and Stanley suggested, in fact, that differences between the experimental and control series be anlalyzed as single group data. Another method is to use an extension of the repeated measures ANOVA discussed above. The specific model is a mixed design with one between-subjects variable and one within-subjects variable (cf. Howell, 1987, pp. 423-435). A third option available in SPSS is to use multiple analysis of variance (MANOVA). An example of this type will be presented in the section on statistics.

The Nonequivalent Control Group Design. Perhaps the most widespread design in educational research is one which utilizes a pretest and posttest with two intact groups. This is the quasi-experimental version of the pretest-posttest control group design described earlier.

```
Y1   X   Y2
- - - - - - -
Y3       Y4
```

Under ideal conditions the researcher assigns the treatment randomly to one of the two groups. However, the assignment of subjects to groups is not under the researcher's control. The groups are typically preassembled and may be self-selected. School classrooms are a prime example of naturally assembled groups used in this design.

The discerning reader may recognize this design as a special case of the two-group time series design shown above. Indeed it is; but because it has only one measurement before and after the treatment, it is not usually treated as a time series design in the literature.

The non-equivalent control group design is similar to its true-experimental cousin in its ability to control most threats to internal validity. Perhaps the most troublesome threat to internal validity is regression. Consider a counseling experiment using marital satisfaction as the dependent variable. If applicants to marriage counseling are used as the experimental group and they are compared with a group of "normal" couples, then the counseling applicants represent an extreme group at the low end of marital satisfaction. They will probably regress upward in their satisfaction scores on a second testing whether or not they receive a therapeutic intervention. A similar phenomenon has been noted in evaluations of compensatory education programs when disadvantaged students are compared with students from a regular program.

Another problem with the non-equivalent control group design involves the possible interaction of selection and treatment. In non-educational settings where testing is uncommon, there might also be a testing-treatment interaction effect. These are both threats to external validity. How does one avoid these threats to validity when a true experiment is not possible? In the psychotherapy example above, differential regression could be avoided by using counseling applicants in both the experimental and control groups. This might be accomplished by using couples on a waiting list vs. couples who have just entered therapy. If the waiting time is long enough, a pre- and posttest could be given to the control group prior to their entry into therapy. A threat to external validity involving selection of subjects is less important in quasi-exerimental research if one does not attempt to over-generalize results. After all, if it can be shown that a particular therapy works well on distressed couples, we need not recommend it to the healthy population at large.

The nonequivalent control group design has received the attention of many statisticians and measurement specialist because of its thorny analysis problems. Kenny (1975) summarized the positions of several authorities as to the proper method of data analysis. He presents four possible methods: (1) the analysis of covariance (ANCOVA) or its multiple regression equivalent, (2) ANCOVA with reliability correction (of the pretest scores), (3) raw change score (gain score) analysis, and (4) standardized change score analysis. Kenny points out that each of these methods has its advocates, and there are some authorities who claim it is not possible to determine treatment effects adequately with any of these methods. Kenny himself favors the use of standardized gain scores. This is a relatively simple procedure in which the pretest and posttest scores are standardized separately across both groups. That is, an overall mean and standard deviation are calculated for the combined group data and used to compute standard scores for each subject (see Chapter 9 for details). This is done separately for pretests and posttests. Finally, the standard scores from the two tests are compared subject by subject, and the difference between the two scores, either positive or negative, becomes the dependent variable for the analysis. A between groups t-test or F-ratio can then be computed to test the hypothesis of group differences.

In summarzing his discussion of this design and quasi-experiments in general, Kenny makes an insightful comment about the state of behavioral research, which serves as an appropriate conclusion to this section of the book:

> ...because the internal validity of quasi-experiments is lower than true experiments, it does not argue against using the judgments of quasi-experiments. We would all prefer to have the testimony about an event from a sighted man over a blind man. But when we have only the blind man, we would not dismiss his testimony, expecially if he were aware of his biases and had developed faculties of touch and hearing that the sighted man could have developed but neglected. The difference between the true experiment and the quasi-experiment is of the magnitude of the difference between sight and blindness. We must often grope in the darkness with quasi-experimental designs, but this blindness both forces us to compensate for biases and helps us develop a newfound sensitivity to the structure of data. Finally, it makes us appreciate the clarity of true experimental inference (Kenny, 1975, p. 360).

Program Evaluation

The purpose of this section is to acquaint the reader with an important subdivision of behavioral research known as program evaluation. A brief history of this emerging field will be presented along with an explanation of purposes and types of program evaluation and how this field differs from other research enterprises. The section will be concluded with an example of educational program evaluation conducted by the author.

Program evalution was "born" in 1965 when the federal government initiated Compensatory Education (Title I) programs through funds made available by the Elementary and Secondary Education Act. The 1965 legislation required school districts receiving federal funds to evaluate the effectiveness of their programs. Because school personnel often lacked the technical skills for evaluation, they turned to the universities for assistance.

The early years of program evaluation were progressive but chaotic. Diverse theories were introduced; the quality of evaluation research was inconsistent and unstandardized. But there was optimism that this new science would improve programmatic quality. The evalution concept grew and was quickly expanded to a whole array of social programs including job training, community health and mental health, residential treatment, group and individual therapy, certification and licensing designed to protect the public from malpractice, economic assistance, law enforcement, drug rehabilitation, public safety, organized political action, urban planning, and environmental protection (Anderson and Ball, 1978).

Program evaluation is defined by Posavac and Carey (1980) as "a collection of methods, skills, and sensitivities necessary to determine whether a human service is needed and likely to be used, whether it is conducted as planned, and whether the human service actually does help people in need" (p. 6). Although the "bottom line" of evaluation is to determine whether a program is worthwhile, most practicing evaluators subscribe to the *formative-summative distinction* proposed by Scriven (1967). While summative evaluation deals with the overall effectiveness of a program, formative evaluation is concerned with the planning and monitoring of programs. Anderson and Ball (1978) point out that some evaluators even specialize in helping improve programs rather than appraising their impact for policy decisions. These authors proposed six major purposes of program evaluation: (1) to contribute to decisions about program installation, (2) to contribute to decisions about program continuation, expansion, or certification, (3) to contribute to decisions about program modification, (4) to obtain evidence to rally support for a program, (5) to obtain evidence to rally opposition to a program, and (6) to contribute to the understanding of basic psychological, social, and other processes. Not all authorities would agree with the 4th and 5th purposes, but there is often a political component in program evaluation.

Though program evaluation is a type of behavioral research, it differs from other types in a number of ways. Evaluation is decision-oriented rather than knowledge-oriented. Evaluation is atheoretical or, at best, eclectic in the source of its methods. Evaluation provides immediate payoff without necesarily supporting or extending theories of behavior. In addition, it is important not to confuse evaluation with individual assessment. Educational and counseling psychologists have traditionally provided diagnostic information for human service organizations. These are often in the form of intelligence, aptitude, achievement, interest, or personality tests. The process of "evaluating" an individual's need for a service is not program evaluation per se, though such a process may be included in program evaluation.

There are several different models of program evaluation, but it is beyond the scope of this book to describe them in detail. The interested reader may find such information in Morris and Fitz-Gibbon (1982) who summarize six evaluation models before describing the CSE Evaluation Model developed by the Center for the Study of Evaluation at UCLA. This author agrees with Fitz-Gibbon and Morris (1978) who stated that "summative evaluations should whenever possible employ experimental designs when examining programs that are to be judged by their results. The very best summative evaluation has all the characteristics of the best research study" (p. 13).

An Example of a Summative Evaluation

From 1975 to 1980 this author acted as principal investigator in a series of annual evalutions of Project SEED, Special Elementary Education for the Disadvantaged. Not to be confused with the special education programs offered by most public school districts, SEED was a special mathematics program targeted for Title I schools. It received funding from a variety of sources,including state and local governments, the federal government, and donations from the private sector (Whalen, 1976).

The originator of Project SEED believed that abstract, conceptually-oriented mathematics is an appropriate subject matter for disadvantaged children in the upper elementary grades (Johntz, 1971). He reasoned that young children in general possess the ability to do abstract mathematical reasoning and to enter into it with enthusiasm when it is presented by means of a questioning, discovery approach by teachers who understand the subject in depth. He further reasoned that abstract mathematics represented a culture-free subject, unencumbered by past failures--that disadvantaged children were on the same footing as their advantaged peers, who are typically superior in language ability, a culturally-based skill.

Project SEED contracted with school districts to provide expert instructors, mostly university master's degree candidates, to teach the SEED program for one hour per day, four days a week. On the fifth day, the instructor was available for inservice training of teachers. The curriculum was designed to minimize rote learning and to encourage discovery of mathematical rules and principles. Topics included exponentiation, summational and matrix algebra, factorization of integers, and inverse operations. Although the program had been tried at a variety of grade levels, the evaluation concerned its implementation in grades 4, 5, and 6.

During the 1975-76 academic year Project SEED was implememted in 57 classrooms in 17 cities in 10 states from New York to California. The evaluation plan utilized a nonequivalent control group design. Thus, there were an additional 54 control classrooms where pre- and posttesting were conducted in the same schools as the experimental classrooms. Although this was a large-scale evaluation, the same techniques can be applied to much smaller programs.

A problem common to many evaluations is the decision about criteria. What aspects of the program should be observed and measured? What is the program supposed to improve? What are the dependent variables? SEED personnel could name many things they thought their program improved including students' self esteem, teachers' enthusiasm, and parents' satisfaction. In fact, these and other variables were included in the first-year evaluation in a separate affective component.

But the heart of the evaluation was the instructional component. How was the instructional program to be measured? SEED personnel argued for a special test to measure the unique characteristics of their program. However, such a test did not exist and the researchers did not have sufficient time or resources to develop it. Finally, a decision was made to use the Comprehensive Test of Basic Skills (CTBS), a standardized test of computation, concepts, and applications of arithmetic. Program personnel were finally convinced that, although the CTBS did not adequately measure the special features of their program, it did validly measure something of considerable importance to all participants. If it could be shown that SEED significantly improved computational skills, then a strong case for its expansion could be made.

Although the evaluation included nine subtests of the CTBS and comparisons between states and school districts, only the total test score results between SEED and Control groups are summarized here. Figure 12.4 shows the status of the two groups at the time of the pretest. The grade equivalent means show a close correspondence between children in the two groups except at the 5th grade level where SEED students were four months ahead of their Control counterparts. Recall that one of the hazards of the nonequivalent control-group design is a possible difference between groups at the start of an experiment. ANOVA, with class means as data points, was used to test for equality. The results are shown at the bottom of Figure 12.4. Note that only the grade level effect is significant, indicating an expected difference between grade levels in math ability. A treatment-by-grade level interaction would have been evidence that a disparity existed at the fifth grade level. But this was not the case.

Figure 12.5 shows the results of CTBS posttesting and ANCOVA summaries for each grade level. Despite the pre-experimental equivalence of groups, the analysis of covariance, with the pretest as a covariate, was used to produce a more powerful test of the treatment effect and to remove the slight inequality that existed on the pretest. This procedure is analogous to handicapping. A group's score is statistically adjusted upward or downward depending on the direction and magnitude of group difference on the pretest.

At the top of Figure 12.5 you can see the raw and adjusted posttest means for each grade level. Notice at grade five that

FIGURE 12.4
CTBS Total Pretest Means and ANOVA Summary
for
SEED and Control Classes

Treatment Group 1

Grade Level		SEED	CONTROL
	4	3.7	3.8
	5	4.6	4.2
	6	4.9	4.8

NOTE: Scores are in grade equivalent units

ANOVA Summary

Source	df.	SS	MS	F-Ratio
Treatment	1	81.69	81.69	1.29
Grade Level	2	1,947.77	973.89	15.36***
T x G	2	169.36	84.68	1.34
Within	98	6,214.56	63.41	
Total	103	8,413.38		

*** Significant at the.001 level.

FIGURE 12.5
CTBS Total Post-Test Means (raw and adjusted)
and ANCOVA Summaries for
Fourth, Fifth and Sixth Grades

Grade Level	SEED Raw	SEED Adj.	CONTROL Raw	CONTROL Adj.
4	4.7	4.8	4.6	4.5
5	5.6	5.4	4.8	5.0
6	6.0	5.9	5.2	5.3

Fourth Grade ANCOVA Summary

Source	df.	SS	MS	F-Ratio
Adj. Means	1	105.56	105.56	11.39**
Zero Slope	1	2,696.51	2,696.51	291.04***
Error	32	296.48	9.27	
Equal. of Slope	1	31.65	31.65	3.70
Error	31	264.83	8.54	

Fifth Grade ANCOVA Summary

Source	df.	SS	MS	F-Ratio
Adj. Means	1	175.34	175.34	4.50*
Zero Slope	1	1,852.17	1,852.17	47.48***
Error	41	1,599.31	39.01	
Equal. of Slope	1	117.98	117.98	3.19
Error	40	1,481.33	37.03	

Sixth Grade ANCOVA Summary

Source	df.	SS	MS	F-Ratio
Adj. Means	1	232.16	232.16	16.60***
Zero Slope	1	988.82	988.82	70.72***
Error	22	307.62	13.98	
Equal. of Slope	1	6.94	6.94	0.48
Error	21	300.68	14.32	

*Significant at the .05 level
**Significant at the .01 level
***Significant at the .001 level

SEED scores were adjusted downward by two months while Control students got a two-month boost. Nevertheless, there remains a four month disparity in favor of SEED on the adjusted posttest means. A similar disparity was found at the other grade levels--three months and six months at grades four and six, respectively. Because the treatment period was only five months in duration, these differences in favor of the SEED program were considered substantial.

The bottom of Figure 12.5 contains the ANCOVA summaries for the tests at each grade level. In each case the F-test for a difference between adjusted means is significant. Two other tests of significance in this model require explanation. The zero slope test is made to determine if the covariate is significantly related to the dependent variable. The results show that at each grade level the pretest was indeed significantly correlated with the posttest. This F-test serves as a check of the covariate's ability to adjust pretest differences between groups. The equality-of-slopes test indicates whether the correlation between pretest and posttest is the same for both SEED and Control classes. If it is not, then an important assumption underlying ANCOVA is not met, and the method should not be used. All of these test were not significant meaning that the regression line describing the relation between pre- and posttest is essentially the same for both SEED and Control classes. The equality-of-slopes assumption was met.

ANCOVA was used a second time in this evaluation to determine how the SEED curriculum affected students in different ability groups. Would an algebra-based program work equally well on high and low ability students, especially disadvantaged ones? To answer this question, SEED students at each grade level were divided into high, medium, and low ability groups. Then their scores were analyzed using the same ANCOVA model as before, except that individual scores were used as data points. Figure 12.6 shows results for the fifth and sixth grades. Note the considerable disparity in raw posttest means between ability groups. Note also how these differences diminish after adjustment. The F-test for the adjusted means was not significant at either grade level. This meant that students in the three ability groups made similar progress in the SEED program. This situation is depicted graphically for the sixth grade in Figure 12.7. The scores at the bottom of the figure are unadjusted means.

Statistics for Experimental Research

This section will present three methods of analysis using SPSS with data from the happiness questionnaire. The reader is well aware that the happiness data are not experimental. The statistics shown here will work equally well on data from experimental or correlational studies.

The Analysis of Covariance (ANCOVA)

The first example pertains to Item 6: How optimistic or pessimistic are you about the future of the country? Responses to this item ranged from very optimistic to very pessimistic on a 6-point scale. Suppose we hypothesize that these responses are related to an individual's age (Item 49) and political philosphy (Item 51). We are aware from a previous analysis that the degree of one's optimism about the country is related to personal optimism (Item 5). Therefore, we would like to study the effects of age and political stance while controlling for personal optimism. In order to translate this problem into an experimental one, you might think of personal optimism as a pretest and optimism about the country as a posttest. Age and political philosophy might be ability level and gender. Then our research question would involve the extent to which a treatment affected males and females at various ability levels, a two-way factorial design.

In a two-way ANCOVA, the analysis is identical to a two-way ANOVA except for the use of residual scores. It is useful to think of ANCOVA as a two-step process. The first step is to determine the relationship between the covariate and dependent variable. All of the scores in all of the subgroups are lumped together, and a regression equation is formulated. This equation is then used to "predict" an outcome score for each subject based on his score on the covariate. In our example, this would mean predicting a score on Item 6 based on a score on Item 5. Once these predicted scores are computed, they are each then compared with a subject's actual response on the dependent variable. The difference between them, known as a residual score, is then computed. Step Two of the analysis is exactly the same as in analysis of variance except that the residual scores are analyzed. This has the effect of removing the influence of the covariate from consideration. In our example it means we can explore the effects of age and politics without worrying about personal optimism. In effect, everyone is equal on personal optimism, just as they would be equal on a pretest used as a covariate.

As in ANOVA, it is often desirous to collapse some categories of the independent variables to avoid small cell sizes. This is accomplished with RECODE statements. ANCOVA is performed by the same SPSS program which performs analysis of variance. The program is shown below:

```
12.     RECODE
12.005 V49 (1=1)(2=2)(3=3)(4 THRU 6=2)/
```

FIGURE 12.6
ANCOVA Summaries for SEED Students:
Ability Group Comparisons

Fifth Grade

	Raw Mean	Adj. Mean
Group I (low)	4.4	6.1
Group II (med.)	5.9	6.4
Group III (high)	7.8	6.6

ANCOVA Summary

Source	df.	SS	MS	F-Ratio
Adj. Means	2	424	212	2.49
Zero Slope	1	14,028	14,028	164.17***
Error	402	34,350	85	
Equal. of Slope	2	489	244	2.89
Error	400	33,861	84	

Sixth Grade

	Raw Mean	Adj. Mean
Group I (low)	4.9	6.4
Group II (med.)	6.6	6.6
Group III (high)	8.4	7.0

ANCOVA Summary

Source	df.	SS	MS	F-Ratio
Adj. Means	2	338	169	2.11
Zero Slope	1	7,462	7,462	92.95***
Error	266	21,355	80	
Equal. of Slope	2	250	125	1.57
Error	264	21,105	79	

***Significant at the .001 level

FIGURE 12.7
Sixth Grade Growth Patterns by Ability Level
(Over a Five Month Treatment Interval)

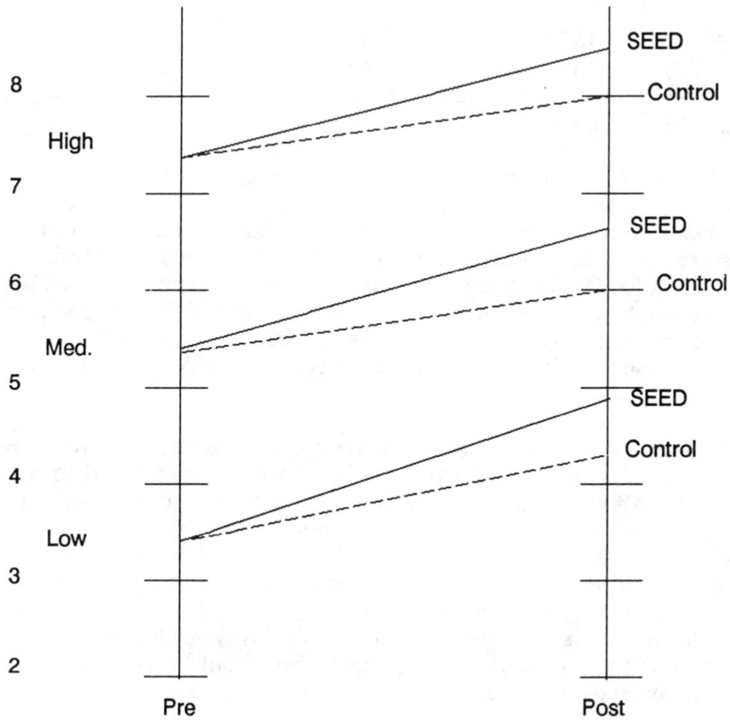

Grade Equivalent Scores

	SEED		CONTROL	
	Pre	Post	Pre	Post
Low Group	3.5	4.9	3.5	4.3
Med. Group	5.5	6.6	5.5	6.0
High Group	7.5	8.4	7.5	7.9

```
12.010 V51 (1 THRU 3=1)(4 THRU 6=2)
15.    ANOVA
15.005 V6 BY V49(1,4), V51(1,2) WITH V5
20.    STATISTICS
20.005 ALL
```

The SPSS-X version is similar:

```
RECODE  V49 (1=1)(2=2)(3=3)(4 THRU 6=2)/
        V51 (1 THRU 3=1)(4 THRU 6=2)
ANOVA   V6 BY V49(1,4), V51(1,2) WITH V5
STATISTICS   ALL
```

The RECODE statements create four age categories: 25 or less, 26-30, 31-35, and over 35. The political variable is collapsed into two categories--liberal and conservative. You should recognize the ANOVA statement from the previous chapter. It has become an ANCOVA statement by adding the keyword WITH followed by V5. Although this example and the one that follows both contain only one covariate, it is possible to use two or more covariates. Their variable names would simply be added after WITH and separated by spaces or commas.

Figure 12.8 shows the ANCOVA summary table. Notice that the covariate, V5, is listed first. Its significant F-ratio indicates that personal optimism is indeed related to optimism about the country. Notice also that V5 accounts for almost as much variance, in sums of squares, as the combined main effects. Both V48, age, and V51, political philosophy, are significantly related to optimism for the country at high levels of significance. The interaction is not significant. An inspection of cell means indicated that subjects over 35 were more optimistic than those in the younger age categories. Conservatives were more optimistic than liberals.

Figure 12.9 shows another part of the printout, the MCA table. Multiple Classification Analysis is the name SPSS gives to the process of adjusting group means. There is a breakdown of the independent variables showing the numbers in each subgroup and their deviations from the grand mean of 3.22. Notice the fairly even distribution in age categories, but the uneven split in politics. There are many more liberals than conservatives in the student sample. Because of this lopsided distribution with uneven cell sizes, it is wise to verify these results through regression analysis. Recall from Chapter 11 that SPSS ANOVA can be run in a regression mode by adding OPTIONS 9 to the program. This was done and the results were the same.

Figure 12.9 shows two sets of deviations. The first is the unadjusted deviation. Notice that subgroup 1 on the age variable, V49, has no deviation from the grand mean of 3.22. Subgroups 2

Figure 12.8
ANCOVA on Happiness Data
Optimism about the Future of the Country

ANOVA TABLE
V6
BY V49
V51
WITH V5

SOURCE OF VARIATION	SUM OF SQUARES	DF	MEAN SQUARE	F	SIGNIF OF F
COVARIATES	49.971	1	49.971	36.474	.001
V5	49.971	1	49.971	36.474	.001
MAIN EFFECTS	53.204	4	13.301	9.709	.001
V49	32.252	3	10.751	7.847	.001
V51	14.543	1	14.543	10.615	.001
2-WAY INTERACTIONS	6.619	3	2.206	1.610	.186
V49 V51	6.619	3	2.206	1.610	.186
EXPLAINED	109.794	8	13.724	10.017	.001
RESIDUAL	531.576	388	1.370		
TOTAL	641.370	396	1.620		

COVARIATE	REGRESSION COEFFICIENT ADJUSTED FOR ALL OTHER COVARIATES
V5	.373

402 CASES WERE PROCESSED
5 CASES (1.2 PCT) WERE MISSING.

FIGURE 12.9
Multiple Classification Analysis
Optimism about the Future of the Country

MCA TABLE
V6
BY V49
V51
WITH V5

GRAND MEAN = 3.22

VARIABLE + CATEGORY		N	UNADJUSTED DEV'N	UNADJUSTED BETA	ADJUSTED FOR INDEPENDENTS DEV'N	ADJUSTED FOR INDEPENDENTS BETA	ADJUSTED FOR INDEPENDENTS + COVARIATES DEV'N	ADJUSTED FOR INDEPENDENTS + COVARIATES BETA
V49								
	1	86	.00				.03	
	2	105	.20				.17	
	3	84	.37				.34	
	4	122	-.43				-.40	
				.24				.23
V51								
	1	313	.13				.10	
	2	84	-.48				-.37	
				.20				.15

MULTIPLE R SQUARED .161
MULTIPLE R .401

CPU TIME REQUIRED 1.053 SECONDS

TOTAL CPU TIME USED 6.555 SECONDS
SPSS/ONLINE AUTO-MODE

and 3 are somewhat above the mean, while subgroup 4, the older subjects, are considerably below the mean. By comparing their deviation of -.43 with the grand mean of 3.22, we can derive their raw mean of 2.79. This translates into a "slightly optimistic" response concerning the future of the country. The other three age groups were less optimistic, although, interestingly, the youngest group was more optimistic than those in the age range of 26 to 35. There is a curvilinear relationship between age and optimism for the country.

The second set of deviations is shown on the right side of Figure 12.9. These are the subgroup means after the effects of the covariate and other independent variables have been removed from them. Notice the slight leveling effect in these means, as compared to the unadjusted deviations. There is less difference among groups. The other statistics in this table are ETA, BETA and the MULTIPLE R. ETA is comparable to E, the correlation ratio. It indicates the degree of correlation between independent and dependent variables. For instance, V49, age, has a correlation of .24 with V6. You may recall from Chapter 10 that beta weights are standardized regression coefficients. Thus, the BETA statistic also provides an estimate of correlation. Note that after adjustment, the correlation between politics and optimism for the country drops from .20 (ETA) to .15 (BETA). The MULTIPLE R indicates the overall correlation of all variables with V6. When this statistic is squared, it indicates the proportion of variance accounted for in the dependent variable. In this case, we have accounted for 16.1%.

It should be noted here that some statisticians prefer multiple regression to the analysis of covariance. The difference between the two is that in multiple regression there is no need to collapse or recode the independent variables. This makes for a more precise analysis because more information is contained in the scores. However, the SPSS package does not contain a straightforward procedure for doing this. The slight loss in precision is more than offset by the ease of conducting ANCOVA.

Because ANCOVA is such a useful analysis tool, a second example is provided here. This problem is a three-way factorial model with one covariate. We will analyze Item 2: Does your level of happiness change or remain fairly constant? This might be termed a moodiness factor. Responses range from "it remains stable" to "it changes very often." One might hypothesize that the stability of one's happiness might fluctuate as a function of the importance one attaches to the happiness of one's spouse (Item 19), satisfaction with one's sex life (Item 41), and frequency of getting drunk or "loaded" (Item 39). Furthermore, if one believes that women are moodier than men, a common societal stereotype, then Item 48, gender, should be a useful covariate.

The SPSS program for this analysis is similar to the one above with the simple addition of a third independent variable in the ANOVA specifiction. The independent variables were recoded into two groups to produce a relatively balanced 2-by-2-by-2 design.

Figure 12.10 shows the ANCOVA summary. Note that the covariate has an F-ratio close to zero. Gender is completely unrelated to moodiness in this sample of 400 students. While this is a finding of considerable interest, it means that the covariate is virtually useless in the analysis. This does not negate the analysis; it simply turns it into a more conventional three-way ANOVA. Two of the main effects are significant. One's use of alcohol or drugs and satisfaction with one's sex life are both significantly related to fluctations in happiness. Less moodiness was reported by students who use drugs and alcohol infrequently and among students who have more satisfying sex lives.

Repeated Measures ANOVA

When conducting a repeated measures analysis with only one group of subjects, the simplest analysis procedure is to use an SPSS program designed to calculate reliability coefficients for measurement scales. Consider an attitude instrument of, say, 25 items all scored on a 5-point Likert scale of agreement. After the scale is given to a group of subjects, a question arises as to how reliably their attitudes were measured. A statistic used for this purpose is the alpha coefficient which is computed by using analysis of variance. With the SPSS RELIABILITY program we can make use of the ANOVA portion to analyze simple time series data.

Turn to Appendix A and review items 7 to 22 on the happiness questionnaire. Notice that these items are measured on a common scale of importance. We could analyze all of them, but let's simplify the exercise by selecting three items--8, 12, and 17. These deal with the perceived importance of being a parent, one's job or primary activity, and one's sex life. The question is: do the sampled subjects consider these three activities of equal importance? Are there differences among the three item means? In order to place the analysis in experimental terms, you might think of Item 8 as a pre-treatment variable on politeness among rapid transit riders. On the day prior to a poster campaign on politeness, observations are made of the number of polite interactions between riders at several stations. Three days after the poster blitz a second observation is made. A month later, a week after the posters have been taken down, a final measurement is made. Thus, we have three measures of politeness behavior (items 8, 12, and 17). Are they of equal magnitude?

The SPSS and SPSS-X programs for this analysis are shown below:

Figure 12.10
ANCOVA on Happiness Data
Constancy of Happiness

ANOVA TABLE

	V2
BY	V19
	V39
	V41
WITH	V48

SOURCE OF VARIATION	SUM OF SQUARES	DF	MEAN SQUARE	F	SIGNIF OF F
COVARIATES	.043	1	.043	.033	.855
V48	.043	1	.043	.033	.855
MAIN EFFECTS	32.475	3	10.825	8.396	.001
V19	1.711	1	1.711	1.327	.250
V39	19.768	1	19.768	15.333	.001
V41	12.130	1	12.130	9.409	.002
2-WAY INTERACTIONS	4.625	3	1.542	1.196	.311
V19 V39	4.258	1	4.258	3.303	.070
V19 V41	.185	1	.185	.143	.705
V39 V41	.134	1	.134	.104	.747
3-WAY INTERACTIONS	.230	1	.230	.179	.673
V19 V39 V41	.230	1	.230	.179	.673
EXPLAINED	37.373	8	4.672	3.624	.001
RESIDUAL	491.201	381	1.289		
TOTAL	528.574	389	1.359		

COVARIATE	REGRESSION COEFFICIENT ADJUSTED FOR ALL OTHER COVARIATES
V48	-.024

402 CASES WERE PROCESSED
12 CASES (3.0 PCT) WERE MISSING.

```
20.    RELIABILITY
20.005 VARIABLES=V8, V12, V17/
20.010 SCALE(ITEMS)=V8, V12, V17
25     STATISTICS
25.005 1, 3, 5, 10
```

```
RELIABILITY   VARIABLES=V8, V12, V17/
              SCALE(ITEMS)=V8, V12, V17
STATISTICS    1, 3, 5, 10
```

Table 12.1 below shows means, SD's and an ANOVA summary for this analysis. It appears that Item 12, with a mean of 5.37, is different from items 8 and 17, with means of 4.63 and 4.66, respectively. Indeed, the between-measures F-ratio of 60.65 verifies that Item 12, job or primary activity, was rated as significantly more important to subjects' happiness than the other two items. At the time they were surveyed, these subjects rated their job or primary activity as more important to their happiness than either their sex life or being a parent. In terms of the hypothetical politeness experiment, these data would have provided evidence for a short-term poster effect, with commuters returning rapidly to pre-treatment politeness levels when the poster campaign was ended.

- -

TABLE 12.1
Single Group Repeated Measures Analysis
Summary Statistics and ANOVA Table

Item No.	Mean	SD	Cases
V8	4.630	1.462	400
V12	5.372	.775	400
V17	4.660	1.001	400

ANOVA Summary Table

Source of Variation	SS	DF	MS	F	P
Between People	563.146	399	1.411		
Within People	1070.667	800	1.338		
Between Measures	141.315	2	70.657	60.665	.000
Residual	929.352	798	1.165		
Total	1633.812	1199	1.363		

- -

The Two-Group Repeated Measures ANOVA

If we add a between-subjects, or between-people source of variance, as it is termed in the summary table above, we have a two-group repeated measures design. We shall add gender, V48, to the analysis, and then determine whether males and females are in agreement on their ratings of the three questionnaire items. That is, do males and females feel the same about the importance of parenting, job, and sex life to their overall happiness?

The authors of SPSS chose to incorporate a mixed-model repeated measures capability in their program for multiple analysis of variance (MANOVA). A mixed model is one which has at least one between-subjects factor, gender in this case, and at least one within-subjects factor, the repeated item measurement in this example. The SPSS and SPSS-X programs for this analysis are shown below:

```
MANOVA
V8, V12, V17 BY V48(1,2)/
WSFACTORS=ITEM(3)/
WSDESIGN=MWITHIN ITEM(1) MWITHIN ITEM(2)
MWITHIN ITEM(3)/
ANALYSIS(REPEATED)/
DESIGN=V48/
PRINT=CELLINFO(MEANS)/
```

```
MANOVA   V8, V12, V17 BY V48(1,2)
   /WSFACTORS=ITEM(3)
   /WSDESIGN=MWITHIN ITEM(1) MWITHIN ITEM(2) MWITHIN ITEM(3)
   /ANALYSIS(REPEATED)
   /DESIGN=V48
   /PRINT=CELLINFO(MEANS)
```

The first line of this program is similar to an ANOVA specification. WSFACTORS specifies the within-subjects source of variance, designated ITEM here. WSDESIGN specifies the within-subjects design. MWITHIN ITEM shows that we want a comparison between the female (1) and male (2) means for each measurement. The ANALYSIS is a type of repeated measures model. DESIGN=V48 specifies the between-subjects factor, gender. Finally, we request that cell information including means and SD's be printed out for the two subgroups.

Figure 12.11 shows the first part of the output for this program, produced by the optional PRINT specification. It appears from the gender breakdown that some differences between the sexes may be significant. Notice the one-half point difference on V8, the importance of parenting. The results of significance tests of the mean differences are shown in Figure 12.12. A separate ANOVA is calculated for each item mean difference. At the top of Figure 12.12 the critical test of a gender difference on Item 8 is given by the F-test for V48 AND MWITHIN ITEM. The F-ratio of 9.591 and its associated significance level of .002 indicate that females rated parenting as significantly more important to their happiness than males. Differences on the other two items were not

FIGURE 12.11
Mixed Model ANOVA
Cell Information

MANOVA

END OF FILE ON FILE HAPPY
AFTER READING 402 CASES FROM SUBFILE NONAME

ANALYSIS OF VARIANCE

CELL MEANS AND STANDARD DEVIATIONS

VARIABLE V8

FACTOR	CODE	MEAN	STD. DEV.	N
V48	1	4.768	1.411	297
V48	2	4.250	1.546	100
FOR ENTIRE SAMPLE		4.637	1.461	397

VARIABLE V12

FACTOR	CODE	MEAN	STD. DEV.	N
V48	1	5.407	.783	297
V48	2	5.270	.750	100
FOR ENTIRE SAMPLE		5.373	.777	397

VARIABLE V17

FACTOR	CODE	MEAN	STD. DEV.	N
V48	1	4.609	1.047	297
V48	2	4.800	.853	100
FOR ENTIRE SAMPLE		4.657	1.004	397

397 CASES ACCEPTED
0 CASES REJECTED BECAUSE OF OUT-OF-RANGE FACTOR VALUES
5 CASES REJECTED BECAUSE OF MISSING DATA
2 NON-EMPTY CELLS

FIGURE 12.12
Mixed Model ANOVA
Summary Tables

TESTS OF SIGNIFICANCE FOR V8 USING SEQUENTIAL SUMS OF SQUARES

SOURCE OF VARIATION	SUM OF SQUARES	DF	MEAN SQUARE	F	SIG OF F
WITHIN CELLS	825.720	395	2.090		
MWITHIN ITEM(1)	8537.232	1	8537.232	4083.960	0
V48 AND MWITHIN ITEM(1)	20.049	1	20.049	9.591	.00210
(MODEL)	8557.280	2	4278.640	2046.776	0
(TOTAL)	9383.000	397	23.635		

TESTS OF SIGNIFICANCE FOR V12 USING SEQUENTIAL SUMS OF SQUARES

SOURCE OF VARIATION	SUM OF SQUARES	DF	MEAN SQUARE	F	SIG OF F
WITHIN CELLS	237.414	395	.601		
MWITHIN ITEM(2)	11460.174	1	11460.174	19067.007	0
V48 AND MWITHIN ITEM(2)	1.412	1	1.412	2.350	.12608
(MODEL)	11461.586	2	5730.793	9534.678	0
(TOTAL)	11699.000	397	29.469		

TESTS OF SIGNIFICANCE FOR V17 USING SEQUENTIAL SUMS OF SQUARES

SOURCE OF VARIATION	SUM OF SQUARES	DF	MEAN SQUARE	F	SIG OF F
WITHIN CELLS	396.694	395	1.004		
MWITHIN ITEM(3)	8611.589	1	8611.589	8574.824	0
V48 AND MWITHIN ITEM(3)	2.717	1	2.717	2.705	.10081
(MODEL)	8614.306	2	4307.153	4288.765	0
(TOTAL)	9011.000	397	22.698		

sufficient to reject the null hypothesis. Males and females had similar views concerning the importance of their jobs and sex lives to their overall happiness.

Recent Developments in Data Analysis

It is appropriate to conclude this text by citing a few techniques which have entered the research literature in relatively recent years. The student who masters the methods presented thus far in the book will have taken a long stride toward research competence. But new techniques are constantly being developed. Here are three of them:

Meta-Analysis. Glass (1977) developed a method of integrating research findings quantitatively which he terms meta-analysis. Meta-analysis refers to the analysis of analyses, the statistical analysis of a large collection of results from individual studies involving similar variables. For example, Glass and his colleague (Smith and Glass, 1977), in one of the first published meta-analyses, summarized over 400 studies on the effectiveness of psychotherapy. They concluded that psychotherpy is effective. On the average, a person who receives psychotherapy is better off than 75% of those who do not receive treatment. The researchers did not find significant differences between various types of therapy.

Two years later these same researchers (Glass & Smith, 1979) turned their attention to the relationship between class size and achievement in public education. They concluded that a significant relationship existed in favor of smaller class sizes. A pupil who would perform at the 50th percentile in a class of 40 would perform at the 65th percentile in a class of ten. Since the pioneering studies of Glass and Smith, many meta-analyses have been done by other researchers. Surprisingly, the methodology is not difficult and should be considered for use by graduate students. An important outgrowth of meta-analysis is that literature reviews are now seen as important in their own right and not simply preliminary to an individual investigation.

Quantitative Synthesis of Intra-Subject Research. Building on the work of Glass and Smith, Center and his colleagues (Center, Skiba & Casey, 1985) have developed a promising method for analyzing time series data from single-subject studies. They call their method quantitative synthesis because, like meta-analysis, it involves the pooling of results from single-case or n-of-one studies of the type common in special education. However, their method could be used as well on large-sample time series data. The specific regression model, which they term a "piecewise" regression technique, has the advantage of testing for both a slope and level change following a treatment. While ANOVA is sufficient to test for changes in level (mean differences), it is not able to adequately test for slope changes of the type shown in Figure 12.3c and e.

Using their piecewise regression technique, Skiba, Casey, and Center (1986) studied the effects of nonaversive behavior modification procedures in the treatment of classroom behavior problems. Although few main effect differences were found between types of treatment, the researchers discovered some interesting interactions which would probably have gone unnoticed in the type of visual analysis previously used on such data. In the words of the authors:

> Despite the failure to find main-effect differences, interaction effects were large and robust. Social, token, and activity reinforcement were clearly superior to simple feedback in group situations, but were somewhat less effective than feedback when given in individual contigency arrangements....By taking both slope and level into account, the (piecewise regression) model uses considerably more data than simple comparisons of means, and probably results in more accurate estimates of effects when linear trends are present in either the baseline or treatment phase....The methodology presented herein offers benefits similar to between-group meta-analysis: Using quantitative rather than qualitative bases for judgment of treatment effectiveness may eliminate some of the subjective biases that can characterize the narrative review (Skiba, et al., 1986, pp. 475-78).

Path Analysis. Although path analysis is not a new technique, it has become quite prominent in non-experimental research in recent years because of the availability of high-speed computers and multiple regression programs. According to Kerlinger (1973), path analysis is "a method for studying the direct and indirect effects of variables taken as causes of variables taken as effects" (p. 305). Path analysis is an attempt to bring correlational research a bit closer to experimental research through the testing of causal models formulated by the researcher. It is a method which promotes more valid theory-testing than conventional correlational procedures.

Path analysis is based on the use of beta weights from multiple regression. These weights, called path coefficients, indicate the unique effect of a presumed causal variable. A path coefficient represents the effect of an independent variable after all other independent variables have been controlled or equalized. Let us view two path models and see how the researchers tested them.

FIGURE 12.13
Path Diagrams*

KEITH AND PAGE

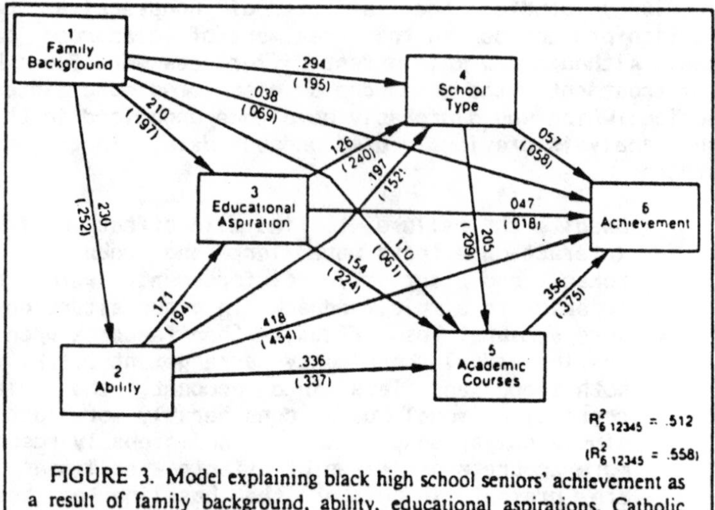

FIGURE 3. Model explaining black high school seniors' achievement as a result of family background, ability, educational aspirations, Catholic schooling, and academic coursework. Paths for Hispanic seniors are shown in parentheses.

*reprinted by permission of the publisher, AERA

TAYLOR DELAIN, PEARSON, AND ANDERSON

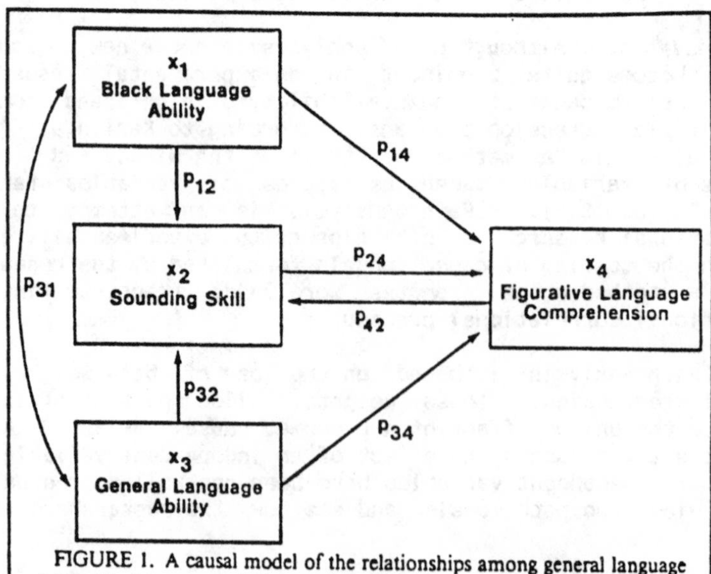

FIGURE 1. A causal model of the relationships among general language ability, black language ability, sounding skill, and figurative language comprehension.

Figure 12.13 (top) shows a model by Keith and Page (1985) to test the effect of parochial vs. public education, a controversial research topic (cf. Page & Keith, 1981; and Coleman, 1981). Using the "High School and Beyond" data set, Keith and Page constructed a theoretical model of academic achievement among minority students who attended either public or private high schools. The path model is an attempt to ascertain the effect of Catholic vs. public schooling while taking into account family background, ability, and educational aspirations of students, as well as the type of coursework they experienced during high school. This model, unlike most, has two sets of path coefficients. The coefficients above the paths are for black high school seniors; those in parentheses below the paths are for Hispanic students. The path arrows indicate the presumed direction of cause and effect. The R squared statistics indicate the proportion of variance accounted for by each model--.512 for black students and .558 for Hispanics.

In drawing conclusions about the path model for black students, the researchers stated the following:

> As can be seen from the very strong path from Academic Courses to Achievement (p=.356), the amount of such coursework seems to have a powerful effect on achievement, even when achievement is measured with only basic reading and math tests. In fact, the only direct influence stronger than that from Academic Courses was from Ability (p=.418). Furthermore, Academic Courses not only had a powerful direct effect on Achievement, but its inclusion in the model (along with Educational Aspirations) substantially reduced the direct effect of School Type from a path of .145 (in a previous model) to a path of .057 (in the present one). Such results, along with the strong path from School Type to Academic Courses (p=.205), suggests that the small but meaningful Catholic School effect found for black seniors is at least in part due to the more academic coursework they take in Catholic Schools (Keith and Page, 1985, p. 344).

The bottom of Figure 12.13 shows another causal model by Taylor Delain, Pearson, and Anderson (1985) representing their theory of the interrelation of language skills for a population of black seventh graders in Tennessee and Illinois. Specifically, they hypothesized that figurative language ability among black children is a product of three variables--general language ability, black language ability, and a third variable they termed sounding skill. "Sounding" is a kind of nonliteral language prevalent among many black children, especially males. It is sometimes called "playing the dozens," or "cracking," or "ranking." The authors described sounding in this way:

> Sounds usually make reference to close relatives, especially the mother. Derogatory allusions are made to the physical attributes, sexual conduct, or other features of that relative. For example, "Your momma so skinny she can dance between raindrops without getting wet," or, "Your sister's like railroad track--been laid coast to coast" (Taylor Delain, et al, 1985, p. 159).

The researchers hypothesized that this kind of language behavior, which is normal and inoffensive among black children, trains them in the use and understanding of metaphorical language, an important component of figurative language comprehension. Without going into the details of measurement and testing procedures, the researchers' strategy was to compute path coefficients to fit their causal model for two separate groups of children--the black seventh graders previously described and a control group of simlilar white children. They then compared the path coefficients and discovered that their model fit the black student data quite well, but it was not a good fit for the white children. In their words:

> Evidence obtained from this study indicates that, for white subjects, understanding of figurative language is accounted for by general verbal ability. For black subjects, on the other hand, the evidence indicates that understanding of figurative language is explained by a combination of skills in general verbal ability, sounding, and black language....
>
> Therefore, it appears that teachers need to appreciate differences in communication strategies in order to foster an environment in the classroom that capitalizes on the strengths of all children. Since this study suggests that skills acquired "in the streets," so to speak, do transfer to school settings, teachers need to develop a respect for, rather than a bias against, the use of such language (Taylor Delain et al., 1985, p. 171).

Concluding Remarks

We have come a long way down the road of research methodology. What is the meaning of our trip? Will the application of these procedures alter human history?

The process of change works slowly. Human nature is resistant to modification. There is some evidence, however, that improvements in method eventually lead to improvements in the human condition. At the beginning of this book I conceded that perhaps behavioral research will never have the solidarity of the physical sciences. A recent investigation questions this thinking. Using a type of meta-analysis common to the physical and behavioral sciences, Hedges (1987) discovered that social science is as empirically cumulative as physics. There is as much consistency in human experimentation as in partical physics. This is a new concept. It was created by the application of a new method of comparison. If this concept is verified, it may permanently alter our view of behavioral research.

We seek truth. Scientific research is a means to that end. It is not a perfect tool, but no one has yet produced a better one. As scientists, our role is a simple one, aptly described by the Bard himself: "To hold, as 'twere, the mirror up to nature; to show virtue her own feature, scorn her own image...."

In conclusion, I offer another quotation which captures the spirit of this book and pays tribute to the students who unknowingly contributed to its creation:

> A professor can never better distinguish himself in his work than by encouraging a clever pupil, for the true discoverers are among them, as comets amongst the stars (Carl Linnaeus, 1707-1778).

APPENDIX A

Happiness Questionnaire

WHAT MAKES YOU HAPPY?

1. In general, how happy or unhappy have you been over the last six months?
   1. Very happy.
   2. Moderately happy.
   3. Slightly happy.
   4. Slightly unhappy.
   5. Moderately unhappy.
   6. Very unhappy.

2. Does your level of happiness change or remain fairly constant?
   1. It remains stable.
   2. It rarely changes.
   3. It changes infrequently.
   4. It sometimes changes.
   5. It changes often.
   6. It changes very often.

3. If you suddenly inherited large fortune, would you continue in your present work (including student)?
   1. Definitely yes.
   2. Probably yes.
   3. Perhaps yes.
   4. Perhaps not.
   5. Probably not.
   6. Definitely not.

4. How confident are you that your guiding values are right for you and will last?
   1. Very confident.
   2. Considerably confident.
   3. Somewhat confident.
   4. Not very confident.
   5. I'm questioning my values constantly.
   6. I don't really have any constant guiding principles.

5. How optimistic or pessimistic about your life would you say you are?
   1. Very optimistic.
   2. Moderately optimistic.
   3. Slightly optimistic.
   4. Slightly pessimistic.
   5. Moderately pessimistic.
   6. Very pessimistic

6. How optimistic or pessimistic are you about the future of the country?
   1. Very optimistic.
   2. Moderately optimistic.
   3. Slightly optimistic.
   4. Slightly pessimistic.
   5. Moderately pessimistic.
   6. Very pessimistic.

For each of the following issues, indicate how important it is to your own happiness
Use the following scale for your answers
   1. Strongly agree.
   2. Moderately agree.
   3. Slighltly agree.
   4. Slightly disagree.
   5. Moderately disagree.
   6. Strongly disagree.

7.	Recognition, success.	1	2	3	4	5	6
8.	Children and being a parent.	1	2	3	4	5	6
9.	Your financial situation.	1	2	3	4	5	6
10.	Your health and physical condition.	1	2	3	4	5	6
11.	Your house, apartment, or living quarters.	1	2	3	4	5	6
12.	Your job or primary activity.	1	2	3	4	5	6
13.	Your personal growth and development.	1	2	3	4	5	6
14.	Exercise and physical recreation.	1	2	3	4	5	6
15.	Religion.	1	2	3	4	5	6
16.	Being in love.	1	2	3	4	5	6
17.	Your sex life.	1	2	3	4	5	6
18.	Marriage or long love relationship.	1	2	3	4	5	6
19.	The happiness of your spouse of partner.	1	2	3	4	5	6
20.	Friends and social life.	1	2	3	4	5	6
21.	Your body and physical attractiveness.	1	2	3	4	5	6
22.	The city or town in which you live.	1	2	3	4	5	6

23. During most of your childhood (to age 17), with whom did you live?
   1. Both natural or adoptive parents.
   2. One natural or adoptive parent and one step parent.
   3. One natural or adoptive parent.
   4. Relatives.
   5. Foster parents.
   6. Institution(s).

24. How would you describe your parents' relationship while they were together?
   1. Very loving.
   3. Slightly hostile.
   4. Slightly hostile.
   5. Moderately hostile.
   6. Very hostile.

25. If your parents were divorced or separated permanently, how old were you when this event occurred?
   1. Three years old or younger.
   2. Four to six.
   3. Seven to 10.
   4. Eleven to 13.
   5. Fourteen to 17.
   6. Over 17 or they did not separate.

26. List you place in family's birth order
   1. First born.
   2. Second born.
   3. Third born.
   4. Fourth born.
   5. Fifth born.
   6. Sixth or later born.

27. When you were growing up, was your family?
   1. Lower class--poverty
   2. Lower class--working
   3. Lower middle class.
   4. Middle class.
   5. Upper middle class.
   6. Upper class.

28. How many times before the age of 18 did you move from one community to another?
1. Never.
2. Once.
3. Twice.
4. Three times.
5. Four times.
6. Five or more times.

29. When you were a child, what were your parents' attitudes toward sex.
1. Very conservative.
2. Moderately conservative.
3. Slightly conservative.
4. Slightly liberal.
5. Moderately liberal.
6. Very liberal.

30. How would you describe your mother's relationship with you?
1. Very supportive.
2. Moderately supportive.
3. Slightly supportive.
4. Slightly rejecting.
5. Moderately rejecting.
6. Very rejecting.

31. How would you describe your father's relationship with you?
1. Very supportive.
2. Moderately supportive.
3. Slightly supportive.
4. Slightly rejecting.
5. Moderately rejecting.
6. Very rejecting.

32. How would you describe your mother's expression of her emotions?
1. Very open.
2. Moderately open.
3. Slightly open.
4. Slightly closed.
5. Moderately closed.
6. Very closed.

33. How would you describe your father's expression of his emotions?
    1. Very open.
    2. Moderately open.
    3. Slightly open.
    4. Slightly closed.
    5. Moderately closed.
    6. Very closed.

34. How happy were you as a child (age one to 12)?
    1. Very happy.
    2. Moderately happy.
    3. Slightly happy.
    4. Slightly unhappy.
    5. Moderately unhappy.
    6. Very unhappy

35. How would you compare your physical attractiveness when you were an adolescent (13-18) with others of your age and sex.
    1. Much more attractive.
    2. Considerably more attractive.
    3. Slightly more attractive.
    4. About the same.
    5. Somewhat less attractive.
    6. Considerably to much less attractive.

36. How happy were you as an adolescent?
    1. Very happy.
    2. Moderately happy.
    3. Slightly happy.
    4. Slightly unhappy.
    5. Moderately unhappy.
    6. Very unhappy.

37. Did you begin to date earlier or later that your same sex schoolmates.
    1. Much earlier.
    2. Somewhat earlier.
    3. About the same time.
    4. Somewhat later.
    5. Much later.
    6. Did not date during adolescence.

38. During your high school years, how did you feel when you were with members of the opposite sex?
   1. Very relaxed and confident.
   2. Moderately relaxed and confident.
   3. Slightly relaxed and confident.
   4. Slightly awkward and unsure.
   5. Moderately awkward and unsure.
   6. Very anxious and unsure.

39. How often do you get drunk and/or "loaded"?
   1. Never.
   2. Rarely.
   3. Once or twice a month.
   4. Once a week or so.
   5. Several times a week.
   6. Every day.

40. How many cigarettes do you smoke in a typical day?
   1. None.
   2. A few.
   3. About half a pack.
   4. A pack or so.
   5. A pack and a half.
   6. Two pack or more.

41. In general, how satisfied are you with your sex life (or lack thereof)?
   1. Very satisfied.
   2. Moderately satisfied.
   3. Slightly satisfied.
   4. Slightly dissatisfied.
   5. Moderately dissatisfied.
   6. Very dissatisfied.

42. With how many partners have you had sexual intercourse?
   1. None.
   2. One.
   3. Two to five.
   4. Six to ten.
   5. Eleven to 20.
   6. More than 20.

43. During the last six months, how often have you had sexual intercourse?
   1. Daily or more often.
   2. Several times a week.
   3. Once or twice a week.
   4. Once or twice a month.
   5. Rarely.
   6. Not at all.

44. How many sexual partners do you think most people of your age and sex have had?
   1. None.
   2. One.
   3. Two to five.
   4. Six to ten.
   5. Eleven to 20.
   6. More than 20.

45. How satisfied do you think most people of your age and sex with their sex lives?
   1. Very satisfied.
   2. Moderately satisfied.
   3. Slightly satisfied.
   4. Slightly dissatisfied.
   5. Moderately dissatisfied.
   6. Very dissatisfied.

46. Which statement best characterizes your belief in God or a supreme being?
   1. I do not believe in the existence of God or a supreme being.
   2. I am not sure whether God or a supreme being exists.
   3. I believe in an impersonal supreme being or spiritual force which does not direct individual lives.
   4. In believe in a personal God who has little or no direct involvement in individual lives.
   5. I believe in a personal God who directs and controls some of my life.
   6. I believe in a personal God who directs and controls most of my life.

47. Do you believe in life after death?
   1. No, I do not believe in any kind of life after this one.
   2. I am unsure.
   3. Yes, I believe there must be something after death.
   4. Yes, I have definite beliefs about life after death.

48. What is your sex?
   1. Female.
   2. Male.

49. What is your age?
    1. 25 or less.
    2. 26 - 30.
    3. 31 - 35.
    4. 36 - 40.
    5. 41 - 45.
    6. Over 45.

50. What is your current living status?
    1. With your husband or wife.
    2. Cohabiting on a long term basis.
    3. Cohabiting on a "temporary" basis.
    4. With one or more persons with whom you have a personal but "non-love" relationship(s).
    5. With one or more persons with whom you have a relatively impersonal relationship(s).
    6. Alone.

51. What is your stance on most political issues?
    1. Radical left.
    2. Very liberal.
    3. Somewhat liberal.
    4. Somewhat conservative.
    5. Very conservative.
    6. Radical right.

Using the following categories, answer questions 52--54.
    1. Rural: up to 10,000 population (not a residential suburb unless population of area served is under 200,00).
    2. Town: 10,000 to 40,000 (not a residential suburb unless population of area served is under 200,000).
    3. Small city: 40,000 to 200,000 (not a residential suburb).
    4. Residential suburb of a city or area with a population over 200,000.
    5. City: 200,00 to 1,000,000.
    6. Large city or metropolis: over 1,000,000.

52.	Where did you live during most of your childhood?	1	2	3	4	5	6
53.	Where do you live now?	1	2	3	4	5	6
54.	If you could live anywhere you wished, where would that be?	1	2	3	4	5	6

55. What was the religious atmosphere in your childhood home?
    1. Religion was very important.
    2. Religion was fairly important.
    3. Religion was slightly important.
    4. There was an atmosphere of neutrality.
    5. One of agnosticism.
    6. One of atheism.

56. What is your (or your family's) total personal income before taxes?
    1. under $4,000.
    2. $4,000 to $6,999.
    3. $7,000 to $10,999.
    4. $11,000 to $15,999.
    5. $16,000 to $25,000.
    6. Over $25,000.

57. How attractive are you compared with others of your age & sex?
    1. Much more attractive.
    2. Considerably more attractive.
    3. Slightly more attractive.
    4. About the same.
    5. Somewhat less attractive.
    6. Considerably too much less attractive.

58. In your opinion how much control do you have over the good or pleasant things that happen to you?
    1. Almost total control.
    2. Mostly under my control.
    3. About half the time I can control the good things.
    4. Somewhat under my control.
    5. slightly under my control.
    6. Almost no control.

59. In your opinion how much control do you have over the bad or unpleasant things in your life?
    1. Almost total control.
    2. Mostly under my control.
    3. About half the time I can control the bad things.
    4. Somewhat under my control.
    5. Slightly under my control.
    6. Almost no control.

To what extent do you agree of disagree with statements 59-66.
Use the following scale for your answers.

1. Strongly agree.
2. Moderately agree.
3. Slightly agree.
4. Slightly disagree.
5. Moderately disagree.
6. Strongly disagree.

60.	I like most of the people I meet.	1	2	3	4	5	6
61.	I feel that my life has meaning and direction.	1	2	3	4	5	6
62.	Barnum was right when he said there's a sucker born every minute.	1	2	3	4	5	6
63.	When I notice things have been going well for me, I get the feelingit just can't last.	1	2	3	4	5	6
64.	I often feel like a phony or a fraud.	1	2	3	4	5	6
65.	When I notice things have been going badly for me, I know the situation won't last for long.	1	2	3	4	5	6
66.	The best way to handle people is to tell them what they want to hear.	1	2	3	4	5	6

67. How do you feel about the pace of your life?
    1. Quite hurried.
    2. Somewhat hurried.
    3. Slightly hurried.
    4. It's a little slow.
    5. It's moderately slow.
    6. It's quite sedate.

68. How satisfied are you with the pace of your life?
    1. Very satisfied.
    2. Moderately satisfied.
    3. Slightly satisfied.
    4. Slightly dissatisfied.
    5. Moderately dissatisfied.
    6. Very dissatisfied.

Use the following answer codes for questions 69-74. Times are hours per day.

1. Less than one hour.
2. One to two hours.
3. Over two but less than four hours.
4. Four through seven hours.
5. Over seven hours but less than nine hours.
6. Over nine hours.

69. Time with your spouse or partner, or, if you have no spouse or partner, your closest friend.	1	2	3	4	5	6
70. Time doing leisure activities, sports, hobbies.	1	2	3	4	5	6
71. Sleeping.	1	2	3	4	5	6
72. Time with friends (if you used closest friend for 69, exclude that individual).	1	2	3	4	5	6
73. Commuting to and from work (round trip).	1	2	3	4	5	6
74. Watching television.	1	2	3	4	5	6

75. How satisfied are you with this allotment of your time?
    1. Very satisfied.
    2. Moderately satisfied.
    3. Slightly satisfied.
    4. Slightly dissatisfied.
    5. Moderately dissatisfied.
    6. Very dissatisfied.

76. If you could change lives with someone, would you do so?
    1. Definitely not.
    2. Probably not.
    3. Perhaps.
    4. Probably yes.
    5. Definitely yes.

77. I have intense experiences of happiness or bliss where my personal boundaries seem to disappear and I become one with humankind and/or nature.
    1. Very often.
    2. Often.
    3. Sometimes.
    4. Occasionally.
    5. Rarely.
    6. Never.

78. I like to withdraw from others for a short while.
    1. Very often.
    2. Often.
    3. Sometimes
    4. Occasionally.
    5. Rarely.
    6. Never.

79. I like to make my decisions spontaneously.
    1. Very often.
    2. Often.
    3. Sometimes.
    4. Occasionally.
    5. Rarely.
    6. Never.

80. I am creative an inventive in at least some areas of my life.
    1. Very often.
    2. Often.
    3. Sometimes.
    4. Occasionally
    5. Rarely.
    6. Never.

APPENDIX B

Graduate Women's Questionnaire

APPENDIX B

GRADUATE WOMEN'S QUESTIONNAIRE

Directions: Please circle the number that best reflects your true feeling.

1. Rate each of the following factors according to its importance to you in deciding to enter graduate school.

		Degree of Importance Not				Very
a.	Desire for personal fulfillment.	1	2	3	4	5
b.	Prepare for a challenging career.	1	2	3	4	5
c.	Enhance feeling of self-worth.	1	2	3	4	5
d.	Raise economic level of self or family.	1	2	3	4	5
e.	Alleviate boredom.	1	2	3	4	5
f.	Other ________________	1	2	3	4	5

2. Indicate the degree of significance of each of the following people in your decision to return to school.

		Not Significant				Very Significant
a.	Husband	1	2	3	4	5
b.	Parents	1	2	3	4	5
c.	Siblings	1	2	3	4	5
d.	Children	1	2	3	4	5
e.	Male friend (other than spouse)	1	2	3	4	5
f.	Female friend	1	2	3	4	5
g.	Academic counselor	1	2	3	4	5
h.	Other: ______________	1	2	3	4	5

3. Please indicate your agreement or disagreement with each of the following statements.
    1. Strongly agree.
    2. Agree with reservations.
    3. Disagree with reservations.
    4. Strongly disagree.

		Agree				Disagree
a.	I feel confident of my ability to succeed in the graduate studies program.	1	2	3	4	5
b.	My studies will take second place to my family obligations.	1	2	3	4	5
c.	I am basically competitive.	1	2	3	4	5
d.	I am easily influenced by others.	1	2	3	4	5
e.	Without the encouragement of people close to me, I would not be in graduate school.	1	2	3	4	5
f.	Keeping house bores me.	1	2	3	4	5
g.	Reading is one of my favorite activities.	1	2	3	4	5
h.	I feel that my family resents the time required by my studies.	1	2	3	4	5
i.	As a result of my school enrollment my family is becoming more independent, more self-reliant	1	2	3	4	5
j.	Since undertaking graudate studies my self-esteem has increased.	1	2	3	4	5
k.	Graduate school is less challenging than I expected.	1	2	3	4	5
l.	The Feminist Movement influenced my decision to enter graduate school.	1	2	3	4	5

4. Circle the letter that represents your current marital status.

   a. Single b. Separated c. Divorced d. Widowed e. married

5. What is your major field of study?

   ____

6. Please respond to the following on the blanks provided.
   a. Your age: ________
   b. Brith rank among siblings: ________
   c. Spouse's age: ________
   d. Number of years married: ________
   e. Number of children: ________
   f. Ages of children: ________

7. Circle the letter that indicates your or your family's gross income last year.

   a. Under $5000
   b. $5000 to $10,000
   c. $10,000 to $15,000
   d. $15,000 to $25,000
   e. More than $25,000

8. Circle the letter or letters that indicate your goals after obtaining your master's degree.

   a. Enter a doctoral program
   b. Apply for a credential
   c. Apply for a license
   d. Seek employment
   e. Other: ________________________________

9. If seeking employment, what would be your first job choice? ________________________________

10. If married, what is your husband's occupation?

    ____

11. Using the letters given below please indicate the educational level of each of the following:

    Husband: ____ Father: ____ Mother: _____

a. Doctoral degree	b. Master's degree
c. Bachelor's degree	d. Associate in Arts
e. High school diploma	f. Grammar school

12. In terms of a ten-rung "ladder of life", with zero representing the worst possible life and ten the best, where do you now place yourself?

    0 1 2 3 4 5 6 7 8 9 10
    worst possible average best possible

13. Where would you have placed yourself on the ladder of life five years ago?

0 1 2 3 4 5 6 7 8 9 10
worst possible average best possible

14. Where do you think you will be on the ladder of life five years from now?

0 1 2 3 4 5 6 7 8 9 10
worst possible average best possible

15. Indicate the degree of importance of each of the following in your decision to attend CSUH.

		Not Important			Very Important	
a.	The school's reputation	1	2	3	4	5
b.	Location	1	2	3	4	5
c.	Faculty	1	2	3	4	5
d.	Cost	1	2	3	4	5
e.	Consultation with an academic counselor	1	2	3	4	5
f.	Recommendation of friends	1	2	3	4	5
g.	Other: ________	1	2	3	4	5

16. To what extent do you feel your graduate studies are meeting your original expectations?

1 2 3 4 5
Not at all Completely

17. Complete this statement using an additional page if necessary:

"I would describe myself as the kind of person who

____

____

18. I am interested in receiving the results of this study.

Yes _____ No _____

APPENDIX C

Critical Values of r
(Pearson Product-Moment
Correlation Coefficient)

Critical values of r (Pearson product-moment correlation coefficient)

df	Level of significance for two-tailed test		
	.10	.05	.01
1	.988	.997	.9999
2	.900	.950	.990
3	.805	.878	.959
4	.729	.811	.917
5	.669	.754	.874
6	.622	.707	.834
7	.582	.666	.798
8	.549	.632	.765
9	.521	.602	.735
10	.497	.576	.708
11	.476	.553	.684
12	.458	.532	.661
13	.441	.514	.641
14	.426	.497	.623
15	.412	.482	.606
16	.400	.468	.590
17	.389	.456	.575
18	.378	.444	.561
19	.369	.433	.549
20	.360	.423	.537
25	.323	.381	.487
30	.296	.349	.449
35	.275	.325	.418
40	.257	.304	.393
45	.243	.288	.372
50	.231	.273	.354
60	.211	.250	.325
70	.195	.232	.303
80	.183	.217	.283
90	.173	.205	.267
100	.164	.195	.254

Source: Cozby, P. (1985) Methods in Behavioral Research, Palo Alto: Mayfield Pub. Co. Reprinted with permission.

APPENDIX D

Fisher's z Transformation of the Pearson r Coefficient of Correlation

Fisher's z Transformation

r	z	r	z	r	z	r	z	r	z
.000	.000	.200	.203	.400	.424	.600	.693	.800	1.099
.010	.010	.210	.213	.410	.436	.610	.709	.810	1.127
.020	.020	.220	.224	.420	.448	.620	.725	.820	1.157
.030	.030	.230	.234	.430	.460	.630	.741	.830	1.188
.040	.040	.240	.245	.440	.472	.640	.758	.840	1.221
.050	.050	.250	.255	.450	.485	.650	.775	.850	1.256
.060	.060	.260	.266	.460	.497	.660	.793	.860	1.293
.070	.070	.270	.277	.470	.510	.670	.811	.870	1.333
.080	.080	.280	.288	.480	.523	.680	.829	.880	1.376
.090	.090	.290	.299	.490	.536	.690	.848	.890	1.422
.100	.100	.300	.310	.500	.549	.700	.867	.900	1.472
.110	.110	.310	.321	.510	.563	.710	.887	.910	1.528
.120	.121	.320	.332	.520	.576	.720	.908	.920	1.589
.130	.131	.330	.343	.530	.590	.730	.929	.930	1.658
.140	.141	.340	.354	.540	.604	.740	.950	.940	1.738
.150	.151	.350	.365	.550	.618	.750	.973	.950	1.832
.160	.161	.360	.377	.560	.633	.760	.996	.960	1.946
.170	.172	.370	.388	.570	.648	.770	1.020	.970	2.092
.180	.182	.380	.400	.580	.662	.780	1.045	.980	2.298
.190	.192	.390	.412	.590	.678	.790	1.071	.990	2.647

Source: Tabled values were computed by the author.

APPENDIX E

Table of Critical t-Ratios

Critical values of *t*

$N_1 + N_2 - 2$ (*df*)	Significance Level* .05 / .10	.025 / .05	.01 / .02	.005 / .01
1	6.314	12.706	31.821	63.657
2	2.920	4.303	6.965	9.925
3	2.353	3.182	4.541	5.841
4	2.132	2.776	3.747	4.604
5	2.015	2.571	3.365	4.032
6	1.943	2.447	3.143	3.707
7	1.895	2.365	2.998	3.499
8	1.860	2.306	2.896	3.355
9	1.833	2.262	2.821	3.250
10	1.812	2.228	2.764	3.169
11	1.796	2.201	2.718	3.106
12	1.782	2.179	2.681	3.055
13	1.771	2.160	2.650	3.012
14	1.761	2.145	2.624	2.977
15	1.753	2.131	2.602	2.947
16	1.746	2.120	2.583	2.921
17	1.740	2.110	2.567	2.898
18	1.734	2.101	2.552	2.878
19	1.729	2.093	2.539	2.861
20	1.725	2.086	2.528	2.845
21	1.721	2.080	2.518	2.831
22	1.717	2.074	2.508	2.819
23	1.714	2.069	2.500	2.807
24	1.711	2.064	2.492	2.797
25	1.708	2.060	2.485	2.787
26	1.706	2.056	2.479	2.779
27	1.703	2.052	2.473	2.771
28	1.701	2.048	2.467	2.763
29	1.699	2.045	2.462	2.756
30	1.697	2.042	2.457	2.750
40	1.684	2.021	2.423	2.704
60	1.671	2.000	2.390	2.660
120	1.658	1.980	2.358	2.617
∞	1.645	1.960	2.326	2.576

*Use the top significance level when you have predicted a specific directional difference (e.g., group 1 will be greater than group 2). Use the bottom significance level when you have only predicted that group 1 will differ from group 2 without specifying the direction of the difference.

APPENDIX F

Table of Critical F-Ratios

Critical values of F

df for denominator (error)	α	*df* for numerator (systematic)											
		1	2	3	4	5	6	7	8	9	10	11	12
1	.25	5.83	7.50	8.20	8.58	8.82	8.98	9.10	9.19	9.26	9.32	9.36	9.41
	.10	39.9	49.5	53.6	55.8	57.2	58.2	58.9	59.4	59.9	60.2	60.5	60.7
	.05	161	200	216	225	230	234	237	239	241	242	243	244
2	.25	2.57	3.00	3.15	3.23	3.28	3.31	3.34	3.35	3.37	3.38	3.39	3.39
	.10	8.53	9.00	9.16	9.24	9.29	9.33	9.35	9.37	9.38	9.39	9.40	9.41
	.05	18.5	19.0	19.2	19.2	19.3	19.3	19.4	19.4	19.4	19.4	19.4	19.4
	.01	98.5	99.0	99.2	99.2	99.3	99.3	99.4	99.4	99.4	99.4	99.4	99.4
3	.25	2.02	2.28	2.36	2.39	2.41	2.42	2.43	2.44	2.44	2.44	2.45	2.45
	.10	5.54	5.46	5.39	5.34	5.31	5.28	5.27	5.25	5.24	5.23	5.22	5.22
	.05	10.1	9.55	9.28	9.12	9.01	8.94	8.89	8.85	8.81	8.79	8.76	8.74
	.01	34.1	30.8	29.5	28.7	28.2	27.9	27.7	27.5	27.3	27.2	27.1	27.1
4	.25	1.81	2.00	2.05	2.06	2.07	2.08	2.08	2.08	2.08	2.08	2.08	2.08
	.10	4.54	4.32	4.19	4.11	4.05	4.01	3.98	3.95	3.94	3.92	3.91	3.90
	.05	7.71	6.94	6.59	6.39	6.26	6.16	6.09	6.04	6.00	5.96	5.94	5.91
	.01	21.2	18.0	16.7	16.0	15.5	15.2	15.0	14.8	14.7	14.5	14.4	14.4
5	.25	1.69	1.85	1.88	1.89	1.89	1.89	1.89	1.89	1.89	1.89	1.89	1.89
	.10	4.06	3.78	3.62	3.52	3.45	3.40	3.37	3.34	3.32	3.30	3.28	3.27
	.05	6.61	5.79	5.41	5.19	5.05	4.95	4.88	4.82	4.77	4.74	4.71	4.68
	.01	16.3	13.3	12.1	11.4	11.0	10.7	10.5	10.3	10.2	10.1	9.96	9.89
6	.25	1.62	1.76	1.78	1.79	1.79	1.78	1.78	1.78	1.77	1.77	1.77	1.77
	.10	3.78	3.46	3.29	3.18	3.11	3.05	3.01	2.98	2.96	2.94	2.92	2.90
	.05	5.99	5.14	4.76	4.53	4.39	4.28	4.21	4.15	4.10	4.06	4.03	4.00
	.01	13.7	10.9	9.78	9.15	8.75	8.47	8.26	8.10	7.98	7.87	7.79	7.72
7	.25	1.57	1.70	1.72	1.72	1.71	1.71	1.70	1.70	1.69	1.69	1.69	1.68
	.10	3.59	3.26	3.07	2.96	2.88	2.83	2.78	2.75	2.72	2.70	2.68	2.67
	.05	5.59	4.74	4.35	4.12	3.97	3.87	3.79	3.73	3.68	3.64	3.60	3.57
	.01	12.2	9.55	8.45	7.85	7.46	7.19	6.99	6.84	6.72	6.62	6.54	6.47
8	.25	1.54	1.66	1.67	1.66	1.66	1.65	1.64	1.64	1.63	1.63	1.63	1.62
	.10	3.46	3.11	2.92	2.81	2.73	2.67	2.62	2.59	2.56	2.54	2.52	2.50
	.05	5.32	4.46	4.07	3.84	3.69	3.58	3.50	3.44	3.39	3.35	3.31	3.28
	.01	11.3	8.65	7.59	7.01	6.63	6.37	6.18	6.03	5.91	5.81	5.73	5.67
9	.25	1.51	1.62	1.63	1.63	1.62	1.61	1.60	1.60	1.59	1.59	1.58	1.58
	.10	3.36	3.01	2.81	2.69	2.61	2.55	2.51	2.47	2.44	2.42	2.40	2.38
	.05	5.12	4.26	3.86	3.63	3.48	3.37	3.29	3.23	3.18	3.14	3.10	3.07
	.01	10.6	8.02	6.99	6.42	6.06	5.80	5.61	5.47	5.35	5.26	5.18	5.11
10	.25	1.49	1.60	1.60	1.59	1.59	1.58	1.57	1.56	1.56	1.55	1.55	1.54
	.10	3.29	2.92	2.73	2.61	2.52	2.46	2.41	2.38	2.35	2.32	2.30	2.28
	.05	4.96	4.10	3.71	3.48	3.33	3.22	3.14	3.07	3.02	2.98	2.94	2.91
	.01	10.0	7.56	6.55	5.99	5.64	5.39	5.20	5.06	4.94	4.85	4.77	4.71

Source: Cozby, P. (1985) Methods in Behavioral Research, Palo Alto: Mayfield Pub. Co. Reprinted with permission.

Critical values of *F* (continued)

df for denominator (error)	α	*df* for numerator (systematic) 1	2	3	4	5	6	7	8	9	10	11	12
11	.25	1.47	1.58	1.58	1.57	1.56	1.55	1.54	1.53	1.53	1.52	1.52	1.51
	.10	3.23	2.86	2.66	2.54	2.45	2.39	2.34	2.30	2.27	2.25	2.23	2.21
	.05	4.84	3.98	3.59	3.36	3.20	3.09	3.01	2.95	2.90	2.85	2.82	2.79
	.01	9.65	7.21	6.22	5.67	5.32	5.07	4.89	4.74	4.63	4.54	4.46	4.40
12	.25	1.46	1.56	1.56	1.55	1.54	1.53	1.52	1.51	1.51	1.50	1.50	1.49
	.10	3.18	2.81	2.61	2.48	2.39	2.33	2.28	2.24	2.21	2.19	2.17	2.15
	.05	4.75	3.89	3.49	3.26	3.11	3.00	2.91	2.85	2.80	2.75	2.72	2.69
	.01	9.33	6.93	5.95	5.41	5.06	4.82	4.64	4.50	4.39	4.30	4.22	4.16
13	.25	1.45	1.55	1.55	1.53	1.52	1.51	1.50	1.49	1.49	1.48	1.47	1.47
	.10	3.14	2.76	2.56	2.43	2.35	2.28	2.23	2.20	2.16	2.14	2.12	2.10
	.05	4.67	3.81	3.41	3.18	3.03	2.92	2.83	2.77	2.71	2.67	2.63	2.60
	.01	9.07	6.70	5.74	5.21	4.86	4.62	4.44	4.30	4.19	4.10	4.02	3.96
14	.25	1.44	1.53	1.53	1.52	1.51	1.50	1.49	1.48	1.47	1.46	1.46	1.45
	.10	3.10	2.73	2.52	2.39	2.31	2.24	2.19	2.15	2.12	2.10	2.08	2.05
	.05	4.60	3.74	3.34	3.11	2.96	2.85	2.76	2.70	2.65	2.60	2.57	2.53
	.01	8.86	6.51	5.56	5.04	4.69	4.46	4.28	4.14	4.03	3.94	3.86	3.80
15	.25	1.43	1.52	1.52	1.51	1.49	1.48	1.47	1.46	1.46	1.45	1.44	1.44
	.10	3.07	2.70	2.49	2.36	2.27	2.21	2.16	2.12	2.09	2.06	2.04	2.02
	.05	4.54	3.68	3.29	3.06	2.90	2.79	2.71	2.64	2.59	2.54	2.51	2.48
	.01	8.68	6.36	5.42	4.89	4.56	4.32	4.14	4.00	3.89	3.80	3.73	3.67
16	.25	1.42	1.51	1.51	1.50	1.48	1.47	1.46	1.45	1.44	1.44	1.44	1.43
	.10	3.05	2.67	2.46	2.33	2.24	2.18	2.13	2.09	2.06	2.03	2.01	1.99
	.05	4.49	3.63	3.24	3.01	2.85	2.74	2.66	2.59	2.54	2.49	2.46	2.42
	.01	8.53	6.23	5.29	4.77	4.44	4.20	4.03	3.89	3.78	3.69	3.62	3.55
17	.25	1.42	1.51	1.50	1.49	1.47	1.46	1.45	1.44	1.43	1.43	1.42	1.41
	.10	3.03	2.64	2.44	2.31	2.22	2.15	2.10	2.06	2.03	2.00	1.98	1.96
	.05	4.45	3.59	3.20	2.96	2.81	2.70	2.61	2.55	2.49	2.45	2.41	2.38
	.01	8.40	6.11	5.18	4.67	4.34	4.10	3.93	3.79	3.68	3.59	3.52	3.46
18	.25	1.41	1.50	1.49	1.48	1.46	1.45	1.44	1.43	1.42	1.42	1.41	1.40
	.10	3.01	2.62	2.42	2.29	2.20	2.13	2.08	2.04	2.00	1.98	1.96	1.93
	.05	4.41	3.55	3.16	2.93	2.77	2.66	2.58	2.51	2.46	2.41	2.37	2.34
	.01	8.29	6.01	5.09	4.58	4.25	4.01	3.84	3.71	3.60	3.51	3.43	3.37
19	.25	1.41	1.49	1.49	1.47	1.46	1.44	1.43	1.42	1.41	1.41	1.40	1.40
	.10	2.99	2.61	2.40	2.27	2.18	2.11	2.06	2.02	1.98	1.96	1.94	1.91
	.05	4.38	3.52	3.13	2.90	2.74	2.63	2.54	2.48	2.42	2.38	2.34	2.31
	.01	8.18	5.93	5.01	4.50	4.17	3.94	3.77	3.63	3.52	3.43	3.36	3.30
20	.25	1.40	1.49	1.48	1.46	1.45	1.44	1.43	1.42	1.41	1.40	1.39	1.39
	.10	2.97	2.59	2.38	2.25	2.16	2.09	2.04	2.00	1.96	1.94	1.92	1.89
	.05	4.35	3.49	3.10	2.87	2.71	2.60	2.51	2.45	2.39	2.35	2.31	2.28
	.01	8.10	5.85	4.94	4.43	4.10	3.87	3.70	3.56	3.46	3.37	3.29	3.23

Critical values of *F* (continued)

df for denominator (error)	α	*df* for numerator (systematic)											
		1	2	3	4	5	6	7	8	9	10	11	12
22	.25	1.40	1.48	1.47	1.45	1.44	1.42	1.41	1.40	1.39	1.39	1.38	1.37
	.10	2.95	2.56	2.35	2.22	2.13	2.06	2.01	1.97	1.93	1.90	1.88	1.86
	.05	4.30	3.44	3.05	2.82	2.66	2.55	2.46	2.40	2.34	2.30	2.26	2.23
	.01	7.95	5.72	4.82	4.31	3.99	3.76	3.59	3.45	3.35	3.26	3.18	3.12
24	.25	1.39	1.47	1.46	1.44	1.43	1.41	1.40	1.39	1.38	1.38	1.37	1.36
	.10	2.93	2.54	2.33	2.19	2.10	2.04	1.98	1.94	1.91	1.88	1.85	1.83
	.05	4.26	3.40	3.01	2.78	2.62	2.51	2.42	2.36	2.30	2.25	2.21	2.18
	.01	7.82	5.61	4.72	4.22	3.90	3.67	3.50	3.36	3.26	3.17	3.09	3.03
26	.25	1.38	1.46	1.45	1.44	1.42	1.41	1.39	1.38	1.37	1.37	1.36	1.35
	.10	2.91	2.52	2.31	2.17	2.08	2.01	1.96	1.92	1.88	1.86	1.84	1.81
	.05	4.23	3.37	2.98	2.74	2.59	2.47	2.39	2.32	2.27	2.22	2.18	2.15
	.01	7.72	5.53	4.64	4.14	3.82	3.59	3.42	3.29	3.18	3.09	3.02	2.96
28	.25	1.38	1.46	1.45	1.43	1.41	1.40	1.39	1.38	1.37	1.36	1.35	1.34
	.10	2.89	2.50	2.29	2.16	2.06	2.00	1.94	1.90	1.87	1.84	1.81	1.79
	.05	4.20	3.34	2.95	2.71	2.56	2.45	2.36	2.29	2.24	2.19	2.15	2.12
	.01	7.64	5.45	4.57	4.07	3.75	3.53	3.36	3.23	3.12	3.03	2.96	2.90
30	.25	1.38	1.45	1.44	1.42	1.41	1.39	1.38	1.37	1.36	1.35	1.35	1.34
	.10	2.88	2.49	2.28	2.14	2.05	1.98	1.93	1.88	1.85	1.82	1.79	1.77
	.05	4.17	3.32	2.92	2.69	2.53	2.42	2.33	2.27	2.21	2.16	2.13	2.09
	.01	7.56	5.39	4.51	4.02	3.70	3.47	3.30	3.17	3.07	2.98	2.91	2.84
40	.25	1.36	1.44	1.42	1.40	1.39	1.37	1.36	1.35	1.34	1.33	1.32	1.31
	.10	2.84	2.44	2.23	2.09	2.00	1.93	1.87	1.83	1.79	1.76	1.73	1.71
	.05	4.08	3.23	2.84	2.61	2.45	2.34	2.25	2.18	2.12	2.08	2.04	2.00
	.01	7.31	5.18	4.31	3.83	3.51	3.29	3.12	2.99	2.89	2.80	2.73	2.66
60	.25	1.35	1.42	1.41	1.38	1.37	1.35	1.33	1.32	1.31	1.30	1.29	1.29
	.10	2.79	2.39	2.18	2.04	1.95	1.87	1.82	1.77	1.74	1.71	1.68	1.66
	.05	4.00	3.15	2.76	2.53	2.37	2.25	2.17	2.10	2.04	1.99	1.95	1.92
	.01	7.08	4.98	4.13	3.65	3.34	3.12	2.95	2.82	2.72	2.63	2.56	2.50
120	.25	1.34	1.40	1.39	1.37	1.35	1.33	1.31	1.30	1.29	1.28	1.27	1.26
	.10	2.75	2.35	2.13	1.99	1.90	1.82	1.77	1.72	1.68	1.65	1.62	1.60
	.05	3.92	3.07	2.68	2.45	2.29	2.17	2.09	2.02	1.96	1.91	1.87	1.83
	.01	6.85	4.79	3.95	3.48	3.17	2.96	2.79	2.66	2.56	2.47	2.40	2.34
200	.25	1.33	1.39	1.38	1.36	1.34	1.32	1.31	1.29	1.28	1.27	1.26	1.25
	.10	2.73	2.33	2.11	1.97	1.88	1.80	1.75	1.70	1.66	1.63	1.60	1.57
	.05	3.89	3.04	2.65	2.42	2.26	2.14	2.06	1.98	1.93	1.88	1.84	1.80
	.01	6.76	4.71	3.88	3.41	3.11	2.89	2.73	2.60	2.50	2.41	2.34	2.27
∞	.25	1.32	1.39	1.37	1.35	1.33	1.31	1.29	1.28	1.27	1.25	1.24	1.24
	.10	2.71	2.30	2.08	1.94	1.85	1.77	1.72	1.67	1.63	1.60	1.57	1.55
	.05	3.84	3.00	2.60	2.37	2.21	2.10	2.01	1.94	1.88	1.83	1.79	1.75
	.01	6.63	4.61	3.78	3.32	3.02	2.80	2.64	2.51	2.41	2.32	2.25	2.18

BIBLIOGRAPHY

American Psychological Association (1982). Ethical principles in the conduct of research with human participants. Washington, D.C.: Author.

Anderson, S. and Ball, S. (1978). The profession and practice of program evaluation. San Francisco: Jossey Bass.

Applebaum, M. & Cramer, E. (1974). Some problems in the non-orthogonal analysis of variance, Psychological Bulletin, 81(6), 335-343.

Ary, D., Jacobs, L., & Razavieh, A. (1979) Introduction to Research in Education (2nd Ed.). New York: Holt.

Babbie, E. (1975). The practice of social research. Belmont, CA: Wadsworth.

Bruning, J. & Kintz,, B. (1977). Computational handbook of statistics (2nd Ed.). Glenview, IL: Scott, Foresman & Co.

Buros, O. (Ed.) (1978). Mental measurements yearbook (8th Ed.) (Vols. 1 & 2). Highland Park, NJ: Gryphon Press.

Calcagno, S. (1979). The prediction of counseling success using occupational and academic predictors. California State University, Hayward: unpublished master's thesis.

Campbell, D. & Stanley, J. (1963). Experimental and quasi-experimental designs for research. In N. Gage (Ed.) Handbook of research on teaching. Chicago: Rand McNally.

Campbell, D. & Stanley, J. (1968). Experimental and quasi-experimental designs for research. Chicago: Rand McNally.

Center, B., Skiba, R., & Casey, A. (1985). A methodology for the quantitative synthesis of intra-subject research. Journal of Special Education. 19(4), 387-400.

Coleman, J. (1981). Reply to Page and Keith. Educational Researcher, 10(7), 18-20.

Consumers Guide (1984). Easy-to-Understand Guide to Home Computers. New York: Beekman House.

Cozby, P. (1984). Using Computers in the Behavioral Sciences. Palo Alto: Mayfield Publishing Co.

Cozby, P. (1985). Methods in behavioral research. Palo Alto, CA: Mayfield.

Davis, D. (1972). The effect of three types of testing procedures on course achievement of graduate students. California State University, Hayward: unpublished master's thesis.

DeLong, J. (1975). An analysis of the motivational factors influencing mature women to enter graduate studies programs. California State University, Hayward: unpublished master's thesis.

Dillon, R. and Goldstein, M. (1984). Multivariate analysis: methods and applications. New York: John Wiley.

Donmoyer, R. (1985). The rescue from relativism: Two failed attempts and an alternative strategy. Educational Reseacher, 14(10), 13-20.

Driscoll, R. (1972). TM as a secondary school subject. Phi Delta Kappan, 54(4), 236-237.

Erickson, F. (1986). Qualitative methods in research on teaching. In Handbook of research on teaching (J.M. Wittrock, Ed.) New York: MacMillan.

Fitz-Gibbon, C. & Morris, L. (1978). How to design a program evaluation. Beverly Hills: Sage.

Frank, J. (1977). Nature and function of belief systems: Humanism and transcendental religion. American Psychologist, 32, 555-559.

Freedman, J., Klevansky, S., & Erlich, P. (1971). The effect of crowding on human task performance. *Journal of Applied Social Psychology,* 1, 7-25.

Frey, D. (1985). *Acalanes longitudinal study, year one: A narrative analysis of demographic characteristics.* Hayward, CA: unpublished evaluation report.

Fried, M. (1972). *Geographic mobility and its effect on student achievement.* California State University, Hayward: unpublished master's thesis.

Gilliland, C. (1967). The relation of pupil mobility to achievement in the elementary school. *Journal of Experimental Education,* 35, 74-80.

Glass, G. (1977) Integrating findings: The meta-analysis of research. *Review of research in education,* 5, 351-379.

Glass, G. & Smith, M. (1979). Meta-analysis of research on the relationship of class size and achievement. *Evaluation and Policy Analysis,* 1, 2-16.

Hahn, H. (1975). *The effects of transcendental meditation on three factors of personal discontent: hostility, anxiety, and depression.* California State University, Hayward: unpublished master's thesis.

Hahn, H. & Whalen, T. (1974). The effects of transcendental meditation on three factors of personal discontent. Paper presented at the meeting of the California Educational Research Association, San Francisco.

Hanley, J. (1976). *A follow-up survey of non-persisters in a master's degree in counseling program.* California State University, Hayward: unpublished master's thesis.

Hayes, J. & Flower, L. (1986). Writing research and the writer. *American Psychologist,* 41(10), 1106-1113.

Hedges, L. (1987). How hard is hard science, how soft is soft science? The empirical cumulativeness of research. *American Psychologist,* 42(5), 443-455.

Helmstadter, G. (1970). *Research concepts in human behavior.* New York: Appleton-Century-Crofts.

Hitt, W. (1969). Two models of man. In *Issues and advances in educational psychology.* (Torrance, E. and White, W., Eds.). Itasca: Peacock, 1975.

Holland, J. (1973). *Making vocational choices: A theory of careers.* Englewood Cliffs: Prentice-Hall.

Howell, D. (1987). *Statistical methods for psychology* (2nd edition). Boston: Duxbury Press.

Hull, C. and Nie, N. (1981). *SPSS Update 7-9: New Procedures and Facilities for Releases 7-9.* New York: McGraw-Hill.

Jensen, A. R. (1981) *Straight talk about mental tests.* New York: The Free Press.

Johnson, O. and Bommarito, J. (1971). *Tests and measurements in child development: A handbook.* San Francisco: Jossey-Bass.

Johntz, W. (1971). Teaching the disadvantaged. In L. Deighton (Ed.), *The encyclopedia of education,* (Vol. 4). New Jersey: MacMillan.

Keith, T. and Page, E. (1985). Do Catholic high schools improve minority student achievement? *American Educational Research Journal,* 22. 337-349.

Kerlinger, F. (1986). *Foundations of behavioral research.* New York: Holt.

Kerlinger, F. and Pedhazur, E. (1973). *Multiple regression in behavioral research.* New York: Holt.

Klecka, W., Nie, N., and Hull, C. (1975). *SPSS Primer: Statistical Package for the Social Sciences Primer.* New York: McGraw-Hill.

Lehmann, I. and Mehrens, W. (1971). *Educational research: Readings in focus.* New York: Holt.

Likert, R. (1932). A technique for the measurement of attitudes. *Archives of Psychology,* 140, 44-53.

Mathon, M. (1986). *A study of possible indicators of emotional problems in adolescents.* California State University, Hayward: unpublished master's thesis.

Mitchell, J. (1986). Measurement scales and statistics: A clash of paradigms. *Psychological Bulletin,* 100 (3), 398-407.

Morris, L. and Fitz-Gibbon, C. (1982). *Evaluator's handbook.* Beverly Hills: Sage.

Mueller, D. (1986). *Measuring social attitudes: A handbook for researchers and practitioners.* New York: Teachers College Press.

Neale, J. and Liebert, R. (1980). *Science and behavior.* Englewood Cliffs: Prentice-Hall.

Nie, N., Hull, C., Jenkins, J., Steinbrenner, K., and Bent, D. (1975). *SPSS: Statistical Package for the Social Sciences* (2nd edition). New York: McGraw-Hill.

Norusis, M. (1982). *SPSS Introductory Guide: Basic Statistics and Operations.* New York: McGraw-Hill.

Norusis, M. (1986). *The SPSS Guide to Data Analysis.* Chicago: SPSS, Inc.

Osgood, C., Suci, G., and Tannenbaum, P. (1957). *The measurement of meaning.* Urbana: University of Illinois Press.

Overall, J. and Spiegel, D. (1969). Concerning least squares analysis of experimental data. Psychological Bulletin, 72., 311-322.

Page, E. and Keith, T. (1981). Effects of U.S. private schools: A technical analysis of two recent claims. Educational Researcher, 10(7), 7-17.

Posavac, E. and Carey, R. (1980). Program evaluation: methods and cases. Englewood Cliffs: Prentice-Hall.

Putnam, H. (1981). Reason, truth, and history. Cambridge: Cambridge University Press.

Robinson, J. and Shaver, P. (1973). Measures of social psychological attitudes. Ann Arbor: Institute for Social Research.

Selkirk, K. (1978). Sampling. Nottingham, England: University of Nottingham School of Education.

Scriven, M. (1967). The methodology of evaluation. Perspectives of Curriculum Evaluation. American Educational Research Association Series on Curriculum Evaluation, No. 1. Chicago: Rand McNally.

Shavelson, R. (1981). Statistical Reasoning for the Behavioral Sciences. Boston: Allyn and Bacon.

Shaver, P. and Freedman, J. (1976). Your pursuit of happiness. Psychology Today, August, 1976.

Siegel, S. (1956). Nonparametric Statistics for the Behavioral Sciences. New York: McGraw-Hill.

Skiba, R., Casey, A., and Center, B. (1986). Nonaversive procedures in the treatment of classroom behavior problems. The Journal of Special Education, 19(4), 459-481.

Slonin, M. (1967). Sampling: A quick, reliable guide to practical statistics. New York: Simon & Schuster.

Smith, J. and Heshusius, L. (1986). Closing down the conversation: The end of the quantitative-qualitative debate among educational inquirers. _Educational Researcher,_ 15(1), 4-12.

Smith, M. and Glass, G. (1977). Meta-analysis of psychotherapy outcome studies. _American Psychologist,_ 32, 752-760.

SPSS-X User's Guide, 2nd Edition (1985). New York: McGraw-Hill.

Stanley, J. and Hopkins, D. (1972). _Educational and psychological measurement and evaluation._ Englewood Cliffs: Prentice-Hall.

Taylor Delain, M., Pearson, P., and Anderson, R. (1985). Reading comprehension and creativity in Black Language use: You stand to gain by playing the sounding game! _American Educational Research Journal,_ 22(2), 155-173.

Tesch, R. (1978). _Phenomenological and Transformative Research._ Santa Barbara: The Fielding Institute.

Test Corporation of America (1984). _Test critiques (Vol. 1)._ Kansas City, Missouri: Westport.

Time (January 3, 1983). Machine of the year: The computer moves in, 14-39.

Traynor, S. (1976). _Predicting success in the educational psychology program at California State University, Hayward._ California State University, Hayward: unpublished master's thesis.

Turney, B. and Robb, G. (1971). _Research in Education: an introduction._ Hinsdale, Illinois: The Dryden Press.

Vernon, P. (1979). _Intelligence: heredity and environment._ San Francisco: W. H. Freeman and Company.

Weiner, E. and Stewart, B. (1984). *Assessing individuals: Psychological and educational tests and measurements.* Boston: Little, Brown.

Whalen, T. (1969). Total English equals writing competence. *Research in the Teaching of English,* 3(1), 52-61.

Whalen, T. and Fried, M. (1973). Geographic mobility and its effect on student achievement. *Journal of Educational Research,* 67(4), 163-165.

Whalen, T. (1976). Project SEED 1975-76 program evaluation, Educational Planners and Evaluators, Associated. Los Gatos, CA: unpublished evaluation report.

ABOUT THE AUTHOR

Thomas E. Whalen received his Ph.D. from the University of Connecticut in 1970. He immediately took a teaching position at California State University, Hayward, where he has been a full professor since 1978. He chaired the Department of Educational Psychology and is currently acting associate dean of the School of Education.

Dr. Whalen teaches graduate level courses in behavioral research methods, program evaluation, research design, appraisal procedures, educational psychology, and computers in education. He has published articles in professional journals and has presented his research findings to various groups such as the American Educational Research Association and the California Psychological Association.

Professor Whalen has served as a consultant in program evaluation to the California State Department of Education, Lawrence Livermore National Laboratory, the City of Hayward Police Department, and several school districts in the San Francisco Bay Area. He served as secretary for the California Association of Program Evaluators and was on the board of directors for both the California Educational Research Association and the Bay Area Council for Measurement and Evaluation in Education, of which he is past president. Dr. Whalen is a member of both the American Educational Research Association and the American Psychological Association.